URBAN TOURISM

URBAN TOURISM

By

David Carr

DISCOVERY PUBLISHING HOUSE PVT. LTD.
NEW DELHI-110 002

Published by:
Tilak Wasan

DISCOVERY PUBLISHING HOUSE PVT. LTD.
4383/4B, Ansari Road, Darya Ganj
New Delhi-110 002 (India)
Phone : +91-11-23279245, 23253475, 43596065
E-mail : discoverypublishinghouse@gmail.com
sales@discoverypublishinggroup.com
web : www.discoverypublishinggroup.com

First Edition: **2011**

Reprinted: **2020**

ISBN: 978-81-8356-947-7

Urban Tourism

Printed at:
Infinity Imaging Systems
Delhi

PREFACE

Urbanization is closely linked to modernization, industrialization, and the sociological process of rationalization. Urbanization can describe a specific condition at a set time, ie. the proportion of total population or area in cities or towns, or the term can describe the increase of this proportion over time. So the term urbanization can represent the level of urban relative to overall population, or it can represent the rate at which the urban proportion is increasing.

Studying urban tourism requires taking seriously leisure activities and transient populations, features of the city that much of past urban theory declines to address. For many cities urban tourism is their number one industry, generating not only rising income but also underpinning many regeneration projects. The University of Gloucestershire (United Kingdom) says in its prospectus that tourism and culture had been catalysts for large-scale urban developments internationally, from cultural facilities such as the Guggenheim Museum, which provides a focal point for urban regeneration in Bilbao, to the Sydney Olympic Games and the Manchester Commonwealth Games as sources of urban renewal.

We've learned much about place and tourism over the last few decades, from movements like ecotourism, cultural tourism, and heritage tourism. Our goal is to integrate these and other approaches, add a strong dose of the public's voice, and "use" tourism as a tool to build healthier communities. If effect, we encourage flipping two paradigms.

Amusement parks evolved in Europe from fairs and pleasure gardens which were created for people's recreation. The oldest amusement park in the world (opened 1583) is Bakken, at Klampenborg, north of Copenhagen, Denmark. In the United States, world's fairs and expositions were another influence on development of the amusement park industry.

The delay of interest in urban tourism can be explained by a neglect in urban studies to assess the importance of leisure, recreation and tourism in an urban environment. Further, there was a lack of understanding of the urban tourism system. The difficulty of separating this from non-tourism functions in the wide range of urban activities and the tendency to explore the issue of urban tourism in case studies rather than by conceptual studies have contributed to the slow progress of urban tourism research.

Shopping centers are locations consisting of retail space. In the U.S. and Canada, these vary from strip malls which refer to collections of buildings sharing a common parking lot, usually built on a high-capacity roadway with commercial functions. Similar developments in the UK are called Retail Parks. Strip malls/retail parks contain a wide variety of retail and non-retail functions that also cater to daily use. Strip malls consisting mostly of big box stores or category killers are sometimes called power centers.

—Author

CONTENTS

UNDERSTANDING URBAN TOURISM

Urban tourism refers to the consumption of city spectacles such as architecture, monuments, and parks and cultural amenities such as museums, restaurants, and performances by visitors. Studying urban tourism requires taking seriously leisure activities and transient populations, features of the city that much of past urban theory declines to address.

However, a number of developments in recent decades have led tourism to assume a larger place in urban scholarship. As industrial manufacturing deserts dense urban areas, entertainment plays an expanded role in many city economies. Leisure and consumption for some means work and profits for others. The attraction and accommodation of visitors has become a central concern for public and private city elites. The sizable but fleeting population of visitors to the city has a surprising influence over local politics, investment choices, and the built environment.

The label "tourist" frequently evokes pejorative connotations, which color not only popular but also scholarly representations. While crude stereotypes of the tourist suggest a plodding brute oblivious to all but the most obvious and pre-packaged attractions of the urban landscape, the leisure activity of tourism in fact contains a wide range of consumption activities and orientations towards the city.

Urban tourism has, in one form or other, been with us since Mesopotamia and Sumeria were spawning the phenomenon of urbanization. People with the means and inclination to do so have been drawn to towns and cities just to visit and experience a multiplicity of things to see and do... These towns and cities were the melting pots of national culture, art, music, literature and of course magnificent architecture and urban design. It was the concentration, variety, and quality of these activities and attributes ... that created their attraction and put certain towns and cities on the tourism map.

Today tourism consumes substantial amounts of space within urban destinations: tourist-historic urban cores, special museums of many kinds, urban waterfronts, theme parks and specialized precincts all contribute to this consumption. Major urban areas perform important functions within the workings of the overall tourism system: for example, they are key "gateways" for both international and domestic tourists and, as key nodes in the air transport system, act as staging posts for multi-destination trips. Many of these functions are often taken for granted and, as a consequence, the requirements for profitable and sustainable tourism development in urban areas are not well understood. While urban tourism has been subject to some research attention in recent years, this effort has arguably not reflected its degree of importance relative to tourism in other types of destinations.

URBAN TOURISM

For many cities urban tourism is their number one industry, generating not only rising income but also underpinning many regeneration projects. The University of Gloucestershire (United Kingdom) says in its prospectus that tourism and culture had been catalysts for large-scale urban developments internationally, from cultural facilities such as the Guggenheim Museum, which provides a focal point for urban regeneration in Bilbao, to the Sydney Olympic Games and the Manchester Commonwealth Games as sources of urban renewal.

New York, which, with more than 40 million tourists per year, is the most visited US city, earned US$220 million through hotel taxes alone in 2004. Direct spending by tourists amounted to $15.1 billion. In total, the tourist industry is worth $23 billion to the New York economy and supports more than 250,000 jobs. International tourists make up 13.3 per cent of all visitors to New York but they are responsible for 40 per cent of visitor spending.

Cities all over the world make special efforts to attract foreign tourists. In his article for City Mayors 'Cologne starts China Offensive to attract tourists and business' Gregor Gosciniak says that for Cologne attracting tourists and business investment are two sides of the same coin. "The tourist office's 'China Offensive' is supported by the chamber of commerce, the Cologne Trade Fair and the airport authority," he writes.

Tourism is also big business for Hong Kong. In October 2005, the city welcomed 2.1 million visitors, with almost half coming from countries other than Mainland China. Overnight visitors spent more than HK$61 million (US$7.9 million). Their spending in October 2004 was HK$48.8 million. The expenditure of cruise passengers shot up by 196 per cent from HK13 million in October 2004 to HK$38 million one year later. Day visitors spent HK$5.6 million.

Civic Tourism Can Help Preserve Historic Towns

Civic Tourism begins with what some consider an outlandish claim, which is that tourism, one of the largest industries in the world, could help communities preserve their quality of life. The industry's argument generally ends with 'economic development,' but we're suggesting tourism could help protect historic neighbourhoods, save the environment, and preserve cultures -- in addition to strengthening the economy. Does it always? No, and some people argue tourism does the opposite, that it ruins 'sense of place,' that it's the problem. We're suggesting tourism can be part of the solution.

For example, Sharlot Hall Museum (Arizona, USA), the sponsor of the Civic Tourism project, could not portrait the region's history as effectively as it does without tourists' dollars. That's true for many museums, parks, and other hometown assets. So, can tourism help protect the things we cherish? Yes. Does it always? No, but remember: the tourism industry, as an 'industry,' is a relatively new phenomenon. It's still learning.

So, is Civic Tourism another exercise in whining about how tourism 'ruined our town'? No, that approach only builds walls we're think of themselves the same way? One answer is to think of place an experience. Consider Nike: they don't sell shoes, you rarely see a sneaker in their ads. They're an experience. Towns can do the same thing – through story.

As more Boomers retire, as Gen-Xers emerge from their Gordon Gecko cocoons, and as the so-called 'Creative Class' surfaces (the theory popularized by Richard Florida, which has huge implications for tourism), it's unique experiences, not assembly-line settings, that will create this connection; and uniqueness is a by-product of the cultural, natural, and historic assets particular to a place.

Extending the Reach

There's one last topic, and that's the how of the conversation – the 'politics' of place. The discussion about how towns 'do' tourism used to be a narrow one: the chamber, city, or convention and visitors bureau. When niches like ecotourism appeared the conversation often broadened to include other voices. The group still missing is the public, the people who live in the places the hospitality industry markets. Including residents is a natural evolution, just as we've seen the same thinking in government, journalism, philanthropy, education, culture, and other industries. Tourism is no different, and as this relatively new business matures we see more avenues for public input in the discussion of how one 'does' tourism – such as 'geotourism or 'community tourism'.

Civic engagement means doing more than talking at citizens; it means giving people who are often the most affected by the tourism industry's decisions a voice in how their town is bundled as an attraction. In broadening the conversation, will the industry be criticized? Most likely, but tourism officials should be big enough to listen, they may learn something, and giving resident ownership in the conversation will help appease anti-tourism sentiments.

We've learned much about place and tourism over the last few decades, from movements like ecotourism, cultural tourism, and heritage tourism. Our goal is to integrate these and other approaches, add a strong dose of the public's voice, and "use" tourism as a tool to build healthier communities. If effect, we encourage flipping two paradigms:

1) Use tourism to serve place (its preservation and maintenance), rather than using place to serve the tourism economy.
2) Build towns to benefit residents, rather than building towns to attract visitors.

Evidence suggests that towns, which focus on building a healthy place for residents will ultimately attract high-value visitors who want to experience livable communities. Conversely, towns that put too much emphasis on attracting tourists risk destroying place, and alienating residents.

A few discussions I've had end like this: "What's your endgame?" We'll be happy if it's another way to think about tourism, and a broader cast of characters to participate in the conversation about place as a tourism product. We're in the product business; this isn't about marketing, but about re-articulating the thing we market; and most importantly, about creating the political will to advocate for appropriate product development.

We've finished a year of research, summits, town halls, and other community meetings, and we'll share our findings – and continue the research – at a national conference in March. We invite you to join the conversation about how communities can think about tourism differently – from an industry that sometimes buries "place" to one that preserves it.

Urban Tourism in Peru: Lima Walks Offers a City Tour on Foot

Who would have thought that Lima is a good place for walking? Judging from other limeños like me, that is something you simply don't do here. But for Dutch editor, Ronald Elward, who's been living in Peru for the last two years, the city is a very exciting place – exactly for that purpose.

Elward recently launched Lima Walks, a program of about nine walks around the city, each two to three hours long, focused on the architectural and historic value of the buildings.

He even went a step further. He labels Lima as "the Americas' best kept secret." It is true that a lot of limeños don't see their city as a place people would love.to walk. But a secret? In the continent? Elward believes there is a tendency to put Lima down.

Here's step one in how visitors manage to ignore Lima: "Lima looks rather off-putting when you first arrive," Elward says. "You see a lot of vey unattractive buildings along the way and you get the idea there is very little to do here."

Step two, Elward explains, happens when "the tour operators take you very quickly out of the city, to Nasca, Cusco, Arequipa. So you think that it is best to ignore Lima."

A visit to Rimac

On the day we meet, we do the Rimac walk. The sun is shining and makes a very welcome change to the bleak Lima winter. As soon as we cross the river to the old Jiron Trujillo, Elward points out to a small, bright-pink building.

"That is the smallest church in Lima," he says, "the church of San Jose del Puente." Funny that it would take a foreigner to tell me things I should know.

"It started as an Inn in the 17th Century," he explains, and here they had a revered image of the Virgin of the Rosary. The devotion grew so much that in time it became a chapel. "Later, this tiny room," he says once inside, "it was transformed in the church it is now."

According to Spanish architect Fernando Palazuelo, owner of Art-Express, the company that has been buying emblematic buildings in the historic center, Lima offers what no other city in Latin America does.

He argues that "the historic center of Lima has a unique range of good architecture of the last 500 years in a relatively small area." (To this, we should add the archaeological legacy of the last 4,000 years that we can find around the city.)

The City Needs its Markers

Step three in disliking Lima: attitude. "The other thing that happens here too often is that limeños always say that you cannot go out, that it is unsafe. So you're not really stimulated to venture too much into the older parts of the city," says Elward.

Step four in disliking Lima: lack of information. You cannot love what you don't know. The fact is that no authority seems to have taken the trouble to let us know what we have. If Lima residents don't walk the city, it's not only because we think the place is unsafe (in fact, many areas are safe for walking) or are too lazy to put on the walking shoes. The average person simply doesn't know what's out there.

While people like Ronald Elward take the trouble to research and find out about our own heritage, the relevant authorities could do their part: What about some basic signs around the city? How about letting tourists and locals know what we have? We could be so much happier.

So far, the Lima Walks are conducted in English, Dutch and German only. "Spanish will come later," Elward adds with a smile, "once limeños start believing in the city they have."

AMUSEMENT PARK

Amusement park and theme park are terms for a group of rides and other entertainment attractions assembled for the purpose of entertaining large numbers of people. An amusement park is more elaborate than a simple city park or playground, usually providing attractions meant to cater to children, teenagers, and adults.

Amusement parks evolved in Europe from fairs and pleasure gardens which were created for people's recreation. The oldest amusement park in the world (opened 1583) is Bakken, at Klampenborg, north of Copenhagen, Denmark. In the United States, world's fairs and expositions were another influence on development of the amusement park industry.

Most amusement parks have a fixed location, as compared to traveling funfairs and carnivals. These temporary types of amusement parks are usually present for a few days or weeks per year, such as funfairs in the United Kingdom, and carnivals (temporarily set up in a vacant lot or parking lots) and fairs (temporarily operated in a fair ground) in the United States. The temporary nature of these fairs helps to convey the feeling that people are in a different place or time.

In common language, Theme Park is often used as a synonym for the term 'Amusement Park'. A 'Theme Park' is actually a distinct style of amusement park, for a theme park has landscaping, buildings, and attractions that are based on one or more specific or central themes. A plurality of themes are not required to be considered a 'Theme' park. Despite the long history of amusement parks, where many parks have traditionally incorporated themes into the evolving design and operation of the park, qualifying a park as a theme park, the first park built with the original intension of promoting a specific (or exclusive set of) theme(s), Santa Claus Land (currently known as Holiday World & Splashin' Safari) located in Santa Claus, Indiana, did not open until 1946. Disneyland, located in Anaheim, California, built around the concept of encapsulating multiple theme parks into a single amusement park is often mistakenly noted as the first themed amusement park.

Periodic fairs, such as the Bartholomew Fair which began in England in 1543, are a parent for the modern amusement park. Beginning in the Elizabethan period the fair had evolved into a center of amusement with entertainment, food, games, and carnival-like freak-show attractions. The seasonal celebration was a natural place for development of amusement attractions.

Oktoberfest is not only a beer festival but also provided amusement park features beginning in 1810, when the first event was held in Munich, Germany. In the United States, the county and state fairs also played a part in the history of amusement parks. These were annual events that were usually held for a short time, a week or two, to celebrate a good harvest. These fairs featured livestock exhibits, baking and cooking competitions.

Amusement parks also grew out of the pleasure gardens that became especially popular at the beginning of the Industrial revolution as an area where one could escape from the grim urban environment. The oldest intact still-surviving amusement park in the world (opened 1583) is Bakken ("The Hill") at Klampenborg, north of Copenhagen, Denmark. The most well known of the parks in London, was Vauxhall Gardens founded in 1661 and closed in 1859. Another long-standing park is Prater in Vienna, Austria, which opened in 1766.

This park was conceived as a place where the common person could enjoy a respite in a pastoral setting and participate in the musical culture of the city. Tivoli Gardens, Copenhagen is another example of a European park, dating from 1843, which still exists. These parks consisted of booths, entertainment, fireworks displays and some "rides" such as introduction to the modern railroad. The parks grew to accommodate the expectations of their customers—who were increasingly familiar with the mechanical wonders of industrialization. Rides became a required part of the pleasure garden and by 1896 there were 65 such pleasure parks in London.

Another type of fair is the exposition or world's fair. World's fairs began in 1851 with the construction of the landmark Crystal Palace in London, England. The purpose of the exposition was to celebrate the industrial achievement of the nations of the world (of which Britain just so happened to be the leader). America cities and business saw the world's fair as a way of demonstrating economic and industrial success.

People particularly point to the World's Columbian Exposition of 1893 in Chicago, Illinois as an early precursor to the modern amusement park. This fair was an enclosed site that merged entertainment, engineering and education to entertain the masses. It set out to bedazzle the visitors, and successfully did so with a blaze of lights from the "White City." To make sure that the fair was a financial success, the planners included a dedicated amusement concessions area called the Midway Plaisance.

Rides from this fair captured imagination of the visitors and of amusement parks around the world, such as the first steel Ferris wheel, which was found in many other amusement areas, such as the Prater by 1896. Also, the experience of the enclosed ideal city with wonder, rides, culture and progress (electricity), was based on the creation of an illusory place. Certainly the precursor of the amusement park experience to come.

The "midway" introduced at the Columbian Exposition would become a standard part of most amusement parks, fairs, carnivals and circuses. The midway contained not only the rides, but other concessions and entertainments such as shooting galleries, penny arcades, games of chance and shows.

Trolley Parks, Atlantic City, and Coney Island

In the final decade of the 19th century, the electric trolley lines were developed in most of the larger American cities. Companies that established the trolley lines were directly responsible for establishing amusement parks — trolley parks — as destinations of these lines. Trolley parks like Atlanta's Ponce de Leon Park, or Reading's Carsonia Park were initially popular natural leisure spots before local streetcar companies purchased the sites, expanding them from picnic groves to include regular entertainments, mechanical amusements, dance halls, sports fields, boats rides, restaurants and other resort facilities. Various sources report the existence of between 1500 and 2000 amusement parks in the United States by 1919.

Some of these parks were developed in resort locations, such as bathing resorts at the seaside in New Jersey and New York. A premiere example in New Jersey was Atlantic City, a then famed bathing resort. Enterprisers erected amusement parks on piers that extended from the boardwalk out over the ocean. The first of several was Ocean Pier in 1891, followed later by Steel Pier in 1898, both of which boasted rides and attractions typical of that time, such as Midway-style games and electric trolley rides. The boardwalk also had the first Roundabout installed in 1892 by William Somers, a wooden predecessor to the Ferris Wheel. Somers installed two others in Asbury Park and Coney Island.

Other such parks were found along rivers and lakes that provided bathing and water sports such as Riverside Park in Massachusetts, which was founded along the Connecticut River in the 1840s, and Lake Compounce in Connecticut, first established as a bathing beach in 1846.

Another such location was Coney Island in Brooklyn, New York, where a horse-drawn streetcar line brought pleasure seekers to the beach beginning in 1829. In 1875, a million passengers rode the Coney Island Railroad, and in 1876 two million reached Coney Island. Hotels and amusements were built to accommodate both the upper-classes and the working-class.

The first carousel was installed in the 1870s, the first roller coaster, the "Switchback Railway", in 1884. It wasn't till 1895 that the first permanent amusement park in North America opened: Sea Lion Park at Coney Island in Brooklyn. This park was one of the first to charge admission to get into the park in addition to sell tickets for rides within the park.

In 1897, Sea Lion Park was joined by Steeplechase Park, the first of three major amusement parks that would open in the Coney

Island area. George Tilyou designed the park to provide thrills and sweep away the restraints of the Victorian crowds. The combination of the nearby population center of New York City and the ease of access to the area made Coney Island the embodiment of the American amusement park.

Often, it is Steeplechase Park that comes to mind when one generically thinks of the heyday of Coney Island, but there was also Luna Park (opened in 1903), and Dreamland (opened in 1904). Coney Island was a huge success and by year 1910 attendance on a Sunday could reach a million people. Fueled by the efforts of Frederick Ingersoll, other "Luna Parks" (starting with ones in Pittsburgh and Cleveland in 1905) were quickly erected worldwide and opened to rave reviews.

Fire was a constant threat in those days, as much of the construction within the amusement parks of the era was wooden. In 1911, Dreamland was the first Coney Island amusement park to completely burn down; in 1944, Luna Park also burned to the ground. Most of Ingersoll's Luna Parks were similarly destroyed (usually by arson) before his death in 1927.

The "Golden Age" of Amusement Parks

During the Gilded Age, many Americans began working fewer hours and had more disposable income. With new-found money and time to spend on leisure activities, Americans sought new venues for entertainment. Amusement parks, set up outside major cities and in rural areas, emerged to meet this new economic opportunity.

These parks reflected the mechanization and efficiency of industrialization while serving as source of fantasy and escape from real life. By the early 1900s, hundreds of amusement parks were operating in the United States and Canada.

Trolley parks (established at the end of the trolley linc by enterprising streetcar companies) stood outside many cities. Parks like Atlanta's Ponce de Leon and Idora Park near Youngstown, OH took passengers to traditionally popular picnic grounds, which by the late 1890s also often included rides like the Giant Swing, Carousel, and Shoot-the-Chutes. These amusement parks were often based on nationally-known parks or world's fairs: they had names like Coney Island, White City, Luna Park, or Dreamland. The American Gilded Age was, in fact, amusement parks' "golden age" that reigned until the late 1920s.

The Golden Age of amusement parks also included the advent of the kiddie park. Founded in 1925, the original Kiddie Park is located in San Antonio, Texas and is still in operation today. The Kiddie Parks became popular all over America after World War II.

This era saw the development of the new innovations in roller coasters that encouraged extreme drops and speeds to thrill the riders. By the end of the First World War, people seemed to want an even more exciting entertainment, a need met by the roller coasters. Although the development of the automobile provided people with more options for satisfying their entertainment needs, the amusement parks after the war continued to be successful, while urban amusement parks saw declining attendance. The 1920s is more properly known as the "Golden Age" of roller coasters, being the decade of frenetic building of these rides.

Depression and Post-World War II Decline

The Great Depression of the 1930s and World War II during the 1940s saw the decline of the amusement park industry. War saw the affluent urban population move to the suburbs, television became a source of entertainment, and families went to amusement parks less often.

By the 1950s, factors such as urban decay, crime, and even desegregation in the ghettos led to changing patterns in how people chose to spend their free time. Many of the older, traditional amusement parks closed or burned to the ground. Many would be taken out by the wrecking ball to make way for suburban living and development. In 1964, Steeplechase Park, once the king of all amusement parks, closed down for good. The traditional amusement parks which survived, for example, Kennywood, in West Mifflin, Pennsylvania, and Cedar Point, in Sandusky, Ohio, did so in spite of the odds.

The Modern Amusement Park

First parks devoted to a particular theme are precursors for the modern amusement park. A Blackgang Chine amusement park, established in 1843 by Victorian entrepreneur Alexander Dabell, on the Isle of Wight, UK can be considered the oldest existing theme park in the world. The first amusement park on Coney Island, Sea Lion Park was built around a nautical theme.

Modern amusement parks now run differently than those of years past. Amusement parks are usually owned by a large corporate conglomerate which allows capital investment unknown by the traditional family-owned parks. Starting with Disneyland in the 1950s, the park experience became part of a larger package, reflected in a television show, movies, lunch boxes, action figures and finally park rides and costumed characters that make up the "theme." These parks offer an ideal world that serves as an escape from the daily grind.

The thrills of the theme parks are often obscured from the outside by high fences or barriers re-enforcing the feeling of escape, they are kept clean and new thrill rides are frequently added to keep people coming back. In addition to this experience, the theme park is either based on a central theme or, divided into several distinctly themed areas, lands or "spaces." Large resorts, such as Walt Disney World in Florida (United States), actually house several different theme parks within their confines.

Today, central Florida and most notably Orlando boasts more theme parks than any other worldwide destination. The northeastern USA region, most notably Pennsylvania, is now a hotbed of traditional surviving amusement parks. In its truest traditional form is Conneaut Lake Park in Conneaut Lake, Pennsylvania. Others include Hersheypark in Hershey, Pennsylvania, Knoebels Groves in Elysburg, Pennsylvania; Kennywood in West Mifflin, Pennsylvania; Idlewild Park in Ligonier, Pennsylvania; Lakemont Park in Altoona, Pennsylvania; Dorney Park & Wildwater Kingdom in Allentown, Pennsylvania; Waldameer Park in Erie, Pennsylvania; and DelGrosso's Amusement Park in Tipton, Pennsylvania.

EDUCATIONAL THEME PARKS

Other parks use outdoor attractions for educational purposes. Epcot center is well known, but there are also Holy Land USA and the Holy Land Experience are theme parks built to inspire Christian piety, Dinosaur World entertains families with dinosaurs in natural settings.

Family-owned Theme Parks

Some theme parks did evolve from more traditional amusement park enterprises, such as Knott's Berry Farm. In the 1920s, Walter Knott and his family sold berries from a roadside stand, which grew to include a restaurant serving fried chicken dinners. Within a few years, lines outside the restaurant were often several hours long. To entertain the waiting crowds, Walter Knott built a Ghost Town in 1940, using buildings relocated from real old west towns such as the Calico, California ghost town and Prescott, Arizona. In 1968, the Knott family fenced the farm, charged admission for the first time, and Knott's Berry Farm officially became an amusement park.

Because of its long history, Knott's Berry Farm currently claims to be "America's First Theme Park." Knott's Berry Farm is now owned by Cedar Fair Entertainment Company. Lake Compounce in Bristol, Connecticut may be the true oldest continuously operating amusement park in the United States, open since 1846

Santa Claus Town, which opened in Santa Claus, Indiana in 1935 and included Santa's Candy Castle and other Santa Claus-themed attractions, is considered the first themed attraction in the United States: a pre-cursor to the modern day theme park. Santa Claus Land (renamed Holiday World in 1984) opened in 1946 in Santa Claus, Indiana and many people will argue that it was the first true Theme Park despite Knott's history.

In the 1950s the Herschend family took over operation of the tourist attraction, Marvel Cave near Branson, Missouri. Over the next decade they modernized the cave, which led to large numbers of people waiting to take the tour. The Herschend family opened a recreation of the old mining town that once existed atop Marvel Cave. The small village eventually became the theme park, Silver Dollar City. The park is still owned and operated by the Herschends and the family has several other parks including Dollywood, Celebration City and Wild Adventures.

Other theme parks include: Children's Fairyland opened in 1950 in Oakland, California. Another variation of the theme park were the animal theme parks that reintroduced the concept of Sea Lion Park such as Marineland of the Pacific which opened in 1954 which paved the way for SeaWorld parks which eventually added thrill rides.

Disneyland and the Corporate-owned Park

Walt Disney, however, is often credited with having originated the concept of the themed amusement park, although he was obviously influenced by Knotts Berry Farm owned by Walter Knott (at the time owner of Calico Ghost town) who brought buildings from Calico to increase business at his berry stand located in nearby Buena Park, CA, as well as Tivoli Gardens in Copenhagen Disney took these influences and melded them with the popular Disney animated characters and his unique vision, and "Disneyland" was born. Disneyland officially opened in Anaheim, California in 1955 and changed the amusement industry forever. Key to the design process of Disney's new park was the replacement of architects with art directors from the film industry.

The years in which Disneyland opened were a sort of stopgap period for the amusement park industry, as many of the older, traditional amusement parks had already closed and many were close to closing their doors. Cedar Point was set to be torn down in the 1950s when local businesspeople were intrigued by the success of Disneyland and saved it from destruction.

Other parks were not as lucky, with Steeplechase Park at Coney Island closing in 1964; Riverview Park, Chicago, closed in 1967. Some traditional parks were able to borrow a page from Disneyland and use television to its advantage, such as Kennywood, a park started in 1898 and continuing to operate to the present which used television advertising and featured television personalities at the park.

The first regional theme park, as well as the first Six Flags park, Six Flags over Texas was officially opened in 1961 in Arlington, Texas near Dallas. The first Six Flags theme park was the vision of Angus Wynne, Jr. and helped create the modern, competitive theme park industry. By 1968, the second Six Flags park, Six Flags Over Georgia, opened, and in 1971, Six Flags Over Mid-America (now Six Flags St. Louis) opened near St. Louis, MIssouri. Also in 1971 was the opening of the Walt Disney World resort complex in Florida, which is still the largest theme park and resort complex in the world with the Magic Kingdom (1971), Epcot (1982), Disney's Hollywood Studios (1989) and Disney's Animal Kingdom (1998).

During the 1970s, the theme park industry started to mature as a combination of revitalized traditional amusement parks and new ventures funded by larger corporations emerged. Magic Mountain (now a Six Flags park) opened in Valencia, California. Regional parks such as Cedar Point and Kings Island, popular amusement parks in Ohio, moved towards the more modern theme park-concept as well as rotating new roller coasters and modern thrill rides.

Also during the mid-1970s, Marriott Corporation built two identical theme parks named "Great America" in northern California and Illinois. The former is now California's Great America and is owned by Cedar Fair, L.P., which now also owns Kings Island and Cedar Point; and the latter is now Six Flags Great America. Many theme parks were hit badly by the Arab oil embargo of 1973 and a number of planned theme parks were scrapped during this time. Most of today's major amusement parks were built in the 1970s.

Perhaps the most indirect evolution of an attraction into a full-fledged theme park is that of Universal Studios Hollywood. Originally just a backlot tram ride tour of the actual studios in Hollywood, the train ride that started in 1964 slowly evolved into a larger attraction with a western stunt show in 1967, "The Parting of the Red Sea" in 1973, a look at props from the movie *Jaws* in 1975, and the *"Conan the Barbarian"* show in 1984. By 1985, the modern era of the Universal Studios Hollywood theme park began with the "King Kong" ride and, in 1990, Universal Studios Florida in Orlando opened. Universal Studios is now the third-largest theme park company in the world, behind Disney and Merlin.

Present and Future of Amusement Parks

Since the 1980s, the amusement park industry has become larger than ever before, with everything from large, worldwide type theme parks such as Disneyworld and Universal Studios Hollywood to smaller and medium-sized theme parks such as the Six Flags parks and countless smaller ventures in many of the states of the U.S. and in countries around the world. Even simpler theme parks directly aimed at smaller children have emerged, including Legoland opened in 1999 in Carlsbad, California (the first Legoland opened in 1968 in Billund, Denmark). The only limit to future theme park ventures is one's imagination.

Amusement parks in shopping malls began in the 1990s, blending traditional amusement park entertainments—roller coasters, water parks, carousels, and live entertainment—with hotels, movie theaters, and shopping facilities. Examples of giant mall parks are West Edmonton Mall, Alberta, Canada; Pier 39, San Francisco; Mall of America, Bloomington, Minnesota.

Amusement park owners are also aware of the need to satisfy their aging baby boomer customer base with more restaurants, landscaping, gardens and live entertainment. Kennywood has created in 1995 the "Lost Kennywood" area with classic rides that recall the possibly more tranquil times of the early twentieth century. In 2001, Disney opened the Disney's California Adventure which includes Paradise Pier, a recreation of the traditional seaside amusement park of yesteryear.

Family fun parks starting as miniature golf courses have begun to grow to include batting cages, go-karts, bumper cars, bumper boats and water slides. Some of these parks have grown to include even roller coasters, and traditional amusement parks now also have these competition areas in addition to their thrill rides.

The popularity of theme parks has led to the increase of theming — "the use of an overarching theme, such as western, to create a holistic and integrated spatial organization of a consumer venue" — in non-theme park venues. While theme restaurants, casinos, and other themed spaces lack the rides and other features of theme parks, they owe much to the legacy of the theme lands and spatial organization that became popular in theme parks.

For several years, there have been the emergence of a new type of theme parks, in which roller coasters are replaced by shows such as Médinat Alzahra in Tunisia and Puy du Fou in France (dealing with History).

Although domestic visitors still make up around 80 percent of admissions to theme and amusement parks, an aging population in the U.S. and a slowing economy in 2008 are forcing The Walt Disney Company and its competitors to seek their fortunes in emerging tourist markets such as in the Middle East and in China. The Walt Disney Company, accounts for around half of the total industry's revenue in the US as a result of more than 50 million adventure seekers pouring through the gates of its U.S.-based attractions each year.

Admission Prices and Admission Policies

Amusement parks collect much of their revenue from admission fees paid by guests attending the park. Other revenue sources include parking fees, food and beverage sales and souvenirs.

Practically all amusement parks operate using one of two admission principles:

Pay-as-you-go

In this format, a guest enters the park at little or no charge. The guest must then purchase rides individually, either at the attraction's entrance or by purchasing ride tickets (or a similar exchange method, like a token). The cost of the attraction is often based on its complexity or popularity. For example, a guest might pay one ticket to ride a carousel but four tickets to ride a roller coaster. The park may allow guests to purchase unlimited admissions to all attractions within the park. A wristband or pass is then shown at the attraction entrance to gain admission.

Disneyland opened in 1955 using the pay-as-you-go format. Initially, guests paid the ride admission fees at the attractions. Within a short time, the problems of handling such large amounts of coins led to the development of a ticket system that, while now out of use, is still part of the amusement-park lexicon. In this new format, guests purchased ticket books that contained a number of tickets, labeled "A," "B" and "C." Rides and attractions using an "A-ticket" were generally simple, with "B-tickets" and "C-tickets" used for the larger, more popular rides. Later, the "D-ticket" was added, then finally the now-famous "E-ticket", which was used on the biggest and most elaborate rides, like Space Mountain. Smaller tickets could be traded up for use on larger rides (i.e., two or three A-tickets would equal a single B-ticket). Disneyland, as well as the Magic Kingdom at Walt Disney World, abandoned this practice in 1982.

The advantages of pay-as-you-go include the following:

- guests pay for only what they choose to experience
- attraction costs can be changed easily to encourage use or capitalize on popularity

The disadvantages of pay-as-you-go include the following:

- guests may get tired of spending money almost continuously
- guests may not spend as much on food or souvenirs

Pay-one-price

An amusement park using the pay-one-price format will charge guests a single, large admission fee. The guest is then entitled to use all or more often almost all of the attractions in the park as often as they wish during their visit. The park usually has some attractions that are not included in the admission charge; these are called "up-charge attractions" and can include bungee jumping or go-kart tracks or games of skill. However, the majority of the park's attractions are included in the admission cost.

The "pay-one-price" ticket was first used by George Tilyou at Steeplechase Park, Coney Island in 1897. The entrance fee was \$0.25 for entrance to the 15-acre (61,000 m^2) park and visitors could enjoy all of the attractions as much as they wanted.

When Angus Wynne, founder of Six Flags Over Texas, first visited Disneyland in 1959, he noted that park's pay-as-you-go format as a reason to make his park pay-one-price. He thought that a family would be more likely to visit his park if they knew, up front, how much it would cost to attend.

The advantages of pay-one-price include:

- guests can more easily budget their visit
- guests may be more likely to experience an attraction they've already paid for
- lower costs for the park operators, since ticket-takers are not needed at each attractions

The disadvantages of pay-one-price include:

- guests will often be paying for attractions that they do not ride or visit
- guests who are simply coming just to be with their families will have to pay anyway

Today's modern theme parks typically charge a single admission fee for admission and unlimited use of attractions, rides, and shows, where as most modern amusement parks offer free admission yet charge separate fees per attraction.

Rides and Attractions

Mechanized thrill machines are what makes an amusement park out of a pastoral, relaxing picnic grove or retreat. Earliest rides include the carousel which was originally developed as a way of practicing and then showing-off expertise at tournament skills such as riding and spearing the ring.

By the 19th century, carousels were common in parks around the world. Another such ride which shaped the future of the amusement park was the roller coaster. Beginning as a winter sport in 17th century Russia, these gravity driven railroads were the beginning of the search for even more thrilling amusement park rides. The Columbian Exposition of 1893 was a particular fertile testing ground for amusement rides. The Ferris wheel is the most recognized product of the fair. Many rides are set round a theme.

Thrill Rides

There is a core set of thrill rides which most amusement parks have, including the enterprise, tilt-a-whirl, the gravitron, chairswing, swinging inverter ship, twister, and the top spin. However, there is constant innovation, with new variations on ways to spin and throw passengers around appearing in an effort to keep attracting customers.

Roller Coasters

Since the late 19th century, amusement parks have featured roller coasters. Roller coasters feature steep drops, sharp curves, and inversions. Roller coasters may be the most attractive aspect of a park, but many people come for other reasons. Amusement parks generally have anywhere from two to seven coasters, depending on space and budget. As of 2009, the record for the most coasters in one park is held by Cedar Point with 17; followed by Six Flags Magic Mountain with 16, and Canada's Wonderland with 15.

Train Rides

Amusement park trains have had long and varied history in American amusement parks as well as overseas.

According to various websites and historians,[who?] the earliest park trains weren't really trains—they were trolleys. The earliest park trains were mostly custom built. Some of the most common manufacturers were:

- Allan Herschfield
- Cagney Brothers
- Chance Rides (C.P. Huntington Train)
- Crown Metal Products
- Custom Locomotives
- Miniature Train Co. (MTC)
- The National Amusement Devices Co.(NAD)
- Ottaway
- Sandley

Water Rides

Amusement parks with water resources generally feature a few water rides, such as the log flume, bumper boats, rapids and rowing boats. Such rides are usually gentler and shorter than roller coasters and many are suitable for all ages. Water rides are especially popular on hot days.

Dark Rides

Overlapping with both train rides and water rides, dark rides are enclosed attractions in which patrons travel in guided vehicles along a predetermined path, through an array of illuminated scenes which may include lighting effects, animation, other special effects, music and recorded dialogue.

Transport Rides

Transport rides are used to take large amounts of guests from one area in the park to another. They usually cost extra, even in parks where rides are free. They are generally popular as they offer an alternative to walking . Transport rides include chairlifts, monorails, and train rides.

Food and Drink

Amusement parks generate a portion of their income through the sale of food and drink to their patrons. Food is routinely sold through food booths, push carts and indoor restaurants. The offerings vary as widely as the amusement parks themselves, and range from common fast food items, like hamburgers, hot dogs, cotton candy, candy apples, donuts and local street foods up to full-service gourmet dishes. Amusement parks with exotic themes may include specialty items or delicacies related to the park's theme. Many restaurants and food stands are operated by the amusement parks themselves, while others are branches of regional or national chains.

Funfair

A funfair or simply "fair" is a small to medium sized traveling show primarily composed of stalls and other amusements. Larger fairs such as the permanent fairs of cities and seaside resorts might be called a *fairground*, although technically this should refer to the land where a fair is traditionally held. The word *fair* comes from the Latin word *feria*, meaning a holiday.

In the UK and much of Europe, individual rides and stalls are run by different, independent showmen who all converge for the duration of the fair, then often go their separate ways to set up at fairs in other towns.

In the United States, regional companies own large numbers of rides and games, and book schedules of fairs with multiple *units* of machinery and staff. They are typically on the road throughout a season that runs from mid-February through December, usually beginning in the southern US and traveling north as summer approaches, then becoming active again in the south with the arrival of cooler fall weather.

The relative costs and profitability of such long-distance operations are largely impacted by fuel prices; when prices are unusually high, smaller operators often resort to spending long stretches in shopping mall parking lots, drumming up what business they can as they accumulate additional funds, or wait for prices to fall.

Attractions

Fairs contain a mixture of attractions which can be divided into the categories of adult, teenager and child; usually including thrill rides, children's rides, sideshows and sidestalls. Originally a fair would also have had a significant number of market stalls, but today this is rare and most sidestalls only offer food or games. The first fairground rides began to appear in the eighteenth century, these were small and made out of wood and propelled by gangs of boys. In 1868, Frederick Savage, an agricultural engineer from Kings Lynn, devised a method of driving rides by steam. His invention, a steam engine mounted in the centre of the ride, transformed the fairground industry.

Thrill Rides

There is a core set of thrill rides which are common at fairs and which most funfairs have. These include the Sizzler Twist, The Gravitron, Booster, Freak Out, Miami and the Top Spin. There is constant innovation, with new variations on ways to spin and throw passengers around, in an effort to attract customers. With the requirement that rides be packed into one or more trailers for travel, there is a limit to the size of the rides, and funfairs struggle to compete with much larger attractions, such as roller coasters, found in amusement parks. See also amusement rides.

Roller Coasters

Some fairs may feature compact roller coasters to attract teenagers and preteens. Roller coasters feature steep drops, sharp curves, and sometimes loops. Roller coasters are generally the most attractive aspect of a fair, but many people come for other reasons. Fairs usually only feature one or two coasters.

Children's Rides

Funfairs are seen as family entertainment, and most include a significant number of children's rides designed for children from 2 – 10 years old. Many of these are smaller, slower versions of the adult rides, such as merry-go-rounds, teacup rides and Ferris wheels. Such rides are usually referred to as "kiddie rides" or "juveniles". Others are simple train rides, slides, mirror mazes and variations on the bouncy castle.

Sideshows

In the 19th century, before the development of mechanical attractions, sideshows were the mainstay of most funfairs. Typical shows included menageries of wild animals, freak shows, wax works, boxing/wrestling challenges and theatrical shows.

Up until the 1960s, boxing shows were a common feature of British fairs, but they went into decline when in 1947 the British Boxing Board of Control prohibited appearances of licensed members in fairground boxing booths. An echo of the boxing booth remains with boxing or punch ball machines being common around fairgrounds. The very last travelling boxing booth was still making annual visits to the Great Dorset Steam Fair until 2006. The owner, Ronnie Taylor, died a few weeks before the 2006 show, and the future of this unique attraction is uncertain.

After World War II, sideshows featuring burlesque and striptease performances also declined with the general relaxation of censorship legislation.

Sidestalls and Games

Most stalls feature games of skill or strength. The most traditional example being the coconut shy in which players throw balls at coconuts balanced on posts, winning the coconut if they manage to dislodge it.

Other sidestalls range from the trivially easy, such as hooking rubber ducks from a water trough in which nearly every player is expected to win a prize, to the deceptively challenging, which includes games which utilize optical illusions or physical relationships that are difficult to judge. In the United States, the funfair is one of the few arenas of public life in which classical hoodwinkery in the form of outright fraud can be perpetrated by the light of day. Highly profitable (and therefore timeless) games include:

- the hoopla, in which a ring can be demonstrated to fit neatly around a wooden block, but when the customer attempts to throw the ring over the block, it is nearly impossible to achieve the perfect angle which the attendant deftly demonstrates. This game is similar to quoits and horseshoe pitching.
- ball-in-the-basket games in which the basket is presented at an angle almost certain to bounce the ball out. (The basket bottom may also be suspiciously springy.)

- basketball-shooting games in which the basket is ovoid in shape and tne basketball literally cannot fit inside the rim under any circumstances, but takes advantage of the oval shape an individual expects to see when directly confronted by a circle presented at an angle nearly parallel with the ground. (The sides of such a game are walled with netting which presumably keeps the ball in play, but the netting is typically covered with the prizes the customer hopes to win, which block the view of the basket from the side and thus exposing the hoax.) Sometimes the basketballs are also inflated to their full capacity, thus allowing the ball to bounce off of the hoop more easily.
- archery, air rifles, and paint ball guns with sometimes misaligned sights, with targets ranging from bullseyes to playing cards.

Much of the true "con artistry" has been driven out of funfairs in the twentieth century, and combined with an increasing emphasis on the role of families and small children in such entertainment, contemporary showmen often find greater profit in pricing their games far above the value of the prizes being offered, with complex formulae for upgrading to the large prizes that advertise the game and instill desire among customers. The rises in pricing of many sidestalls must often reflect the overheads of running fairground equipment - the cost of swag (see below), diesel, staff and rents.

Typical prizes change to reflect popular tastes. A traditional fairground prize used to be a goldfish in a small plastic bag, but these have fallen out of favor, partly because goldfish are no longer seen as exotic, but also because of animal welfare concerns. Many stalls offer cuddly toys as prizes — many teenage romances are established at funfairs, where thrill rides provide ample excuse for embracing. Displays of skill at shooting and winning a cuddly toy for your girlfriend is a rite of passage for many young men. In showland, the prizes are known as swag and are supplied by a swagman.

Food Booths

Food is routinely sold through food booths and the offerings range from common fast food items to indigenous street food, and may include specialty items or delicacies depending on the nature of the festival and availability of ingredients.

In North America and Europe a funfair generally includes:

- Pizza
- Hot dogs
- Corn dogs
- Hamburgers
- Fried chicken
- French fries
- Funnel cake
- Cotton candy
- Ice cream
- Fried dough
- Nachos
- Popcorn
- Giant Pretzels
- Candy Apples
- Lollipops
- Soda

British Funfairs

In the United Kingdom, many larger towns host travelling fairs at specific times of the year (for example Mop Fairs). Frequently the fairground is on an area of common land and has a history extending back to the Middle Ages. For example, St Giles' Fair has been held in St Giles', Oxford since the consecration of St Giles' Church in 1200. In Cambridge, the Midsummer Fair is held on Midsummer Common, an ancient area of common land to the northeast of the city centre.

Funfairs in England, Scotland and Wales are not the property of one owner, but a collaborative effort between families of fairground travellers. Descended from the medieval strollers and players of mainly Romani descent who have followed this way of life for generations, they have a distinct culture related to their trade and nomadic existence. The routes they travel are usually inherited and are much the same from year to year.

The average fairground is made up when a Lessee (usually the owner of a large ride) sublets ground and pitches to other showmen who bring their own rides, stalls and shows to make up a fair. This may involve negotiation and bargaining over who gets to put their stalls and rides where, although in many well established fairs 'standing rights' are recognized and passed down through the generations.

Once the fair is over, the families go their separate ways, but will cross each other's paths regularly. Their sense of community is strong and few 'marry out' of the trade. Showmen, as they are known, are proud of their heritage and have their own language, Parlyaree (a mixture of Lingua Franca, Romani, Yiddish, Thieves' Cant, sailor slang, and backslang) e.g. words such as *flatty* or *joskin* (meaning someone not from the showman community). Those showmen who don't travel with the fair still remain showmen, being said just to be settled down. The community is clannish and somewhat insular, the received wisdom being that one cannot just become a showman, but must be born into it.

This by definition makes running fairgrounds a family business, and family names are synonymous with fairgrounds in certain areas. e.g. Breeze, Hirst, Fleming, Vanner, Hatwell, Atha, Danter, Marshalls, etc., in the North, and Thurston's, Stocks, Harris and Hedges in the South. The Show/Fairground community is close knit, with multiple ties often existing between the older families and a vibrant social scene centered both around the summer fairs and the various sites and yards used as winter quarters.

Hosting an estimated 80% of all Scottish showfamilies, Glasgow is believed to have the largest concentration of Showmen in winter quarters in Europe, centered mostly in Whiteinch, Shettleston and Carntyne. However, new zoning laws and planning difficulties posed by Glasgow City Council look set to push many of these long-established facilities out of the city in the near future.

Since the late 19th century, fairgrounds in the UK have been run by a guild known as the Showmen's Guild of Great Britain. This lays down rules for managing and running fairs, helps them organize fairs and settle member disputes and serves to protect them from deleterious legislation. Unusual for an industrial body, membership is awarded exclusively on a hereditary basis.

A new breed of showmen is now appearing. These people are usually fairground enthusiasts and can own preserved older rides. They are connected to the Show communities around Britain but only loosely and they, therefore, have their own organizations such as the Society of Independent Roundabout Proprietors.

Fairgrounds are common at British seaside resorts, usually run by travelling fairground families who have decided to settle down, in whole or part. Showmen who run fair equipment at the seaside are referred to as sand scratchers.

An interesting annual attraction in the North Wales resort of Llandudno is the *Victorian Extravaganza* held over the May Day Bank Holiday weekend.

In regard to confectionery, candy floss stalls are especially associated with funfairs. Sweets are known as fairings and include such things as brandy snaps, toffee apples and at Nottingham Goose Fair, cocks on sticks. Of savoury food, the mainstays are hot dogs, burgers and, in the Midlands and the North of England, hot peas served with mint sauce.

Fairgrounds have sharply declined in popularity over the last few decades, although many families continue to follow their unusual lifestyle.

The largest British (and European) fairground is The Hoppings on Newcastle Town Moor, which is held annually in the last two weeks of June. The second largest fair, the largest travelling fair, is Nottingham Goose Fair held annually in October.

Historically, travelling showmen and the gypsy community had close links, necessitated by the heavy reliance of the business on horsepower. Intermarrying and sharing the same land was not uncommon, although they remained two distinct groups. Nowadays, however, there is often friction between the two communities, and travelling showmen have been known to distance themselves from the gypsy community (by not using Polari, for example) because they feel that the negative stereotype that the British public holds towards the gypsy community could adversely affect their business. The word "gypsy" is often used to refer to travelling showmen, but it is not a phrase that they would use to refer to themselves (the usual term is "traveller") and in fact many would regard this as a slur.

German Funfairs

Most things said about British funfairs apply to Germany. Rides include roller coasters, dark rides and log flumes that often eclipse many theme park equivalents in terms of both size and quality. The language of German showmen contains elements of Sintitikes, Rotwelsch, Yiddish and other old minority languages. Their children are almost always sent to a small set of showmen-friendly boarding schools where they can remain in contact with other showmen's children; during school holidays, they travel with their parents.

In the west of the country, there is some overlap with Dutch showmen. A relatively small number of "showmen dynasties" run most of the medium- to large size amusement rides at funfairs around the country. There have been some allegations of forced marriages among them in recent years.

In Catholic areas of the country, it is still customary for most villages and small towns to hold their annual funfair on or near the saint's day of the patron saint of the local church.

Very common are the so called "Volksfeste", which are mainly held in the larger cities. They consist of a funfair and a beer festival at the same place. The largest and best known of them is the Oktoberfest in Munich, the largest fair of the world. The second largest is the Cranger Kirmes in Herne in the eastern part of the Ruhr Area. Another famous "Volksfest" is the Cannstatter Wasen in Stuttgart and the Rheinkirmes in Düsseldorf. One of the oldest is the Annaberger Kät held in the Ore Mountains of East Germany since 1520.

Canadian Funfairs (exhibitions)

North America's (and the world's) largest, and one of longest running exhibitions is Toronto's Canadian National Exhibition, it takes place at Exhibition Place from late August to early September. Most carnival fairs are run by traveling companies that move town to town with their rides and exhibits. Conklin Shows is the largest and oldest organization of its type in North America.Other notable fairs are the Pacific National Exhibition in Vancouver and the Calgary Stampede.

Tent Boxing

Tent boxing, an amusement commonly seen at agricultural shows throughout Australia between the 1920s and the 1960s is an old Australian tradition that is barely kept alive today. Born in England, now banned in America, the outback is today the only place such an attraction can survive.

Traveling boxing troupes of professional fighters would travel the mining towns and outback of the country, following fairs and carnivals, putting up big top tents and taking on all-comers for cash in the ring.

Among the more famous of tent boxing troupes, are Roy Bell's, Jimmy Sharman's and lastly, Fred Brophy's, which today is the last surviving tent boxing troupe in the world. Fred Brophy, who owns the Cracow Hotel in Cracow, Queensland, still travels with his troupe across Australia with his wife, Sandi, and son, Fred Brophy Jnr- the world's only fourth generation tent boxer.

Only Jimmy Sharman's troupe travelled for longer, starting his famous boxing troupe in Wagga Wagga in 1911 and touring the shows and country towns for six decades.

A Dangerous Sport

Largely unreported on, little is known about early tent boxers and events due to participants and spectators being largely illiterate. In more modern times, very few photographs exist of the movement as organisers disapprove of media involvement.

Fred Brophy insists he will continue travelling with his tent boxing troupe, until he dies, even though the sport was banned in 1971 by the government, due to health concerns.

In 2010, filmmaker Mark Shea made an online film about Brophy's Troupe for Australia's National Broadcaster, the ABC.

In 2011, a new documentary on Fred Brophy's final boxing tour in 2010 will air on the Special Broadcasting Service (SBS). Produced by Isabel Perez under production company Mindful Media, the 2-part documentary is written and directed by Paul Scott. Episode one premieres on Tuesday, January 11th at 8:30pm while part two will air on Tuesday, January 18th at 8:30pm.

Traveling Carnival

A traveling carnival is an amusement show that may be made up of amusement rides, food vendors, merchandise vendors, games of chance and skill, thrill acts, animal acts or sideshow curiosities. A traveling carnival is not set up at a permanent location, like an amusement park, but is moved from place to place. Its roots are similar to the 19th century circus with both being set up in open fields near or in town and moving to a new location after a period of time. Unlike traditional carnival celebrations, the North American traveling carnival is not usually tied to a religious observance.

In 1893 the Chicago's World's Columbian Exposition (also called the Chicago World's Fair) was the catalyst for the development of the traveling carnival. The Chicago World's Fair had an area that included rides, games of chance, freak shows and burlesque. After the Chicago World's Fair, traveling carnival companies began touring the United States. Due to the type of acts featured along with sometimes using dishonest business practices, the traveling carnivals were often looked down upon.

Modern traveling carnivals play both state and county fairs along with smaller venues such as church bazaars, volunteer fire department fund raisers and civic celebrations. Traditionally, on the evening of the last day of the events, the sponsoring organization will often pay for a fireworks display that signals the end of the day's festivities.

Through most of the history of the 19th century, rural North America enjoyed the entertainment of traveling shows. These shows could include a circus, vaudeville show, burlesque show or a magic lantern show. It is believed that the 1893 Chicago World's Fair was the catalyst that brought about the modern traveling carnival. At the Chicago World's Fair was an avenue at the edge of the grounds called the Midway Plaisance. This avenue of the fair had games of chance, freak shows, wild west shows (including Buffalo Bill whose show was set up near the fairground) and burlesque shows. It also featured the first Ferris wheel constructed by George Washington Gale Ferris, Jr. Following the Chicago World's Fair, the term "midway" was adopted from the Midway Plaisance to denote the area at county and state fairs where sideshow entertainment was located.

Otto Schmitt, who was a showman at the world's fair, formed Chicago Midway Plaisance Amusement Company. The company featured thirteen acts, including some from the World's Fair, and began a tour of the northeast United States. His company closed due to poor business practices before completing their first tour. Some members of his company formed their own successful traveling carnivals after Otto Schmitt's company closed .

The appeal of this new type of entertainment was embraced. In 1902 there were seventeen traveling carnivals in the United States. The number grew to forty-six in 1905 and by 1937 there was an estimated 300 carnivals touring the country. One such show, The "IT Shows" set up yearly on probably every empty sandlot in NY's Brooklyn,Queens and surrounds.

Carnival Operations

Worldwide there are many different traveling carnival companies. Most carnivals are not made up of just one operator of rides, food or games. Many of these venues are operated by independent owners who contract (or "book") with the carnival. These independent owners are contract to pay the carnival operator a percentage of what their ride or stand gross in sales. A large carnival operator, however, usually owns the majority of the rides and possibly a few special interest items (i.e. food wagons or games) with the rest being booked with the independents.

Many carnival operators are so big that they have carnival "Units" or divisions. Each of these Units may consist of six or more major rides. By having these units a carnival operator can have a carnival operating in many different areas during the same week.

Transporting carnival rides and stands are generally done by truck. The rides generally have wheels mounted on the base and the rest of the ride is then dismantled and folded up to allow for over the road transport. Food stands are usually tow-behind trailers, although there are still some booths that require complete take down and packing. Some large carnival operators use the railroad to transport their equipment from one location to another.

A traveling carnival operator may schedule their carnival for certain seasons. They will have their carnivals in warm climate southern areas and then move into northern regions during the warmer months. A traditional winter home is Florida for carnival operators. Gibsonton, Florida became a famous winter home community for carnival workers (slang term: carny) to live.

Admission is free to many carnivals. A larger carnival, at an events like county and state fair, may charge an admission fee. Tickets or all-day passes are usually sold for rides. Exhibits or displays may charge their own entry fee. Some entertainment acts (such as a music concert, tractor pulling or a demolition derby) may also require the purchase of a separate ticket to see them.

Carnival Food

At many carnivals, there are also concessionaires who run food stands. Depending on the size of the carnival, there may be one or more concessionaires on site. These independent concessionaires, like the independent ride owners, "book" their stands with the carnival operator or venue. The food stands serve a variety of food and beverages. Some examples are snack items like cotton candy, ice cream, fried dough, funnel cake, candy or caramel apples and french fries.

Meal items may include pizza, hamburgers, hot dogs and chicken. Beverages may include soda, coffee, tea and lemonade. Local and regional specialties, along with ethnic foods, are often available at carnivals. Many carnivals, as of the early 2000s, offer Empanadas and Tacos. At Autumn carnivals, drinks like hot cider or hot chocolate may be featured along with harvest items.

Items like deep fried candy bars, the deep-fried Twinkie, Dippin' Dots ice cream and the blooming onion are some of the food items found at a carnival.

Carnival Games

At many traveling carnivals are games of chance and skill. Games like the "Crossbow Shoot" game or the "Balloon and Darts" game will test an individuals target shooting ability. Other games, such as the "Water gun" game, will pit a group of individuals against each other to win the game. Chance is involved in games like the "Duck Pond" game or the "Pingpong Ball and Fishbowl" game. Most games offer a small prize to the winner. Prizes may be stuffed animals, toys, posters, etc. Continued play is encouraged as multiple small prizes may traded in for a larger prize. Some more difficult games, including the "Baseball and Basket" or "Stand the Bottle" game, may offer a large prize to any winner.

While the majority of game operators run honest games, some people are wary of carnival games. This may be because carnival games in the past gained a reputation for being dishonest. It is interesting to note the term **"mark"** (slang term: "sucker") originated with the carnival.

When dishonest carnival game operators found someone who they could entice to keep playing their "rigged" (slang term: "gaffed") game, they would then **"mark"** the player by patting their back with a hand that had chalk on it. Other game operators would then look for these chalk marks and entice the individual to also play their rigged game. In many areas, local law enforcement will test the carnival games prior to and during the carnival to help eliminate rigged games. Learning about how carnival games work can help an individual from being cheated.

Carnival Rides

Many traveling carnivals bring with them an assortment of rides. Some rides are for young children and may include a carousel, ridable miniature railway, miniature roller coaster or an inflatable bounce house. For older children and adults there can be many different types of rides. These rides are designed to use height, speed, g-force or centrifugal force to appeal to the riders' senses. Some examples are the Chair-O-Planes, Ferris wheel, Zipper ride and the Tilt-A-Whirl.

Carnival rides are generally painted in bright vibrant colors such as red, yellow and orange. Multicolored lighting is also used to enhance the rides' appearance at night. Each ride also plays its own music: a carousel may have calliope music playing while the ride next to it may have rock music for its riders. The music for each ride is usually upbeat; however, a ride such as a ghost train will have more somber music.

These rides are designed to be quickly set up and taken down, thus helping the carnival operator in moving them. All state governments inspect carnival rides before the start of the carnival to insure the safety of the riders. In the past, many traveling carnivals also had a sideshow that accompanied them. Admission to see these curosites or exhibits was an extra fee. Some sideshows featured a single exhibit, but there were sideshows that had multiple act or exhibits under one tent.

Human acts may include people with multiple arms or legs, midgets, extremely tall people, obese people, people born with facial or other deformities, and tattooed people. The term used for this type of show was called a freak show. Animals oddities such as the two headed calf, the dwarf miniature horse, etc. were featured in the freak show as well. Changing public opinions and increased medical knowledge have led to a decline of these type of shows.

CONTEMPORARY URBAN TOURISM

For a long time, tourism was associated with centrifugal flows of urban residents going to the countryside or the seaside for a holiday or an excursion. The concept of urban tourism only entered the research agenda in the 1980s, when it became obvious that many cities were developing into important destinations. Business travel and city trips have always existed, but the leisure motives have become more important and the numbers of urban tourists have increased considerably.

The delay of interest in urban tourism can be explained by a neglect in urban studies to assess the importance of leisure, recreation and tourism in an urban environment. Further, there was a lack of understanding of the urban tourism system. The difficulty of separating this from non-tourism functions in the wide range of urban activities and the tendency to explore the issue of urban tourism in case studies rather than by conceptual studies have contributed to the slow progress of urban tourism research.

Contrary to other destinations, where the product (the supply side) as well as the range of activities could be well described, in the multifunctional urban system the identification of the tourism function and the multipurpose character of many visits is far more complicated.

Understanding urban tourism and the product life cycle of urban destinations implies an integrated approach in the analysis of forms and functions. Research into new methods to identify the role of tourism and tourists in the urban environment is now in full progress and is the objective of many comparative studies.

The recent popularity of publications on urban tourism covers aspects such as trends in demand, creating urban attractions and clusters, urban planning and policy issues, impact studies, product-place marketing and resource and visitor management. The concepts which were introduced to understand tourism as a system needed to be adapted to the urban context. Cities can be seen as a spatially concentrated spectrum of opportunities (the Tourist Opportunity Spectrum, also referred to as recreation opportunity spectrum) in which one can distinguish core elements and secondary elements.

The first group refers to the mix of attractions which are unique and interesting and thus capable of attracting tourists to the place, whereas the second group includes the range of urban facilities which support the touristic experience, without being a first motive for the visit. The group of primary elements of the urban product includes both the setting of the place (urban morphology, built heritage, green spaces, waterfronts) and the offer of facilities which allow for different activities, such as the cultural resources (museums, theatres, exhibition halls and so on), sport facilities, the amusement sector (such as casinos and theme parks) and the agenda of festivals and events.

These core attractions are supported by facilities in the hospitality sector (hotels, restaurants, pubs) and in the retail trade, including shopping facilities and street markets. The latter group can be considered to be the added value to the urban tourist experience. In some cities, the shopping opportunities are becoming so attractive to the extent that they can be considered as a core product for the market of shopping tourism (the Mall of America in Minneapolis, USA, is quickly assuming this core position).

In most cities the core products belong to the public domain, whereas the supporting facilities result from initiatives in the private sector. This interdependency partners is typical for the supply side of the urban tourism product.

Historic cities, in particular, hold many opportunities to develop tourism products based on cultural heritage resources. The trend towards tourismification of cultural heritage responds to a growing market for cultural tourism. The markets for city trips and for cultural tourism and shopping tourism are growing and are strongly interrelated. Several surveys indicate in the ranking of motives of urban tourists, the predominant role of visiting a unique and interesting place. Visiting museums, discovering interesting architecture, learning about the history of a place and, above all, seeing the well-known landmarks have become important aspects in the experience. This type of behaviour is typical for city trips and short breaks and also penetrates in the market of business travel. However, distinguishing the market segments in urban tourism remains a difficult exercise because of the complexity of motives and behaviour patterns.

Seeing the high potentials of urban tourism and the wide range of facilities which benefit from such earnings, many cities are now exploring the possibilities of developing tourism as a lever to diversify and stimulate for the urban economy. This has become a key instrument in many urban revitalisation projects, in urban waterfront development plans, in the upgrading of cultural activities (such as festivals and events), in the conservation of historical heritage and even an incentive to redesign urban shopping areas. The success of the urban product mix has even led to a stage of saturation in the product life cycle of several historic cities. The issue of carrying capacity and sustainable development has become a major concern in urban management policies. In addition, this market of urban destinations, particularly in Europe, is becoming highly competitive. The traditional top destinations such as London and Paris are now competing with numerous 'new' urban choices, such as Berlin, Barcelona, Munich, Prague and Dublin.

Gradually the focus of tourism research is moving from the place-marketing issues towards a discussion on resource and management strategies. The competitive advantage and, as such, the chances of the sustainability of the urban forms and function now lie in developing cultural tourism products with a strong local identity (sense of place capacity) and with the image of uniqueness and authenticity, despite the strong globalisation trends in the tourism market.

The combination of sustainable development in which the physical and social impacts of tourism can be monitored and the economic benefits optimised requires a new approach in urban planning, a strategic marketing and management policy and a better understanding of the touristic experiences in the urban environment. Understanding the synergy between tourism activities and other urban functions is necessary in order to develop and sustain urban destinations of a high quality both for these temporary and permanent populations.

Throughout the nineteenth century, American cities experienced a great surge in tourism as they grew to become great metropolises. During the early 1800s, the tourist industry targeted wealthier people because this was the only group that could afford to travel for pleasure. After the mid-1800s, however, the middle class became interested in urban travel as well as they grew more prosperous and as the cities themselves became more accessible due to the usage of sight-seeing cars and trolleys. Essential to this transformation was the city guidebook, which changed the way people viewed American cities. First, they attempted to personify urban areas by characterizing them with unique "personalities."

Second, they emphasized the beauty of the city's architecture, likening it to the natural splendor of the countryside. Third, the guidebooks tended to create for each city a "heroic history," highlighting its importance in both local and national history. Lastly, they promoted trips to ethnic localities in these urban areas, downplaying the class and ethnic conflicts of the time. The city guidebook was a microcosm of the greater tourist industry, representing its nationalization and the rise of the American consumer culture-.

IN YOUR POCKET CITY GUIDES

In Your Pocket (IYP) is a European city guide publisher and online tourist information provider. As of April 2008 it publishes city guides to 68 destinations and provides free online information to over 100 cities in 23 countries in Europe, from Athens to Zurich, Ljubljana, Belfast to Bucharest, Tallinn to Tirana and St. Petersburg to Sofia.

Distributed locally, mainly in hotels and newsstands, the entire content of most guides can also be downloaded from the website free of charge as a PDF document which allows travellers to read and print out the full guide before departure.

The first In Your Pocket city guide, *Vilnius In Your Pocket* was written in late 1991 by German journalist Matthias Lüfkens and Belgian brothers George, Oliver and Nicolas Ortiz in Vilnius, Lithuania.

Since then the four founders have franchised the *In Your Pocket* guides, which cover key tourist cities as well as obscure off-beat destinations such as Athens, Belfast, Berlin, Bra°ov, Bucharest, Èeský Krumlov, Derry, Dublin, Dubrovnik, Frankfurt, Gdañsk, Gdynia, Haapsalu, Kaliningrad, Kaunas, Kiev, Klaipëda, Korça, Kraków, Leipzig, Liepaja, Ljubljana, £ódŸ, Lviv, Minsk, Moscow, Narva, Odessa, Palanga, Pärnu, Peæ, Poiana Bra°ov, Poznan, Prague, Pristina, Prizren, Riga, Rijeka, s'Hertogenbosch, Shkodra, Siauliai, Sofia, Sopot, Saint Petersburg, Tallinn, Tarnów, Tartu, Tirana, Utrecht, Vilnius, Warsaw, Wroc³aw, Zadar, Zagreb and Zurich.

In June 2006 *In Your Pocket* published print and online city guides to all the Football World Cup venues in Germany.

In September 2010 *In Your Pocket* published its first iPhone applications. They are currently available in 20 cities.

The guidebooks have received much praise in the international media.

The International Herald Tribune described them as *"an Eastern European publishing phenomenon"*

The Times claimed there are *"The best guides to Eastern Europe"*

, adding that *"the website is a (literally) priceless first stop before your holiday"*

. The New York Times notes it is *"a good all-around information site"*

The Independent lists their website among the *"ten best travel websites"* because *"the writers/compilers live locally and the guides are frequently updated"*

. The Guardian observes that *"InYourPocket.com was the first online travel guide to come up with the idea of offering free downloadable city guides in printable (PDF) format."*

noting that it *"is a brilliant resource written by excellent writers whose slant is always 'off the trail'."*

The Observer says it is *"the most reliable source"*

The guides are frequently mentioned in traditional guidesbooks such as Lonely Planet, Let's Go Travel Guides or Rough Guides

The city guidebook was an important development in the tourist industry and changed the way people viewed American cities. In the 1870s, companies published increasing numbers of these guidebooks. Based on the travel writings and urban descriptions from earlier in the century, they introduced new ways of approaching and getting around the city. City guidebooks distinguished tourists as a social group separate from city residents. This is because they allowed visitors to appreciate the city as a site of leisure without having to experience the aggravations of daily life.

Guidebooks attempted to portray a city as having its own distinct "personality," which derived from its setting and manmade environment as well as the overall character of its citizens. Describing urban areas with respect to these aspects gave potential visitors a single, unique reason to travel there. For example, one author states, "Soaring skyscrapers, frenetic hustle, and up-to-dateness stood for New York and its residents."

Therefore, if one wanted to experience these characteristics firsthand, then he or she would know to travel to New York City. This personality became evident to tourists through the city's fast-paced lifestyle, but during the Hudson-Fulton Celebration of 1909, New York wanted to present itself as a city of history and culture.

During the 1800s, city landscapes were seen more and more to be as beautiful as the natural scenery of the countryside. Guidebooks and postcards illustrated instantly recognizable skylines, which tourists were eager to view from the observation decks of tall buildings. Tourists were also able to get quick and closer looks at the architecture of a city's buildings through new forms of mass transportation, such as the stagecoach.

On Fifth Avenue, stagecoaches allowed visitors to gawk at the opulent mansions of some the city's wealthiest residents. Though riding some modes of public transportation forced tourists to experience the social and physical discomforts of urban life (such as overpopulation), the tourist industry began to use sightseeing cars and trolleys. These vehicles were specifically designed for tourists. They did not follow the regular routes of residents between work and home and instead brought tourists to popular landmarks and commercial areas.

The formation of a heroic history and the romanticization of ethnic minorities also greatly affected the American perspective of urban areas. Many cities publicized positive aspects of the past and emphasized the prominence of their roles in the nation's history. Furthermore, they downplayed class and ethnic conflicts in order to idealize their history and "peasantry." By doing so, they attempted to become more European because American cities wanted to be on the same rich cultural level as Europe.

Interest in creating a heroic history did not arise until after the Civil War. This event was the country's first national tragedy and forced Americans on both sides of the war to reflect on their struggles and sacrifices. Later, Decoration or Memorial Day was established to remember those who died in the war. Furthermore, prior to the Civil War, the United States was too new for most Americans to think about their history. Some citizens could still remember the birth of the nation in the late eighteenth century throughout a large part of the nineteenth century.

With the cultivation of a heroic history for major cities came the preservation of aging landmarks. While some people tried to cleanse and modernize city, others attempted to preserve historic buildings and other structures, and still others erected new public monuments celebrating significant moments and people from the past.

Historical walking tours became popular because they taught tourists forgotten aspects of a city's history. For example, one might learn on a walking tour the origins of the street names within a city. As a result of this effort to preserve cities, they were viewed as surviving artifacts rather than as mere locations or social organizations. New York City in 1909, for example, attempted to preserve and celebrate its Dutch roots.

The city's slums and ghettos were no longer seen as dangerous. Guidebooks for major cities noted companies specializing in slumming tours, which became more respectable fora broader range of people and therefore diminished the dangerous thrill that these less refined neighborhoods once offered. Residents of slums, who were typically immigrants, became commodities for the touring public. Guidebooks claimed that Little Italy and Chinatown were identical to actual cities in Italy and China, with the minorities who lived there representing natives from "exotic" countries.

Americans were curious about these foreign cultures and, bored with American food such as plainly cooked roasts, boiled and fried vegetables, fried and baked cakes and breads, they increasingly ate in ethnic restaurants. The commercialization of ethnic slumming and the romanticization of minorities relieved the boredom and stress of wealthy white Americans.

The structure of guidebooks transformed over time, reflecting the nationalization of the tourist industry as well as the emerging consumer culture. Earlier urban sketches were written from the perspective of aknown author who personally invited readers to experience the fine culture of a city with him. Such is the case with New Cosmopolis by James Huneker, a prominent American music writer and critic.

This chapter describes author's stay in New York and several European cities. Though it was published in 1915, it follows the guidebook format of the nineteenth century in which a well-known author invites readers to join him on his urban journey. An editor or publisher compiled later urban handbooks with certain economic and social interests. He tried to promote a particular business within the city. Even later, handbooks focused more on the tourist and the city's amusements and landmarks.

They stressed the importance of efficiency to the reader in order that he might be able to make the most out of his traveling experience. Though these later guidebooks were more accessible to a wider public, the identity of the author decreased in importance. Instead, the publisher greeted readers with a generic and formal voice.

One example of a city guidebook is the Historical Guide to the City of New York, which was compiled by Frank Bergen Kelley and published in 1909. The preface states that the book is "the result of prolonged efforts . . . to direct attention to the yet visible traces of earlier times which lie hidden within and are fast disappearing from the city today." Thus the historical fervor that came with the Hudson-Fulton Celebration of 1909 also affected New York's guidebooks. The Historical Guide gives in-depth historical narratives of different areas within the city, such as the Battery, Wall Street, Union Square, and Murray Hill. Like this book, the next section of this essay will take the reader on a "historical walking tour" of 1909 Fifth Avenue, a road imperative not only to New York's tourist industry, but also to the city's history, culture, and its development as a metropolis.

Global City

A global city is also called world city or sometimes alpha city or world center. It is a city deemed to be an important node point in the global economic system. The concept comes from geography and urban studies and rests on the idea that globalization can be understood as largely created, facilitated and enacted in strategic geographic locales according to a hierarchy of importance to the operation of the global system of finance and trade.

The most complex of these entities is the "global city", whereby the linkages binding a city have a direct and tangible effect on global affairs through socio-economic means. The terminology of "global city", as opposed to megacity, was *popularized* (not coined or invented) by the sociologist Saskia Sassen in reference to her 1991 work, "*The Global City: New York, London, Tokyo*" though the term "world city" to describe cities which control a disproportionate amount of global business dates to at least May 1886, to a description of Liverpool by the *Illustrated London News*. Patrick Geddes also used the term "world city" later in 1915. Cities can fall from such categorization, as in the case of cities that have become less cosmopolitan and less internationally renowned in the current era, e.g., Kaliningrad, Russia; Thessaloniki, Greece; and Alexandria, Egypt.

Global City or world city status is seen as beneficial, and because of this many groups have tried to classify and rank which cities are seen as 'world cities' or 'non-world cities'. Although there is a consensus upon leading world cities, the criteria upon which a classification is made can affect which other cities are included. The criteria for identification tend either to be based on a "yardstick value" ("e.g., if the producer-service sector is the largest sector, then city X is a world city") or on an "imminent determination" ("if the producer-service sector of city X is greater than the producer-service sector of N other cities, then city X is a world city").

Economic Characteristics

The New York Stock Exchange

- Corporate headquarters for multinational corporations, international financial institutions, law firms, conglomerates, and stock exchanges that have influence over the world economy.
- Significant financial capacity/output: city/regional GDP
- Stock market indices/market capitalisation
- Financial service provision; e.g., banks, accountancy
- Costs of living personal wealth; e.g., number of billionaires

Political Characteristics

- Active influence on and participation in international events and world affairs; for example, Washington, London, Paris, Tokyo, Berlin, Rome, Moscow, or Beijing are major capitals of influential nations or unions.
- Hosting headquarters for international organizations (World Bank), NATO headquarters
- A large proper, population of the municipality (the centre of a metropolitan area, typically several million) or agglomeration
- Diverse demographic constituencies based on various indicators: population, habitat, mobility, and urbanisation
- Quality of life standards or city development
- Expatriate communities

Cultural Characteristics

- International, first-name familiarity. For example, New York City is commonly referred to as just "New York" without needing to specify that it is in the state of New York or even the United States.
- Renowned cultural institutions (often with high endowments), such as notable museums and galleries, notable opera, orchestras, notable film centres and theatre centres. A lively cultural scene, including film festivals (such as the Toronto International Film Festival), premieres, a thriving music scene, nightlife, an opera company, art galleries, street performers, and annual parades.
- Several influential media outlets with an international reach, such as the BBC, Reuters, *The New York Times*, or Agence France-Presse.
- A strong sporting community, including major sports facilities, home teams in major league sports, and the ability and historical experience to host international sporting events such as the Olympic Games, FIFA World Cup, or Grand Slam tennis events.
- Educational institutions; e.g., universities, international student attendance, research facilities
- Sites of pilgrimage for world religions (for example, Mecca, Jerusalem or Rome)
- Cities containing World Heritage Sites of historical and cultural significance
- Tourism throughput
- City as site or subject in Arts and Media, television, film, video games, music, literature, magazines, articles, documentary
- City as an often repeated historic reference, showcase, or symbolic actions

Infrastructural Characteristics

- An advanced transportation system that includes several highways and/or a large mass transit network offering multiple modes of transportation (rapid transit, light rail, regional rail, ferry, or bus), for example the London Underground.

- Extensive and popular mass transit systems, prominent rail usage, road vehicle usage, major seaports
- A major international airport that serves as an established hub for several international airlines, for example, London. Airports with significant passenger traffic and international passengers traffic or cargo movements.
- An advanced communications infrastructure on which modern trans-national corporations rely, such as fiberoptics, Wi-Fi networks, cellular phone services, and other high-speed lines of communications. For example, Seoul and Tokyo are known as the digital and technology capitals of the world.
- Health facilities; e.g., hospitals, medical laboratories
- Prominent skylines/skyscrapers (for example Shanghai or Hong Kong)
- Cities' telephone and mail services, airport flights-range, traffic congestion, availability of water, train facilities, nearby parks, hospitals, libraries, police stations, etc.

Studies

GaWC Studies

The first attempt to define, categorize, and rank global cities using 'relational data' was made in 1998 by Jon Beaverstock, Richard G Smith and Peter Taylor, who all worked at that time at Loughborough University in the United Kingdom. Together they established the Globalization and World Cities Research Network. A roster of world cities was outlined in the *GaWC Research Bulletin* 5 and ranked cities based on their connectivity through four "advanced producer services": accountancy, advertising, banking/ finance, and law. The GaWC inventory identifies three levels of global cities and several sub-ranks. This roster generally denotes cities in which there are offices of certain multinational corporations providing financial and consulting services rather than denoting other cultural, political, and economic centres.

The 2004 rankings acknowledged several new indicators while continuing to rank city economics more heavily than political or cultural factors. The 2008 roster, similar to the 1998 version, is sorted into categories of "Alpha" world cities (with four sub-categories), "Beta" world cities (three sub-categories), "Gamma" world cities (three sub-categories), and additional cities with "High sufficiency" or "Sufficiency" world city presence.

The 2008 roster of leading Alpha, Beta and Gamma world cities is reproduced below; see the source for the complete roster:

- Alpha++ world cities:

  New York, London
- Alpha+ world cities:

  Hong Kong, Paris, Singapore, Tokyo, Sydney, Milan, Shanghai, Beijing
- Alpha world cities:

  Madrid, Moscow, Seoul, Toronto, Brussels, Buenos Aires, Mumbai, Kuala Lumpur, Chicago
- Alpha" world cities:

  Warsaw, São Paulo, Zurich, Amsterdam, Mexico City, Jakarta, Dublin, Bangkok, Taipei, Istanbul, Rome, Lisbon, Frankfurt am Main, Stockholm, Prague, Vienna, Budapest, Athens, Caracas, Auckland, Santiago, Los Angeles
- Beta+ world cities:

  Washington, Melbourne, Johannesburg, Tel Aviv, Barcelona, San Francisco, Atlanta, Manila, Bogotá, New Delhi, Dubai, Bucharest
- Beta world cities:

  Oslo, Berlin, Helsinki, Geneva, Copenhagen, Riyadh, Hamburg, Cairo, Luxembourg, Bangalore, Dallas, Kuwait City, Boston
- Beta" world cities:

  Munich, Jeddah, Miami, Lima, Kiev, Houston, Guangzhou, Beirut, Karachi, Düsseldorf, Sofia, Montevideo, Nicosia, Rio de Janeiro, Ho Chi Minh City
- Gamma+ world cities:

  Montreal, Nairobi, Bratislava, Panama City, Chennai, Brisbane, Casablanca, Denver, Quito, Stuttgart, Vancouver, Zagreb, Manama, Guatemala City, Cape Town, San José, Minneapolis, Santo Domingo, Seattle

- Gamma world cities:

  Ljubljana, Shenzhen, Perth, Kolkata, Guadalajara, Antwerp, Philadelphia, Rotterdam, Amman, Portland, Lagos

- Gamma" world cities:

  Detroit, Manchester, Wellington, Riga, Guayaquil, Edinburgh, Porto, San Salvador, St. Petersburg, Tallinn, Port Louis, San Diego, Islamabad, Birmingham, Doha, Calgary, Almaty, Columbus

Global Cities Index

In 2008, the American journal *Foreign Policy*, in conjunction with consulting firm A.T. Kearney and the Chicago Council on Global Affairs, published a ranking of global cities, based on consultation with Saskia Sassen, Witold Rybczynski, and others. *Foreign Policy* noted that "the world's biggest, most interconnected cities help set global agendas, weather transnational dangers, and serve as the hubs of global integration. They are the engines of growth for their countries and the gateways to the resources of their regions."

In 2010 the index was updated, and the top thirty ranked were:

Rank	City
1	New York City
2	London
3	Tokyo
4	Paris
5	Hong Kong
6	Chicago
7	Los Angeles
8	Singapore
9	Sydney
10	Seoul
11	Brussels
12	San Francisco
13	Washington, D.C.
14	Toronto

Rank	City
15	Beijing
16	Berlin
17	Madrid
18	Vienna
19	Boston
20	Frankfurt am Main
20	Shanghai
22	Buenos Aires
23	Stockholm
24	Zurich
25	Moscow
26	Barcelona
27	Dubai
28	Rome
29	Amsterdam
30	Mexico City

Global Power City Index

The Institute for Urban Strategies at The Mori Memorial Foundation in Tokyo, Japan issued a comprehensive study of global cities in 2009. The ranking is based on six overall categories, "Economy", "Research & Development", "Cultural Interaction", "Livability", "Ecology & Natural Environment", and "Accessibility", with 69 individual indicators among them. This Japanese ranking also breaks down top ten world cities ranked in subjective categories such as "manager, researcher, artist, visitor and resident."

Rank	City	Score	Best category (position)
1	New York City	330.4	Economy (1.) Research & Development (1.)
2	London	322.3	Cultural Interaction (1.)
3	Paris	317.8	Livability (1.) Accessibility (1.)

Rank	City	Score	Best category (position)
4	Tokyo	305.6	Economy (2.) Research & Development (2.)
5	Singapore	274.4	Economy (5.) Cultural Interaction (5.)
6	Berlin	259.3	Livability (2.)
7	Vienna	255.1	Ecology & Natural Environment (3.)
8	Amsterdam	250.5	Accessibility (3.)
9	Zurich	242.5	Ecology & Natural Environment (2.)
10	Hong Kong	242.5	Economy (4.)
11	Madrid	242.5	Ecology & Natural Environment (7.) Accessibility (7.)
12	Seoul	242.1	Research & Development (4.)
13	Los Angeles	240.0	Research & Development (5.)
14	Sydney	237.3	Ecology & Natural Environment (9.)
15	Toronto	234.6	Livability (5.)
16	Frankfurt am Main	232.9	Accessibility (5.)
17	Copenhagen	231.7	Economy (9.) Livability (9.)
18	Brussels	229.9	Livability (8.)
19	Geneva	229.7	Ecology & Natural Environment (1.)
20	Boston	226.2	Research & Development(6.)

World City Survey

In 2010 the London based consultant firm Knight Frank LLP together with the Citibank published a survey of world cities. The Wealth Report 2010, which includes the World City Survey, assesses four parameters - economic activity, political power, knowledge and influence and quality of life. The list aimed to rank the world's most influential cities. New York tops the list in Ecomomic activity, political power and knowledge and Paris tops it in quality of life. London and Paris get the same aggregate ranking of 149, making them de facto world's 2nd and 3rd most prominent cities.

Rank	City	Best category	Score
1	New York	Economic activity	151
2	London	Economic activity	149
3	Paris	Quality of life	149
4	Tokyo	Economic activity	144
5	Los Angeles	Knowledge and influence	122
6	Brussels	Political power	121
7	Singapore	Economic activity	119
8	Berlin	Quality of life	113
9	Beijing	Political power	113
10	Toronto	Quality of life	112
11	Chicago	Knowledge and influence	111
12	Washington, D.C.	Political power	111
13	Seoul	Economic activity	103
14	Hong Kong	Knowledge and influence	96
15	Frankfurt	Quality of life	96
16	Sydney	Knowledge and influence	92
17	San Francisco	Quality of life	90
18	Bangkok	Political power	83
19	Shanghai	Economic activity	83
20	Zurich	Quality of life	79

URBAN TOURISM AND POST-MODERNITY

A shopping mall, shopping centre, shopping precinct or simply mall is one or more buildings forming a complex of shops representing merchandisers, with interconnecting walkways enabling visitors to easily walk from unit to unit, along with a parking area – a modern, indoor version of the traditional marketplace.

Modern "car-friendly" strip malls developed from the 1920s, and shopping malls corresponded with the rise of suburban living in many parts of the Western World, especially the United States, after World War II. From early on, the design tended to be inward-facing, with malls following theories of how customers could best be enticed in a controlled environment. Similar, the concept of a mall having one or more "anchor" or "big box" stores was pioneered early, with individual stores or smaller-scale chain stores intended to benefit from the shoppers attracted by the big stores.

In most of the world the term *shopping centre* is used, especially in Europe, Australasia and South America; however *shopping mall* is also used, predominantly in North America and the Philippines. Outside of North America, *shopping precinct* and *shopping arcade* are also used. In North America, the term *shopping mall* is usually applied to enclosed retail structures (and is generally abbreviated to simply *mall*), while *shopping center* usually refers to open-air retail complexes; both types of facilities usually have large parking lots, face major traffic arterials and have few pedestrian connections to surrounding neighborhoods.

Superb Shopping arcade in Tokyo, Japan

Shopping centres in the United Kingdom can be referred to as "shopping centres", "shopping precincts", or "town centres". The standard British pronunciation of the word "mall" is as in *"The Mall, London"* – the tree-lined avenue leading to Buckingham Palace, London and also like *"pal"* (friend). *Mall* can refer to either a shopping mall – a place where a collection of shops all adjoin a pedestrian area – or an exclusively pedestrianised street that allows shoppers to walk without interference from vehicle traffic.

Mall is generally used in North America to refer to a large shopping area usually composed of a single building which contains multiple shops, usually "anchored" by one or more department stores surrounded by a parking lot, while the term *arcade* is more often used, especially in Britain, to refer to a narrow pedestrian-only street, often covered or between closely spaced buildings. A larger, often partly covered and exclusively pedestrian shopping area is in Britain also termed a *shopping centre*, *shopping precinct*, or *pedestrian precinct*.

The majority of British shopping centres are in town centres, usually inserted into old shopping districts and surrounded by subsidiary open air shopping streets. A number of large out-of-town "regional malls" such as Meadowhall, Sheffield and the Trafford Centre, Manchester were built in the 1980s and 1990s, but planning regulations prohibit the construction of any more.

Out-of-town shopping developments in the UK are now focused on retail parks, which consist of groups of warehouse style shops with individual entrances from outdoors. Planning policy prioritizes the development of existing town centres, although with patchy success. The MetroCentre, in Gateshead (near Newcastle upon Tyne), is the largest shopping centre in Europe with over 330 shops, 50 restaurants and an 11 screen cinema and Westfield London is the largest inner-city shopping centre in Europe. Bullring, Birmingham is the busiest shopping centre in the UK welcoming over 36.5 million shoppers in its opening year.

SHOPPING MALL IN PRESENT DAY

The first structure resembling what is considered to be a "shopping mall" in the present-day is located in The City of Damascus, the capital city of Syria. It is called Al-Hamidiyah Souq in old Damascus and dates back to the seventh century. Isfahan's Grand Bazaar, which is largely covered, dates from the 10th century. The 10 kilometer long covered Tehran's Grand Bazaar also has a long history. The Grand Bazaar of Istanbul was built in the 15th century and is still one of the largest covered markets in the world, with more than 58 streets and 4,000 shops.

Gostiny Dvor in St. Petersburg, which opened in 1785, may be regarded as one of the first purposely-built mall-type shopping complexes, as it consisted of more than 100 shops covering an area of over 53,000 m^2 (570,000 sq ft).

The Oxford Covered Market in Oxford, England opened in 1774 and still runs today. The Burlington Arcade in London was opened in 1819. The Arcade in Providence, Rhode Island introduced the retail arcade concept to the United States in 1828. This was a forerunner of today's shopping mall The Galleria Vittorio Emanuele II in Milan, Italy followed in the 1870s and is closer to large modern malls in spaciousness. Other large cities created arcades and shopping centres in the late 19th century and early 20th century, including the Cleveland Arcade, Dayton (Ohio) Arcade and Moscow's GUM, which opened in 1890. Early shopping centers designed for the automobile include Market Square, Lake Forest, Illinois (1916) and Country Club Plaza, Kansas City, Missouri (1924).

An early indoor mall prototype in the United States was the Lake View Store at Morgan Park, Duluth, Minnesota, which was built in 1915 and held its grand opening on July 20, 1916. The architect was Dean and Dean from Chicago and the building contractor was George H. Lounsberry from Duluth. The building is two stories with a full basement, and shops were originally located on all three levels. All of the stores were located within the interior of the mall; some shops were accessible from inside and out.

In the mid-20th century, with the rise of the suburb and automobile culture in the United States, a new style of shopping centre was created away from downtown.

Indoor Shopping Arcades

The Arcade of Cleveland was among the first indoor shopping arcades in the US and an architectural triumph. When the building opened in 1890, two sides of the arcade had 1,600 panes of glass set in iron framing.

An early shopping center in the United States was Country Club Plaza, which opened in 1924 in Kansas City, Missouri. Other important shopping centers built in the 1920s and early 1930s are the Highland Park Village in Dallas, Texas; River Oaks in Houston, Texas; and Park and Shop in Washington, D.C..

The suburban shopping mall, as Americans -and the world- came to know it, debuted in King County (Seattle), Washington in April 1950. Originally known as Northgate Center (now as Northgate Mall), it was an open-air complex of eighty stores and services, anchored by a Seattle-based The Bon Marche. This idea was quickly copied in several American cities, such as with Lakewood Center (1951), in Lakewood, California, Shoppers' World (1951), In Framingham, Massachusetts, Stonestown Center (now Stonestown Galleria) (1952) in San Francisco, California and Northland Center (1954), in Southfield, Michigan. Open-air-type malls were also built in Canada and Australia. Don Mills Convenience Centre (now Shops at Don Mills) opened in 1955, in Toronto, Ontario. Top Ryde Drive-In Shopping Centre (now Top Ryde City), started trading to the public in 1957, in the environs of Sydney, New South Wales.

The fully-enclosed shopping mall did not appear until the mid-1950s. The idea of a regional-sized, fully-enclosed shopping complex was pioneered in 1956 by the Austrian-born architect and American immigrant Victor Gruen. This new generation of regional-sized shopping centers began with the Gruen-designed Southdale Center, which opened in the Twin Cities suburb of Edina, Minnesota, USA in October 1956. For pioneering the soon-to-be enormously popular mall concept in this form, Gruen has been called the "most influential architect of the twentieth century".

The first retail complex to be promoted as a "mall," as it were, was Paramus, New Jersey's The Outlets at Bergen Town Center. The center, which opened with an open-air-format in 1957, was enclosed in 1973. Aside from Southdale Center, significant early enclosed shopping malls were Harundale Mall (1958), in Glen Burnie, Maryland, Big Town Mall (1959), in Mesquite, Texas, Chris-Town Mall (1961), in Phoenix, Arizona, and Randhurst Center (1962), in Mount Propect, Illinois.

The early malls moved retailing away from the dense, commercial downtowns into the largely residential suburbs. This formula (enclosed space with stores attached, away from downtown, and accessible only by automobile) became a popular way to build retail across the world. Gruen himself came to abhor this effect of his new design; he decried the creation of enormous "land wasting seas of parking" and the spread of suburban sprawl.

In the UK, Chrisp Street Market was the first pedestrian shopping area built with a road at the shop fronts. Developers such as Alfred Taubman of Taubman Centers extended the concept further, with terrazzo tiles at the Mall at Short Hills in New Jersey, indoor fountains, and two levels allowing a shopper to make a circuit of all the stores. Taubman believed carpeting increased friction, slowing down customers, so it was removed. Fading daylight through glass panels was supplemented by gradually increased electric lighting, making it seem like the afternoon was lasting longer, which encouraged shoppers to linger.

Ala Moana Center In Honolulu, Hawaii is currently the largest open-air mall in the world and was the largest mall in the states when it was built in 1957. It is currently the sixteenth largest in the country. The Outlets at Bergen Town Center, the oldest enclosed mall in New Jersey, opened in Paramus on November 14, 1957, with Dave Garroway, hcst of *The Today Show*, serving as master of ceremonies.

The mall, located just outside New York City, was planned in 1955 by Allied Stores to have 100 stores and 8,600 parking spaces in a 1,500,000 sq ft (139,000 m^2) mall that would include a 300,000 sq ft (28,000 m^2) Stern's store and two other 150,000 sq ft (14,000 m^2) department stores as part of the design. Allied's chairman B. Earl Puckett confidently announced The Outlets at Bergen Town Center as the largest of ten proposed centers, stating that there were 25 cities that could support such centers and that no more than 50 malls of this type would ever be built nationwide.

Largest Examples

The largest mall ever is South China Mall in Dongguan, China with gross floor area of 892,000 m^2 (9,600,000 sq ft). The world's second-largest shopping mall is the Golden Resources Mall in Beijing, China with gross floor area of 680,000 m^2 (7,300,000 sq ft). The SM City North EDSA in the Philippines, which opened in November 1985, is the world's third-largest at 460,000 m^2 (5,000,000 sq ft) of gross floor area, and SM Mall of Asia in the Philippines, opened in May 2006, is the world's fourth largest at 386,000 m^2 (4,150,000 sq ft) of gross floor area.

Previously, the title of the largest enclosed shopping mall was with the West Edmonton Mall in Edmonton, Alberta, Canada from 1986–2004. It is now the fifth largest mall. Two of the largest malls are in China, South China Mall and Jin Yuan. Dubai Mall is the largest mall in Middle East, currently ranked seventh in the world. The current largest shopping centre in Europe is the Dolce Vita Tejo in Lisbon, Portugal, while the largest in Australia is Chadstone Shopping Centre in Melbourne.

One of the world's largest shopping complexes in one location is the two-mall agglomeration of the Plaza at King of Prussia and the Court at King of Prussia in the Philadelphia suburb of King of Prussia, Pennsylvania, United States. The King of Prussia mall has the most shopping per square foot in the U.S.

The most visited shopping mall in the world and largest mall in the United States is the Mall of America, located near the Twin Cities in Bloomington, Minnesota. However, several Asian malls are advertised as having more visitors, including Mal Taman Anggrek, Kelapa Gading Mall and Pluit Village, all in Jakarta-Indonesia, Berjaya Times Square in Malaysia and SM Megamall in the Philippines. The largest mall in South Asia is Mantri Square in Bangalore, India.

Classes

In many cases, regional and super-regional malls exist as parts of large superstructures which often also include office space, residential space, amusement parks and so forth. This trend can be seen in the construction and design of many modern supermalls such as Cevahir Mall in Turkey. The International Council of Shopping Centers' 1999 definitions were not restricted to shopping centers in any particular country, but later editions were made specific to the U.S. with a separate set for Europe.

Regional

A regional mall is, per the International Council of Shopping Centers, in the United States, a shopping mall which is designed to service a larger area (15 miles) than a conventional shopping mall. As such, it is typically larger with 400,000 sq ft (37,000 m^2) to 800,000 sq ft (74,000 m^2) gross leasable area with at least two anchor stores and offers a wider selection of stores. Given their wider service area, these malls tend to have higher-end stores that need a larger area in order for their services to be profitable but may have discount department stores. Regional malls are also found as tourist attractions in vacation areas.

Super Regional

A super regional mall is, per the International Council of Shopping Centers, in the U.S. a shopping mall with over 800,000 sq ft (74,000 m^2) of gross leasable area, three or more anchors, mass merchant, more variety, fashion apparel, and serves as the dominant shopping venue for the region (25 miles) in which it is located.

Outlet

An outlet mall (or outlet centre) is a type of shopping mall in which manufacturers sell their products directly to the public through their own stores. Other stores in outlet malls are operated by retailers selling returned goods and discontinued products, often at heavily reduced prices. Outlet stores were found as early as

1936, but the first multi-store outlet mall, Vanity Fair, located in Reading, PA did not open until 1974. Belz Enterprises opened the first enclosed factory outlet mall in 1979, in Lakeland, TN, a suburb of Memphis.

HIGH STREET

High Street is a metonym for the generic name of the primary business street of towns or cities, especially in the United Kingdom. It is usually a focal point for shops and retailers in city centres, and is most often used in reference to retailing. However in recent times, the phrase "high street banks" has been widely used to refer to the retail banking sector in the United Kingdom.

High Street in Gillingham, Kent, England

Main Street is used in many smaller towns and villages. For example, the OSI North Leinster Town Maps book lists 16 Main Streets and only two High Streets in its index of street names (of 30 towns). Similarly, the OSI Dublin Street Guide, covering all of Dublin City and County Dublin, lists 20 Main Streets, but only two High Streets. Killarney is one of the few large Irish towns in which the shopping street is named High Street. Nonetheless, the term *high street* is still often used today in the Irish media in a generic sense to refer to shopping streets, in what could probably be considered as a misapplied metonym (see start of article).

The equivalent in the United States, Canada, and Ireland is Main Street, a term also used in smaller towns and villages in Scotland. In Jamaica, North East England, and some sections of Canada and the United States, the usual term is Front Street. In Cornwall and some places in Devon, the equivalent is Fore Street; in south Lancashire (historic county) the most common name for a "main street" is Market Street. In Canada King Street and Queen Street are often used instead of Main Street, which is more predominant in the United States

Fort William High Street, Scotland.

In recent years, although the term "High Street" is still used to refer to commerce, shopping has begun to shift to purpose-built out-of-town shopping centres and supermarkets. However compared to the United States town and city centre shopping remains widespread. The town centre of many larger British towns combines a group of outdoor shopping streets, one or more of which may be pedestrianised, with an adjacent indoor shopping centre.

High Street is the most common street name in the UK. According to a survey by the Halifax, there are 5,410 High Streets, compared to 3,811 Station Roads, and 2,702 Main Streets. Starting at least 10 centuries ago, the word 'high' gradually evolved to also mean something excellent or of superior rank, as evidenced in high sheriff and high society. It was applied to roads as they improved, and the word highway has been recorded from the early 9th century. "High Street" began to be used to describe the thoroughfares containing the main retail areas in villages and towns.

The large presence of chain stores on High Streets repeated in settlements around the UK is part of the clone town theory, which has among its concerns the loss of "sociability" offered by traditional shopping: "the demise of the small shop would mean that people will not just be disadvantaged in their role as consumers but also as members of communities – the erosion of small shops is viewed as the erosion of the 'social glue' that binds communities together, entrenching social exclusion in the UK."

Irish Usage

The term is far less common in Ireland. Neither of Dublin's two main shopping streets (Grafton Street and Henry Street) carry this name, nor does its main thoroughfare, O'Connell Street. While Dublin does indeed have a street named "High Street", near Christchurch, it is not a shopping street. Cork's main shopping street is St. Patrick's Street and Limerick's is also O'Connell Street, which is also used in a number of other Irish towns (after Daniel O'Connell).

Use

The term "High Street" is often used to describe common stores found on a typical high street, to differentiate them from more specialist or less common outlets. For example, someone might refer to "High Street banks" or "High Street shops".

Food Court

A common feature of shopping malls is a food court: this typically consists of a number of fast food vendors of various types, surrounding a shared seating area.

Department Stores

When the shopping mall format was developed by Victor Gruen in the mid-1950s, signing larger department stores was necessary for the financial stability of the projects, and to draw retail traffic that would result in visits to the smaller stores in the mall as well. These larger stores are termed anchor store or draw tenant. Anchors generally have their rents heavily discounted, and may even receive cash inducements from the mall to remain open. In physical configuration, anchor stores are normally located as far from each other as possible to maximize the amount of traffic from one anchor to another.

Stand-alone Stores

Frequently, a shopping mall or shopping center will have satellite buildings located either on the same tract of land or on one abutting it, on which will be located *stand-alone stores*, which may or may not be legally connected to the central facility through contract or ownership. These stores may have their own parking lots, or their lots may interconnect with those of the mall or center. The existence of the stand-alone store may have been planned by the mall's developer, or may have come about through opportunistic actions by others, but visually the central facility – the mall or shopping center – and the satellite buildings will often be perceived as being a single "unit", even in circumstances where the outlying buildings are not officially or legally connected to the mall in any way.

Dead Malls

In the U.S, as more modern facilities are built, many early malls have become abandoned, due to decreased traffic and tenancy. These "dead malls" have failed to attract new business and often sit unused for many years until restored or demolished. Interesting examples of architecture and urban design, these structures often attract people who explore and photograph them. This phenomenon of dead and dying malls is examined in detail by the website Deadmalls.com, which hosts many such photographs, as well as historical accounts. Until the mid-1990s, the trend was to build enclosed malls and to renovate older outdoor malls into enclosed ones. Such malls had advantages such as temperature control. Since then, the trend has turned and it is once again fashionable to build open-air malls. According to the International Council of Shopping Centers, only one new enclosed mall has been built in the United States since 2006.

Some enclosed malls have been opened up, such as the Sherman Oaks Galleria. In addition, some malls, when replacing an empty anchor location, have replaced the former anchor store building with the more modern outdoor design, leaving the remainder of the indoor mall intact, such as the Del Amo Fashion Center in Torrance, California.

New Trends

In parts of Canada, it is now rare for new shopping malls to be built. The Vaughan Mills Shopping Centre, opened in 2004, and Crossiron Mills, opened in 2009, are the only malls built in Canada since 1992. Outdoor outlet malls or big box shopping areas known as power centres are now favored, although the traditional enclosed shopping mall is still in demand by those seeking weather-protected, all-under-one-roof shopping. In addition the enclosed interconnections between downtown multi story shopping malls continue to grow in the Underground city of Montreal (32 kilometres of passageway), the PATH system of Toronto (27 km (17 mi) of passageway) and the Plus15 system of Calgary (16 km (9.9 mi) of overhead passageway).

Vertical Malls

High land prices in populous cities have led to the concept of the "vertical mall," in which space allocated to retail is configured over a number of stories accessible by elevators and/or escalators linking the different levels of the mall. The challenge of this type of mall is to overcome the natural tendency of shoppers to move horizontally and encourage shoppers to move upwards and downwards.

The concept of a vertical mall was originally conceived in the late 1960s by the Mafco Company, former shopping center development division of Marshall Field & Co. The Water Tower Place skyscraper, Chicago, Illinois, was built in 1975 by Urban Retail Properties. It contains a hotel, luxury condominiums, and office space and sits atop a block-long base containing an eight-level atrium-style retail mall that fronts on the Magnificent Mile.

Vertical malls are common in densely populated conurbations such as Hong Kong and Bangkok. Times Square in Hong Kong is a principal example. A vertical mall may also be built where the geography prevents building outward or there are other restrictions on construction, such as historical buildings or significant archeology.

The Darwin Shopping Centre and associated malls in Shrewsbury, UK, are built on the side of a steep hill, around the former outer walls of the nearby medieval castle; consequently the shopping centre is split over seven floors vertically – two locations horizontally – connected by elevators, escalators and bridge walkways. Some establishments incorporate such design into their layout, such as Shrewsbury's McDonalds restaurant, split into four stories with multiple mezzanines which feature medieval castle vaults – complete with arrowslits – in the basement dining rooms.

Shopping Property Management Firms

A shopping property management firm is a company that specializes in owning and managing shopping malls. Most shopping property management firms own at least 20 malls. Some firms use a similar naming scheme for most of their malls; for example, Mills Corporation puts "Mills" in most of their mall names and SM Prime Holdings of the Philippines puts "SM" in all of their malls, as well as anchor stores such as SM Department Store, SM Appliance Center, SM Hypermarket, SM Cinema, and SM Supermarket. In the UK, The Mall Fund changes the name of any centre they buy to *"The Mall (location)"*, using their pink-M logo; when they sell a mall it reverts to its own name and branding, such as the Ashley Centre in Epsom.

New Towns

Many new towns in the United Kingdom – including Livingston, Cumbernauld, Glenrothes, East Kilbride, Milton Keynes, Washington, Coventry, Newton Aycliffe, Peterlee and Telford – did not incorporate a traditional style town centre but instead developed a shopping centre. Unlike the shopping centres which were developing in established towns and cities, these also contained many civic functions and other community facilities such as libraries, pubs and community centres. As the towns grew, other facilities were usually developed around the centres, effectively enlarging the town centres.

Outlet Store

An outlet store or factory outlet is a brick and mortar or online retail store in which manufacturers sell their stock directly to the public. Traditionally, a factory outlet was a store attached to a factory or warehouse, sometimes allowing customers to watch the production process like in the original L.L. Bean store. In modern usage, outlet stores are typically manufacturer-branded stores like Gap grouped together in outlet malls. The invention of the factory outlet store is often credited to Harold Alfond, founder of the Dexter Shoe Company.

There may be variances in quality and price when comparing true factory stores with general outlet stores. The latter may have higher instances of manufacturers' "overruns" and unmarked seconds and blemished merchandise. Factory stores usually mark any seconds and blemished merchandise as such, and tend to offer newer models.

Plaza

Plaza is a Spanish word related to "field" which describes an open urban public space, such as a city square. All through Spanish America, the plaza mayor of each center of administration held three closely related institutions: the cathedral, the *cabildo* or administrative center, which might be incorporated in a wing of a governor's palace, and the *audiencia* or law court. The plaza might be large enough to serve as a military parade ground. At times of crisis or fiesta, it was the space where a large crowd might gather. Like the Italian piazza, the plaza remains a center of community life that is only equaled by the market-place.

Most colonial cities in Spanish America and the Philippines were planned around a square *plaza de armas*, where troops could be mustered, as the name implies, surrounded by the governor's palace and the main church. A *plaza de toros* is a bullring.

In modern usage, a plaza can be any gathering place on a street or between buildings, a street intersection with a statue, etc. Thus contemporary metropolitan landscapes often incorporate the "plaza" as a design element, or as an outcome of zoning regulations, building budgetary constraints, and the like. Sociologist William H. Whyte conducted an extensive study of plazas in New York City: his study humanized the way modern urban plazas are conceptualized, and helped usher in significant design changes in the making of plazas.

The Italian cognate is *Piazza*, the Portuguese *Praça*, the French *Place*, the Romanian *Piaa*, the German *Platz* and the Greek.

The first purpose-built shopping center in the United States, opened in Kansas City, Missouri in 1922, knowingly took the name of "Country Club Plaza" and adopted Spanish architectural details. More recently *plaza* has been used to describe a shopping complex, similar to a shopping mall, borrowing its connotations of a center of cultural life. The name is currently even applied to a single building with some semi-public street-level areas, often with a hotel or office tower above, while *mall* more often refers to multiple buildings or a street.

Lifestyle Center (retail)

A lifestyle center is a shopping center or mixed-used commercial development that combines the traditional retail functions of a shopping mall but with leisure amenities oriented towards upscale consumers. Lifestyle centers, which were first labeled as such by Memphis developers Poag and McEwen in the late 1980s and emerged as a retailing trend in the late 1990s, are sometimes labeled "boutique malls". They are often located in affluent suburban areas.

Lifestyle centers vs. traditional malls

The proliferation of lifestyle centers in the United States accelerated in the 2000s, with number going from 30 in 2002 to 120 at the end of 2004. Lifestyle centers are sometimes depicted as occupying the upscale end of the spectrum of commercial development, at the opposite end of the outlet mall, which typically caters to a wider range of income with bargain prices. The growth of lifestyle centers has occurred concurrently with an acceleration of the shutting down of traditional shopping malls, which typically require large sites over 70 acres (283,000 m²) at a time when land prices are escalating.

Lifestyle centers usually require less land and generate higher revenue margins, often generating close to 500 dollars per square foot, compared to an average of 330 dollars per square foot for a traditional mall, according to the president of Poag and McEwen. Other advantages lifestyle centers have over traditional enclosed malls are savings on heating and cooling and quicker access for busy customers. Typical amenities at lifestyle centers include plush chairs instead of traditional plastic seating in common areas.

Town Square

A town square is an open public space commonly found in the heart of a traditional town used for community gatherings. Other names for *town square* are *civic center*, *city square*, *urban square*, *market square*, *public square*, *town green*, *platz* (from German), *plaza* (from Spanish), *piazza* (from Italian), *place* (from French), *praça* (from Portuguese), *plac* (from Polish) and *maydan* (from Persian and Arabic).

Most town squares are hardscapes suitable for open markets, music concerts, political rallies, and other events that require firm ground. Being centrally located, town squares are usually surrounded by small shops such as bakeries, meat markets, cheese stores, and clothing stores. At their center is often a fountain, well, monument, or statue. Many of those with fountains are actually named Fountain Square.

Urban Planning

In urban planning, a city square or urban square is a planned open area in a city, usually or originally rectangular in shape. Some city squares are large enough that they act as a sort of "national square".

The first urban formations started appearing at least 6000 years ago. Within urban areas open public space always existed and it served a very important purpose. Along with the development of human society and the development of cities, the squares acquired more and more functions. At first, the squares were established at the crossroads of important trade routes where exchange of goods as well as ideas took place. For example, Phoenician trades–people invented numerical and linguistic pictographic inscriptions out of the need to record transactions. Another very important function of the public square was that it served as an opportunity to exercise the power of rulers with military processions and parades.

Wars and inventions of dangerous weapons, where the ambition was not only to capture women and goods, but to destroy enemies, led to cities surrounded by thick walls and elaborate systems of defense. These became very densely populated, but even under these conditions there was always room for an open public space. Its functions were expanding too. Major places of worship were placed there, squares were used as permanent or temporary markets, monuments to important predecessors were erected and revolutions or contra-revolutions were staged. The squares became the location of royal courts, government buildings and city halls as manifestations of wealth and power. They were also used for races, like the Palio race in Siena, bull fights, executions, or even just to collect rain water in large underground cisterns.

In recent times, theaters, restaurants and museums are also finding their place on the squares. Cities themselves, are actually becoming museums, a collection of human experiences that preserve numerous cultural values. Particularly since the invention of motorized traffic, the individual vehicle has almost destroyed most of the open public spaces. A car parking at one point had more value than the accumulated historical inheritance – human cooperation, technological processes, architectural and urban planning – that a square embodies.

Red Square in Moscow was originally used as an outdoor marketplace and later became the stage for Soviet military parades and May Day demonstrations.

Palace Square in St Petersburg was designed to be the central square of Imperial Russia and ironically became the setting of revolutionary protests that led to the overthrow of monarchy during the February Revolution of 1917.

Similarly, Beijing's Tiananmen Square was the scene of both communist parades and anti-government protests.

John-F.-Kennedy-Platz (formerly Rudolph-Wilde-Platz) was the site of the West Berlin town hall and John F. Kennedy's famous Ich bin ein Berliner speech.

New York City's Times Square as well as Bryant Park and Washington, D.C.'s National Mall often fill this role for the United States.

Trafalgar Square in London does the same for the United Kingdom.

Dundas Square in Toronto is a renowned and famous square in Canada.

Dam Square in Amsterdam for the Netherlands.

Three squares: Main Market Square, Kraków, Town Square in Piotrków Trybunalski and Castle Square, Warsaw for Poland.

The City Hall Square, Copenhagen for Denmark

Trg Republike, Belgrade for Serbia

USA

In the United States, a town square typically consists of a park or plaza in front of the original county courthouse or town hall. In some cities, especially in New England in the U.S., the term "square" (as its Spanish equivalent, *Plaza*) is applied to a commercial area (e.g., Central Square, Cambridge, Massachusetts), usually formed around the intersection of three or more streets, and which originally consisted of some open area (many of which have been filled in with traffic islands and other traffic calming features).

UNITED KINGDOM

In the United Kingdom, and especially in London and Edinburgh, a "square" has a wider meaning. There are public squares of the type described above but the term is also used for formal open spaces surrounded by houses with private gardens at the centre, sometimes known as garden squares.

Most of these were built in the 18th and 19th centuries. In some cases the gardens are now open to the public. See the Squares in London category. Additionally, many public squares were created in towns and cities across the UK as part of urban redevelopment following the blitz. Squares can also be quite small and resemble courtyards, especially in the City of London.

China

In Mainland China, People's Square is a common designation for the central town square of modern Chinese cities, established as part of urban modernization within the last few decades. These squares are the site of government buildings, museums and other public buildings.

Russia

In Russia, *central square* is a common term for an open area in the heart of the town used for community gatherings. Often it has no official name or is informally referred to as *central square.* The name of the town can be added to specify the meaning. *Central squares* are usually located opposite the administration building or some major landmark, e.g. a Great Patriotic War memorial or a cathedral.

Carnival

Carnival is a festive season which occurs immediately before Lent; the main events are usually during February. Carnival typically involves a public celebration or parade combining some elements of a circus, mask and public street party. People often dress up or masquerade during the celebrations, which mark an overturning of daily life.

Carnival is a festival traditionally held in Roman Catholic and, to a lesser extent, Eastern Orthodox societies. Protestant areas usually do not have carnival celebrations or have modified traditions, such as the Danish Carnival or other Shrove Tuesday events. The Brazilian Carnaval is one of the best-known celebrations today, but many cities and regions worldwide celebrate with large, popular, and days-long events.

Carnival in Specific Countries

In India, Carnival is celebrated in the states of Goa, Gujarat, Odisha and Kerala. In Goa, Carnival is known as 'Intruz', and the largest celebration takes place in the city of Loutolim. The three-day-long festival of music and dancing in the streets culminates in a parade on Fat Tuesday. Crowds follow their partying with a buffet dinner of Goan cuisine.

This takes place on Fat Tuesday. Organized by Catholic churches, the *Raasa* involves a public Mass and a parade of religious artifacts, including large copper vessels, a golden cross and a silver cross, and the Papal and Catholicate flag. For the "Chembeduppu" ceremony, people eat raw or half-boiled rice out of the copper vessels. Although many Christians participate only in the parade, Hindus and Muslims join in the other festivities, which often include fireworks.

In Odisha the carnival is celebrated in Sambalpur, it is famous by the name of Sitalsasthi. It attracts tourists from adjoining states as well as outside India. The marriage of Shiva and Parvati is celebrated as Sitalsasthi for several years from now. No one for sure knows when actually it started. However, from the records it is known that for the last 300 years it has been celebrated. This can be the oldest carnival celebrated in India. The Kutch district in northern Gujarat celebrates the Kutch Carnival, also known as Rann Utshav.

Europe

"Karneval" redirects here. For the manga, see Karneval_(manga).

Belgium

Many parts of Belgium celebrate Carnival, typically with costume parades, partying and fireworks. These areas include heist, Binche, Aalst and Malmedy.

The Carnival of Binche has a history dating back at least to the 16th century. Parades are held over the three days before Lent; the most important participants are the Gilles, who go out in traditional costumes on Shrove Tuesday and throw blood oranges to the crowd. In 2003, the Carnival of Binche was recognised as one of the Masterpieces of the Oral and Intangible Heritage of Humanity. The Carnival at Aalst, which is celebrated for the full week preceding Ash Wednesday, is expected to receive the same recognition in 2010.

Some Belgian cities hold carnivals later during Lent. One of the best-known is Stavelot, where the *Carnaval de la Laetare* takes place on Laetare Sunday, the fourth Sunday of Lent. The participants include the *Blancs-Moussis*, who dress in white with long red noses, and parade through town attacking bystanders with confetti and dried pig bladders. The town of Halle also celebrates on Laetare Sunday.

Bosnia and Herzegovina

In Bosnia and Herzegovina, the city of Ljubuški holds a traditional carnival (Bosnian: *Karneval*). Ljubuški is a member of the Federation of European Carnival Cities (FECC).

Croatia

Carla del Ponte as witch at the Rijeka Carnival

The most famous Croatian carnival (Croatian: "karneval", also called "maškare") is the Rijeka Carnival, during which the mayor of Rijeka hands over the keys to the city to the Carnival master ("meštar od karnevala") and the spirit of the Carnival takes over completely. The festival includes several different events, culminating on the final Sunday in a masked procession including participants from many different countries. (A similar procession for children takes place on the previous day.)

Many other towns in Croatia's Kvarner region (and in other parts of the country) observe the Carnival period, often incorporating local traditions and celebrating local culture. Just before the end of Carnival, every Kvarner town burns a man-like doll called a "mesopust," who is blamed for all the strife of the previous year. Another famous tradition of "Karneval" are the Zvonèari, or bell-ringers, who wear bells and large head regalia representing their areas of origin (for example, those from Halubje wear regalia in the shape of animal heads). The traditional Carnival food is fritule, a pastry. This festival can also be called Poklade.

Masks are central to the Carnival celebration, and worn to many of the festivities, including concerts and parties. Children and teachers are commonly allowed to wear masks to school for a day, and also wear masks at school dances or while trick-or-treating. There are also summer carnivals. One of the most famous is the Senj Summer Carnival - the first was 1968. and the tradition stayed. Many other towns in the surroundings also organise Summer Carnivals (Mali Lošinj, Pag, Novi Vinodolski, Fužine, etc.).

Cyprus

Carnival has been celebrated on the island of Cyprus for centuries, and the tradition is believed to have been established under Venetian rule around the 16th century. It may also have been influenced by Greek traditions, such as festivities for deities such as Dionysus. The celebration originally involved dressing in fancy costumes and holding masked balls or visiting friends. For approximately the past century, it has taken the form of an organized festival held during the 10 days preceding Lent (according to the Greek Orthodox calendar). The festival is celebrated almost exclusively in the city of Limassol.

Three main parades take place during Carnival. The first is held on the first day, during which the "Carnival King" (either a person in costume or an effigy) rides through the city on his carriage. The second is held on the first Sunday of the festival and the participants are mainly children. The third and largest takes place on the last day of Carnival, and involves hundreds of people walking in costume alone the town's longest avenue. The latter two parades are open to anyone who wishes to participate.

Czech Republic

In the Czech Republic, the Masopust festival takes place from Epiphany (*Den tøí králù*) through Ash Wednesday (*Popeleènl støeda*). The word *masopust* translates literally from old Czech to mean "meat fast", and the festival often includes a pork feast in preparation for Lent. The tradition is most common in Moravia but does occur in Bohemia as well. While practices vary from region to region, masks and costumes are present everywhere.

Denmark

Carnival in Denmark is called *Fastelavn*, and is held on the Sunday or Monday before Ash Wednesday. The holiday is sometimes described as a Nordic Halloween, with children dressing in costume and gathering treats for the *Fastelavn* feast. One popular custom is the *fastelavnsris*, a switch that children use to flog their parents to wake them up on Fastelavns Sunday.

England

In England, the season immediately before Lent was called Shrovetide. It was a time for confessing sins (*shriving*) with fewer festivities than the Continental Carnivals. Today, Shrove Tuesday is celebrated as Pancake Day, but little else of the Lent-related Shrovetide survived the 16th-century English Reformation. Possibly the only Shrovetide carnival in the United Kingdom is celebrated in Cowes and East Cowes on the Isle of Wight; it is the first carnival on the island's long and busy calendar.

France

The two major carnivals of France are the Nice Carnival and the Paris Carnival. The Nice Carnival was held as far back as 1294, and is still held annually, attracting over a million visitors yearly during the two weeks preceding Lent. The Paris Carnival occurs after the Feast of Fools and dates back to the 16th century or earlier, although it was not held between 1952 and 1957.

Germany, Switzerland and Austria

Although the festival and party season in Germany starts on 11 November at 11:11 am, the actual Carnival week begins on the Thursday before Ash Wednesday. German Carnival parades are held on the weekend before and especially on Rose Monday, and occasionally on Shrove Tuesday as well in the suburbs of larger cities. The carnival session begins each year on 11 November at

11:11 am and finishes on Ash Wednesday with the main festivities occurring around Rosenmontag; this time is also called the "Fifth Season."

In German-speaking countries, two distinct varieties of Carnivals are held. The Rhenish Carnival is held in the west of Germany, mainly in the states of North Rhine-Westphalia, Baden-Württemberg, Rhineland Palatinate, and is famous for celebrations such as parades and costume balls. Cologne Carnival is the largest and most famous. On Carnival Thursday (called "Old Women Day" or "The Women's Day"), in commemoration of an 1824 revolt by washer-women, women storm city halls, cut men's ties, and are allowed to kiss any man who passes their way.

The "Swabian-Alemannic" carnival, known as Fastnacht, takes place in Baden and Swabia (Southwestern Germany), Switzerland, Alsace and Vorarlberg (Western Austria). It traditionally represents the time of year when the reign of the cold, grim winter spirits is over and these spirits are being hunted down and expelled.

Greece

Patras Carnival: the float of King Carnival

The carnival season in Greece is also known as the *Apokriés* (Greek: ÁðïêñéÝò, "saying goodbye to meat"), or the season of the "Opening of the Triodion", so named after the liturgical book used by the church from then until the Holy Week. One of the season's high points is *Tsiknopémpt½* ("Smoke Thursday"), when celebrants enjoy roast beef dinners at taverns or friends' homes;

the ritual is repeated the following Sunday. The following week, the last before Lent, is called *Tyrinç* (Greek: Ôõñéíþ, "cheese [week]") because eating meat is not allowed, but dairy products are. The Great Lent begins on "Clean Monday", the day after "Cheese Sunday". Throughout the carnival season, people disguise themselves as *maskarádes* ("masqueraders") and engage in pranks and general revelry.

Patras holds the largest annual carnival in Greece; the famous Patras Carnival is a 3-day spectacle replete with concerts, *balles masqués*, parading troupes, floats, a treasure hunt and many events for children. The grand parade of masked troupes and floats is held at noon on *Tyrine* Sunday, and culminates in the ceremonial burning of the effigy of King Carnival at the Patras harbour.

In many other regions, festivities of smaller extent are organized, focused on the reenactment of traditional carnevalic customs; for example those held in Tyrnavos (Thessaly), Kozani (West Macedonia), Rethymno (Crete) and in Xanthi (East Macedonia and Thrace). Specifically Tyrnavos holds an annual Phallus festival, a traditional "phallkloric" event in which giant, gaudily painted effigies of phalluses made of papier maché are paraded, and which all women present are asked to touch, or kiss, their reward for doing so being a shot of the famous local tsipouro alcohol spirit. Also every year, to the very beginning (from 1st to 8th of January), mostly in regions of the Western Macedonia, there are carnaval fiestas and festivals. The most known of them is the Kastorian Carnaval or "Ragoutsaria" (Gr. *"ÑáãêïõôóÜñéá"*) [tags: Kastoria, KAstorian Carnaval, Ragoutsaria, Ñáãêïõôóáñéá, ÊáóôïñéÜ]. It is taking place from 6 to 8 of January with a mass participation of the local population and thousands of visitors under the sounds of big brass bands, pipises, macedonian and grand casa drums. It is an ancient celebration of natures' rebirth (fiestas for Dionysus (Dionysia) and Kronos (Saturnalia)), which ends the third day in a huge dance in the medieval square Ntoltso where all the bands are playing the same time and all the people are dancing too.

Hungary

In Mohács, Hungary, the Busójárás is a celebration held at the end of the Carnival season, and involves locals dressing up in woolly costumes, with scary masks and noise-makers. They perform a burial ritual to symbolise the end of winter and spike doughnuts on weapons to symbolise the defeat of Ottomans.

Italy

Decorated floats at the Carnival of Viareggio

The most famous carnivals of Italy are those held in Venice, Viareggio, Ivrea and Acireale. The carnival in Venice was first recorded in 1268. The subversive nature of the festival is reflected in Italy's many laws over the past several centuries attempting to restrict celebrations and the wearing of masks, a central feature of the carnival. Carnival celebrations in Venice were halted for many years after the city fell under Austrian control in 1798, but were revived in the late 20th century.

The month-long carnival of Viareggio is one of the most renowned in Europe, and is characterized mainly by its parade of floats and marks caricaturizing popular figures. In 2001, the town built a new "Carnival citadel" dedicated to carnival preparations and entertainment.

The carnival of Ivrea is famous for its *Battle of the Oranges* fought with citruses between the people by foot and the troops of the tyrant on the carts, to remember the wars that really happened during the Middle Ages.

In the most part of the Archdiocese of Milan the Carnival lasts four more days, ending on the Saturday after Ash Wednesday, because of the Ambrosian rite.

Macedonia

The most popular carnivals in the Republic of Macedonia are held in Vevèani and Strumica.

The Vevèani Carnival (Macedonian: Âåâ÷àíñêè Kàðíåâàë, translated *Vevchanski Karneval*) has been held for over 1,400 years, and takes place on 13 and 14 January (New Year's Eve and New Year's Day by the old calendar). During the carnival, the village becomes a live theatre where costumed actors improvise on the streets in roles such as the traditional "August the Stupid."

The Strumica Carnival (Macedonian: Ñòðóìè÷êè Êàðíåâàë, translated *Strumichki Karneval*) has been held since at least 1670, when the Turkish author Evlija Chelebija wrote while staying there, "I came into a town located in the foothills of a high hillock and what I saw that night was masked people running house–to–house, with laughter, scream and song." The carnival has taken place in an organized form since 1991; in 1994, Strumica became a member of FECC and in 1998 hosted the XVIII International Congress of Carnival Cities. The Strumica carnival opens on a Saturday night at a masked ball where the Prince and Princess are chosen; the main carnival night is on Tuesday, when masked participants (including groups from abroad) compete in various subjects. As of 2000, the Festival of Caricatures and Aphorisms has been held as part of Strumica's carnival celebrations.

Malta

Carnival in Malta (Maltese: *il-Karnival ta' Malta*) has had an important place on the Maltese cultural calendar for just under five centuries, having been introduced to the Islands by Grand Master Piero de Ponte in 1535. It is held during the week leading up to Ash Wednesday, and typically includes masked balls, fancy dress and grotesque mask competitions, lavish late-night parties, a colourful, ticker-tape parade of allegorical floats presided over by King Carnival (Maltese: *ir-Re tal-Karnival*), marching bands and costumed revellers.

Today the largest of the carnival celebrations takes place in and around the capital city of Valletta and Floriana; however, several more "spontaneous" carnivals take place in more remote areas. The Nadur Carnival is notable for its darker and more risqué themes including cross-dressing, ghost costumes, political figures and revellers dressed up as scantily clad clergyfolk. In 2005, the Nadur Carnival hosted the largest-ever gathering of international Carnival organizers for the FECC's global summit.

Traditional dances include the *parata*, which is a lighthearted re-enactment of the 1565 victory of the Knights over the Turks, and an 18th century court dance known as *il-Maltija*. Food eaten at the carnival includes *perlini* (multi-coloured, sugar-coated almonds) and the *prinjolata*, which is a towering assembly of sponge cake, biscuits, almonds and citrus fruits, topped with cream and pine nuts.

Netherlands

Carnival in the Netherlands is also called "Vastenavond" or "Vastelaovend", and is most celebrated in Catholic regions, mainly the southern provinces North Brabant and Limburg. Dutch Carnival is celebrated on the Saturday through Tuesday preceding Ash Wednesday. Although traditions vary from town to town, some common characteristics of Dutch Carnival include a parade, a "prince" plus cortège ("Council of 11"), a farmer's wedding (*boerenbruiloft*), and eating herring (*haring happen*) on Ash Wednesday.

One variant of Dutch Carnival is known as the *Rijnlandsche Carnival*, which can be seen in the province of Limburg. The province's capital of Maastricht holds a street carnival featuring elaborate costumes that resemble some South American and Venetian influences. Intentionally amateurish marching bands ('Zaate Hermeniekes' or 'Drunken Marching Bands') traditionally perform on the streets. In recent years samba bands have become more popular.

The oldest-known Dutch carnival festivities date from 1385 in 's-Hertogenbosch. They are depicted in several paintings of the 15th-century painter Jheronimus Bosch. For the three days of the carnival, 's-Hertogenbosch changes its name to "Oeteldonk," which means "Frog Hill." This name changing tradition is common in and around North Brabant.

Poland

The Polish Carnival Season includes Fat Thursday (Polish: *T³usty Czwartek*), when *p¹czki* (doughnuts) are eaten, and *Œledzik*

(Shrove Tuesday) or Herring Day. The Tuesday before the start of Lent is also often called *Ostatki* (literally "lasts"), meaning the last day to party before the Lenten season.

The traditional way to celebrate Carnival is the *kulig*, a horse-drawn sleigh ride through the snow-covered countryside. In modern times, Carnival is increasingly seen as an excuse for intensive partying and night-clubbing, and has become more commercialized with stores offering Carnival-season sales.

Portugal

Carnival in Portugal is celebrated throughout the country, most famously in Ovar, Madeira, Loulé, Nazaré, and Torres Vedras. The carnivals in Podence and Lazarim incorporate pagan traditions such as the careto, while the Torres Vedras celebration is probably the most typical Portuguese carnival.

Ironically, although Portugal introduced Christianity and the customs related to Catholic practice to Brazil, the country has begun to adopt some aspects of Brazilian-style Carnival celebrations, in particular those of Rio de Janeiro with sumptuous parades, samba and other Brazilian musical elements.

Carnaval is celebrated throughout Portugal, but each region puts its own unique take on the festival.

In Lazarim, a municipality of Lamego, celebrations follow the pagan tradition of the Roman Saturnalias. This rustic town celebrates Carnaval by burning colorful effigies and dressing in carefully crafted, home-made costumes. The region is celebrated for its wood craftsmanship and is most for the locals' heavy, hand-made wooden masks worn during Carnaval. The masks of Lazarim are effigies of both men and women, but both roles are performed by men. They are distinguished by their clothes, which ridiculously characterize different attributes of both men and women.

The Lazarim Carnaval cycle encompasses two periods, the first starting on the fifth Sunday before Fat Sunday. Masked figures and people wearing large sculpted heads walk through the town. The locals also feast on a wide variety of meats, above all pork. The second cycle, held on Sundays preceding Ash Wednesday, incorporates the tradition of the Compadres and Comadres, with men and women displaying light-hearted authority over the other.

Over the course of the five weeks, men prepare large masked heads and women raise funds to pay for the mannequins that will be sacrificed in a public bonfire. This is one of the key events and is a Carnaval tradition unique to Portugal. During the bonfire, a girl reads the Compadre's will and a boy reads the Comadre's will. The executors of the will are named, a donkey is symbolically distributed to both female and male "heirs," and then the final reckoning in which the Entrudo, or Carnaval doll, is burned.

In Estarreja in the Central region of Portugal, the town's first references to Carnaval are noted in the 14th Century, with "Flower Battles," or richly decorated floats which paraded through Estarreja's streets. In the beginning of the twentieth century these festivities ended with the death of its main promoters only to reappear again in the sixties to become one of the many important Carnaval festivals in Portugal.

In the Northern region of Podence children appear from Sunday to Tuesday with tin masks and colorful multilayered costumes made from red, green and yellow wool. And in the Central Portugal towns of Nelas and Canas de Senhorim, Carnaval is one of the most important tourist events in the region, attracting thousands of visitors yearly. Nelas and Canas de Senhorim are host to the four festive parades that promise visitors colorful and creative costumes: The Bairro da Igreja and the Cimo do Povo in Nelas and the do Paço and the do Rossio in Canas de Senhorim.

One of the most famous Carnaval events in Portugal is in the town Ovar near Porto. Organized in 1952 it is the largest festivity of the region drawing thousands of visitors. It is well known for its creative designs, which they display in the Carnaval Parade. Participants and their families work year-round to prepare their elaborate and humorous costumes, masks, decorations and floats. Its Carnaval parade features troupes with themed costumes and music, ranging from the traditional to modern pop culture.

In Lisbon, Portugal's largest city, Carnaval is a more cosmopolitan affair. Parades, dances and festivities throughout the week feature famous stars from Portugal and Brazil. The Loures Carnaval is a highlight of Lisbon's festivities which celebrates the country's folk traditions, including the "enterro do bacalhau" or burial of the cod, which symbolizes the end of Carnaval and the festivities.

North of Lisbon is the famous Torres Vedras Carnaval, described as the "most Portuguese in Portugal." Those looking for a less touristy Carnaval experience should visit this town where the locals are the stars. The celebration highlight is a parade of creatively decorated streetcars satirizing society and politics.

Other Central Portugal towns, such as Fatima and Leiria, offer colorful, family-friendly takes on Carnaval. In these towns everyone dresses up as if it were Halloween. Children and adults wear masks and enjoy the towns' enthusiastic parades.

In the Algarve region along the southern coast of Portugal, several of the posh resorts towns offer their own traditional takes on the Carnaval parades. Besides the themed floats and cars, the Carnaval festivities include "samba" groups, bands, dances and plenty of music and liveliness. In the city of Loulé, the Carnaval parade annually attracts thousands of national and foreign tourists to the region.

Azores

The Islands of the Azores have their own take on the Carnaval festivities, but like on the mainland, many local clubs and Carnaval groups create colorful and creative costumes that take a jab at the political or cultural characters of the times.

On São Miguel Island, Carnaval has a sweet taste with street vendors selling fried dough, called a Malassada. The festival on the Azores biggest island starts off with a black tie grand ball, then and heats up with Latin music at the recently restored Coliseu Micaelense. There is a children's parade in the streets of Ponta Delgada with children from each school district coming in costume. Then a massive Carnaval parade fills the streets into the wee hours ending in fireworks.

Some of the islands' more unique aspects to Carnaval are the theatre performances and dances. In the "Danças de Entrudo" hundreds of people follow the dancers around the island. Throughout the show the dancers, who are guided by a "master," act out dramas from everyday life. The "Dances de Carnaval" are allegorical and comedic tales acted out in the streets throughout the festival. The largest is in "Angra do Heroísmo," with more than 30 Carnaval groups performing. During this festival, it is said there are more Portuguese-language theatrical performances occurring here than anywhere else in the world.

The Carnaval festivities end on Ash Wednesday, when locals sit down for the "Batatada" or potato feast, in which the main dish is salted cod with potatoes, eggs, mint, bread and wine. After, residents head into the streets for the burning of the "Carnaval clown," signaling the end of the Carnaval.

Madeira

On the Island of Madeira, Carnaval maintains its distinctive local roots as well. Funchal, the island's capital, wakes up on the Friday morning before Ash Wednesday to the sound of brass bands and Carnaval parades throughout the downtown area. That night festivities continue with concerts and shows in the Praça do Município for five consecutive days. The Main Carnaval street parade takes place on Saturday evening with thousands of Samba dancers flooding the streets of Funchal. The traditional public street Carnaval takes place on Tuesday, where the island's population displays its ingenuity and imagination by creating daring caricatures for the parade.

Russia

Carnival in Saint Petersburg, Russia

Maslenitsa (also called *Pancake Week* or "Cheese Week") is a Russian folk holiday that incorporates some traditions that date back to pagan times. It is celebrated during the last week before Lent. The essential element of Maslenitsa celebration is bliny, Russian pancakes, popularly taken to symbolize the sun. Round and golden, they are made from the rich foods still allowed during that week by the Orthodox traditions: butter, eggs, and milk (in the tradition of Orthodox lent, the consumption of meat ceases one week before the consumption of milk and eggs).

Maslenitsa also includes masquerades, snowball fights, sledding, swinging on swings and sleigh rides. The mascot of the celebration is usually a brightly dressed straw effigy of *Lady Maslenitsa*, formerly known as Kostroma. As the culmination of the celebration, on Sunday evening, *Lady Maslenitsa* is stripped of her finery, and put to the flames of a bonfire.

In Saint Petersburg the modern celebration of the festival is organized by the city to fall on a fixed date annually (at Sunday, closest to 27 May).

Slovakia

In Slovakia, the Fašiangy (*fašiang*, *fašangy*) takes place from Three Kings' Day (*Traja králi*) until the midnight before Ash Wednesday (*Škaredá streda* or *Popolcová streda*). At the midnight marking the end of fašiangy, a symbolic burial ceremony for the contrabass is performed, because music has to cease for the Lent.

Slovenia

Slovenia has a rich and diverse annual cycle of holidays. Much ethnic heritage has been preserved through widely attended tourist events.

The Slovenian countryside displays a variety of disguised groups and individual characters among which the most popular and characteristic is the Kurent (plural: *Kurenti*), a monstrous and demon-like, but fluffy figure. The most significant ethonological Carnival festival is traditionally held in annually in the town of Ptuj (see: Kurentovanje). The special feature of the event of Ptuj itself and its surrounding area are the Kurents themselves, magical creatures from the other world, who visit all major events throughout the country, members of parliament, the president and mayors, trying to banish the winter and announce the arrival of the spring, fertility, and new life with loud noise and dancing. The origin of the Kurent is a mystery, and not much is known of the times, beliefs, or purposes connected with its first appearance. The origin of the name itself is obscure.

Another town, equal in importance to Ptuj, where the carnival tradition is alive is Cerknica. The carnival is heralded by a figure called "Poganjiè" carrying a whip. In the carnival procession, organised by the "Pust society", a monstrous witch named Uršula is driven from Mt. Slivnica, to be burned at the stake on Ash Wednesday. Unique to this region is a group of dormice, driven by the Devil, and a huge fire-breathing dragon. Cerkno and its surrounding area is known for the *Laufarji*, carnival figures with artistically carved wooden masks.

The *Maèkare* from Dobrepolje used to represent a triple character: the beautiful, the ugly (among which the most important represented by an old man, an old woman, a hunchback, and a *Korant*), and the noble (imitating the urban elite).

The major part of the population, especially the young and children, dress up in ordinary non-ethnic costumes, going to school, work, and organized events, where prizes are given for the best and most original costumes. Costumed children sometimes go from house to house asking for treats in an imitation of American Halloween.

Spain

Arguably the most famous locales in Spain are Santa Cruz de Tenerife, Sitges, Vilanova i la Geltrú, Tarragona, Solsona , Cádiz, Badajoz, Bielsa (an ancestral carnival celebration), Plan, San Juan de Plan, Laza, Verín, Viana and Xinžo de Limia.

Andalusia

In Cádiz the costumes worn are often related to recent news, such as the bird flu epidemic in 2006, during which many people were disguised as chickens. The feeling of this carnival is the sharp criticism, the funny play on words and the imagination in the costumes, more than the glamorous dressings. It is traditional to paint the face with lipstick as a humble substitute of a mask.

The most famous groups are the chirigotas, choirs and comparsas. The chirigotas are well known witty, satiric popular groups who sing about politics, new times and household topics, wearing the same costume, which they train for the whole year. The Choirs (*coros*) are wider groups that go on open carts through the streets singing with a little orchestra of guitars and lutes. Their characteristic composition is the "Carnival Tango", and they alternate comical and serious repertory. The comparsas are the serious counterpart of the chirigota in Cádiz, and the poetical lyrics and the criticism are their main ingredients. They have a more elaborated polyphony, being easily recognizable by the typical countertenor voice.

Canary Islands

The Santa Cruz de Tenerife is together with the Carnival of Cadiz, the most important festival for Spanish tourism and Spain's largest carnival. In 1980 it was declared a Festival Tourist International Interest, by the Secretariat of State for the Tourism. Every February, Santa Cruz de Tenerife, the capital of the largest of the Canary Islands, hosts the event, attracting around a million people. The celebrations could be declared by UNESCO as Heritage of Mankind in 2011. Carnival of Santa Cruz de Tenerife now aspires to become a World Heritage Site.

In 1980 it was declared a Festival Tourist International Interest, by the Secretariat of State for the Tourism and it is one of the most important carnivals of the World. The Carnival of Santa Cruz de Tenerife now aspires to become a World Heritage Site. This declaration by UNESCO will, occur, further promoting international had Santa Cruz de Tenerife, being the first Carnival of Spain to obtain this recognition, for its permanent in time and it would reach the five continents through UNESCO. In 1987 went to the "Carnival Chicharrero" Cuban singer Celia Cruz with orchestra Billo's Caracas Boys, attended by 250,000 people, was registered in the Guinness of Records as the largest gathering of people in an outdoor plaza to attend a concert, a record she holds today.

Catalonia

In Catalonia people dress up and organise parties for a week but particularly on the weekend. Despite it being winter, parties are open air, beginning with a *cercavila* to call everybody to come. *Rues* of people dance along the streets. On Thursday *Dijous Gras* is celebrated, also called 'the omelette day' (el *dia de la truita*), *coques* (*de llardons, butifarra d'ou, butifarra*) and omelettes are eaten. Parties end by burning Mr. Carnestoltes and with *enterrament de la sardina* (sardine's funeral).

Carnaval de Solsona takes place in Solsona, Lleida in central Catalonia. It is one of the longest carnivals in Catalonia; free events in the streets, and concerts every night, run for more than a week. The carnival is known for a legend that explains some people hung a donkey at the tower bell, because the animal wanted to eat some grass which grew on the top of the tower. To remember this legend, every year people in Solsona hang a donkey at the tower, while the animal pisses above the excited people. This event is the most important of Solsona's Carnival and takes place on Saturday night. For this reason, the inhabitants of Solsona are called "matarrucs" ("donkey killers"). Photo:

Another characteristic of the carnival is its giants. Crazy Giants will pursue and try to hit revellers with their articulated arms and legs. The Crazy Giants were created in 1978 by the giant-making master Manel Casserras i Boix. Photo:

"Comparses" groups organize free activities in the streets. They are groups of friends who create and personalize a uniformed suit which is worn every year during the festivities. Website: http://www.carnavalsolsona.com/

Sitges: This carnival is one of the most famous carnivals in Catalonia. Special food includes *xatonades* (a *xató* is a traditional local salad of Sitges) served with omelettes. Two important moments are the *Rua de la Disbauxa* (Debauchery Parade) on Sunday night and the *Rua de l'Extermini* (Extermination Parade) on Tuesday night. Around 40 floats with more than 2,500 participants parade in Sitges.

The carnival of Vilanova i la Geltrú is notable for *Les Comparses* (on Sunday), in which good-humoured rival groups throw boiled sweets (candies) at each other. Vinanova's and Sitge's carnival are rivals.

Tarragona has one of the most complete ritual sequences of the Catalan carnivals. The events start with the building of a huge barrel and end with its burning together with the effigies of the carnival King and Queen. On Saturday, the main parade takes place. There are masked groups, zoomorphic figures, music and percussion bands, and groups with fireworks (the devils, the dragon, the ox, the female dragon). Carnival groups stand out for their clothes full of elegance, showing brilliant examples of fabric crafts, at the Saturday and Sunday parades. About 5,000 people are members of the parade groups.

North America

Caribbean

Most of the islands in the Caribbean celebrate Carnival. The largest and most well-known celebration is held in Trinidad and Tobago. The Dominican Republic, Antigua, Aruba, Cayman Islands, Curaçao, Barbados, Haiti, Dominica, Grenada, Jamaica, Sint Maarten, Saint Lucia, Saint Kitts, Saint Thomas and Saint Vincent and the Grenadines are also known for lengthy carnival seasons and large celebrations.

Carnival is an important cultural event on the Dutch Antilles islands of Aruba, Curaçao, Sint Maarten, Saba, Sint Eustatius (Statia), and Bonaire. Festivities include "jump-up" parades with beautifully colored costumes, floats, and live bands as well as beauty contests and other competitions. Carnival on these islands also includes a middle-of-the-night j'ouvert (juvé) parade that ends at sunrise with the burning of a straw King Momo, cleansing the island of sins and bad luck. On Statia he is called Prince Stupid.

Carnival has also been celebrated in Cuba since the 18th century. The costumes, dances and pageantry grew with each passing year, with the participants donning costumes from the cultural and ethnic variety on the island. After Fidel Castro's Communist Revolution, carnival's religious overture was suppressed. The events remained, albeit frowned upon by the state. Carnival celebrations have been in decline throughout Cuba since 1960.

Aruba

Carnival means weeks of events that bring you colourfully decorated floats, contagiously throbbing music, luxuriously costumed groups of celebrants of all ages, King & Queen elections, electrifying jump ups and torch light parades that wind their way through the streets at night, the Jouvert morning: the Children's Parades and finally the Grand Parade. Aruba's biggest celebration of the year is a month-long celebration consisting of festive "jump-ups" (street parades), spectacular parades and creative contests.

Music and flamboyant costumes play a central role, from the Queen elections to the Grand Parade, which winds it ways down city avenues to the delight of thousands of spectators. Street parades are held in various districts throughout the month, allowing everyone an opportunity to participate and dance to the season's most popular brass band, steel band and roadmarch tunes. On the evening before the start of Lent, Carnival officially comes to end with the symbolic burning of "King Momo."

Antigua

The Antiguan Carnival is a celebration of music and dance held annually from the end of July to the first Tuesday in August. The most important day is that of the j'ouvert (or juvé), in which brass and steel bands perform for much of the island's population. Barbuda's Carnival, held in June, is known as Caribana. The Antiguan and Barbudan Carnivals replaced the Old Time Christmas Festival in 1957, with hopes of inspiring tourism in Antigua and Barbuda. Some elements of the Christmas Festival remain in the modern Carnival celebrations, which are otherwise largely based on the Trinidadian Carnival. The carnival consists of mass playing, steel pan music and various shows such as calypso shows and pageants.

Barbados

Carnival in Barbados is known as Crop Over. Crop Over is Barbados' biggest festival, having had its early beginnings on the sugar cane plantations during the colonial period. The crop over tradition began in 1688, and featured singing, dancing and accompaniment by bottles filled with water, shak-shak, banjo, triangle, fiddle, guitar, and bones. Other traditions included climbing a greased pole, feasting and drinking competitions. Originally a celebration signaling the end of the yearly sugar cane harvest, it has since evolved into a national festival rivaling New Orleans Mardi Gras and Trinidad Carnival in Trinidad. In the late 20th Century, the general schematic of Crop Over began to closely mirror the Trinidad Carnival. Beginning in June, Crop Over it runs until the first Monday in August when it culminates in the finale, The Grand Kadooment.

For the entire two months life for many islanders is one big party with a major feature of crop over being the calypso competition. Calypso music, originating in Trinidad, uses syncopated rhythm and topical lyrics and gives its exponents a medium in which to satirise local politics and comment on the issues of the day, while taking nothing away from the general bacchanal. Calypso tents, also originating in Trinidad, feature their cadre of calypsonians who perform biting social commentaries on the happenings of the past year, political exposés or rousing exhortations to wuk dah waistline and roll dat bumper. There are craft markets, food tents and stalls, street parties and cavalcades every week supplemented by daily events at Tim's on the Highway, the new home of the Barbados Cropover Festival.

Competition "tents" ring with the fierce battle of calypsonians for the coveted Calypso Monarch Award and the air is redolent with the exotic smells of Bajan cooking during the Bridgetown Market Street Fair. Rich with the spirit of local culture, the Cohobblopot Festival blends dance and drama and music with the crowning of the King and Queen of costume bands. Every evening the "Pic-o-de-Crop" Show is performed when finally the King of Calypso is crowned. The climax of the festival is Kadooment Day celebrated with a national holiday when costume bands fill the streets with pulsating Barbadian rhythms and fireworks that ignite the sky.

Haiti

Haiti Kanaval has up to 1,000,000 people jamming the streets of downtown Port-au-Prince's Champs de Marse rock to Meringues (Haitian carnival melodies) on the Beton (the street course where the floats pass through).The many different genres of Haitian Music are fully represented with the different bands that blaze through the beton New styles with foreign influence emerge continuously mixing Haitian sounds with techno, hip-hop, reggae, zouk, Fand soukous to name a few.

The 20 bands in the seven-hour parade play as the chars creep through the wild crowds until 4 am The dancers before and after the floats, dance the ga gun, an aggressive dance that can be as competitive as it is celebrative. Everybody knows the songs; every line, every chant has the audience ecstatic, with the floats themselves bouncing in time to the music. Condoms, thrown from floats and from the stands, were blown up like balloons. And long lines of people dance elaborate dances, turning the sensuality of the music into movement.

Combined, the depth of the music and dance suggests Haiti's enormous cultural power as a reservoir of African and Creole culture, underscoring its importance as one of the major producers of art in the Caribbean. And in its intensity, its Carnival is clearly one of the more important events in the African diaspora in the Americas.

Trinidad and Tobago

In Trinidad & Tobago, Carnival is a holiday season that lasts over a month and culminates in large celebrations in Port of Spain which is the capital of Trinidad, on the Sunday, Monday, and Tuesday before Ash Wednesday with Dimanche Gras, J'ouvert, and Mas (masquerade). Tobago's celebrations also culminates on Monday and Tuesday but on a much smaller scale in its capital Scarborough. Carnival is a festive time of costumes, dance, music, competitions, rum, and partying (also referred to as fete-ing). Music styles associated with Carnival include soca, calypso

The annual Carnival steel pan competition known as the National Panorama competition is held in the weeks preceding Carnival with the finals held on the Saturday before the main event. Pan players compete in various categories such as "Conventional Steel band" or "Single Pan" by performing renditions of the current year's calypsos. Preliminary judging of this event for "Conventional Steel Bands" has been recently moved to the individual pan yards where steel bands practice their selections for the competition.

Carnival Monday involves the parade of the mass bands, but on a casual or relaxed scale. Usually revelers wear only parts of their costumes, and the purpose of the day is more one of fun than display or competition. Also on Carnival Monday, Monday Night Mas is popular in most towns and especially the capital, where smaller bands participate in competition.

Carnival Tuesday is when the main events of the carnival take place. On this day full costume is worn complete with make up and body paints/adornments. Each band has their costume presentation based on a particular theme, and contain various sections (some consisting of thousands of revelers) which reflect these themes. Here the street parade and eventual crowning of the best bands take place.

After following a route where various judging points are located, the mas bands eventually converge on the Queen's Park Savannah to pass "on the stage" to be judged once and for all. Also taking place on this day is the crowning of the Road March king or queen, where the singer of the most played song over the two days of the carnival is crowned winner, complete with prize money and usually a vehicle.

This parading and revelry goes on into the night of the Tuesday. Ash Wednesday itself, whilst not an official holiday, is marked by most by visiting the beaches that abound both Trinidad and Tobago. The most populated being Maracas beach and Manzanilla beach, where huge beach parties take place every Ash Wednesday. These provide a cool down from the previous five days of hectic partying, parades and competitions, and are usually attended by the whole family.

Guatemala

The largest Carnival celebration in Guatemala is in Mazatenango. During the month of February, Mazatenango is famous for its eight day Carnival Feast. Locals and visitors alike look forward to the days of food, music, parades, games, etc. that bring the streets of the capital city of the department of Suchitepéquez to life.

As one Guatemalan website states, "To mention the carnival of Mazatenango is to bring to mind moments of a happy and cordial party. In the eight days of this celebration's duration the local residents have kept alive the traditions of the Department."

Honduras

In La Ceiba in Honduras, Carnival is held on the fourth Saturday of every May to commemorate San Isidro. It is the largest Carnival celebration in Central America.

Nicaragua

In the Caribbean coast of Nicaragua, in the city of Bluefields, the *carnival*, better known as Palo de Mayo (or Mayo Ya!), is celebrated every day of May.

In the Nicaragua's capital city, Managua, it is only celebrated for 2 days. The *carnival* in Managua is named *"Alegria por la vida"* translated to *"Joy for Life"* and features a different theme each year.

Mexico

In Mexico, Carnival is celebrated in many cities and towns, most notably in Mazatlán, Sinaloa, Mérida, Yucatán, and in the city of Veracruz, where Carnival is celebrated with traditional music, folklore, arts and dances. People dress in bright, feathered costumes resembling the indigenous traditions, and create a series of performances on the streets as well as on stages. In most cases there is a large set-up of fair games and roller coasters. Both Mazatlán's and Veracruz's celebrations are often compared to the carnival of Rio de Janeiro or New Orleans. In Copándaro de Galeana, Michoacán carnival is celebrated with lively parades often surrounding bull riding, cockfights and dancing.

In some of the central to northern regions the popular Norteña and Mexican rodeo influences are very present, whereas in the coastal or southern regions, carnivals represent a more indigenous rendition. Each one will include many region-specific food dishes and drinks.

Panama

The Panamanian Carnival is the second biggest festival in the world. Traditionally beginning on Friday and ending on the Tuesday before Ash Wednesday, "los carnavales", as Panamanians refer to the days of carnival, are celebrated in almost the whole country. Carnival Week in Panama is specially popular because of the luxury and magnitude of the Las Tablas Carnival as well as the carnival celebrations in Panama City and almost all of the Azuero Peninsula. The Panamanian Carnival is also popular because of the great number of concerts by national and international artists held on different stages in the most visited areas of the country.

Canada

Caribana, held in Toronto on the first weekend of August, has its origins in the carnival traditions of the Caribbean, notably Trinidad and Tobago. Due to climatic imperatives, Caribana is held in the summer when Caribbean costumes may be paraded comfortably, rather than adhering to the traditional winter dates of the other carnivals in which the festival is strongly rooted. Attendance at the Caribana parade typically exceeds one million people.

The Quebec Winter Carnival is the biggest winter-themed carnival in the world. It depends on good snowfalls and very cold weather, to keep snowy ski trails in good condition and the many ice sculptures intact. For this reason it does not coincide with the pre-Lent celebration but is fixed instead to the last days of January and first days of February. In the Ottawa-Gatineau region, Winterlude takes place during the first four weeks of February.

United States

Carnival is celebrated in New York City in the Borough of Brooklyn. As in the UK, the timing of carnival has been separated from the Christian calendar and is celebrated on Labor Day Monday, in September. It is called the West Indian Day Parade or West Indian Day Carnival, and was founded by immigrants from Trinidad, one of the West Indian islands that has one of the largest Carnivals of the Caribbean region. In the mid twentieth century, West Indians moved the timing of the New York area Carnival from the beginning of Lent to the Labor Day weekend.

The West Indian Day Carnival is one of the largest parades and street festivals in New York with usually over one million people participating or attending. The parade, which consists of steel bands, floats, elaborate carnival costumes and sound trucks proceeds down Brooklyn's Eastern Parkway in the Crown Heights neighborhood.

Louisiana

The best-known, most elaborate, and most popular events are in New Orleans, while other South Louisiana cities such as Lafayette, Mamou, Houma,and Thibodaux all of which were under French control at one time or another, are the sites of famous Carnival celebrations of their own.

Major Mardi Gras celebrations are spreading to other parts of the United States, such as the Mississippi Valley region of St. Louis, Missouri, Orlando, Florida in Universal Studios, and in the Gaslamp Quarter of San Diego, California.

South America

Argentina

In Argentina, the most representative carnival performed is the so called Murga, although other famous carnival, more Brazilian stylized, are held in the Argentine Mesopotamia and the North-East. Gualeguaychú in the east of Entre Ríos province is the most important carnival city and has one of the largest parades, with a similar afro-American musical background to Brazilian or Uruguayan Carnival. Corrientes is another city with a lively carnival tradition. Chamame, a kind of polka is played during the carnivals. In all major cities and many towns throughout the country, Carnival is also celebrated, but less famous than in the above mentioned places.

As carnival coincides with summer, in many parts of Argentina children play with water. The 19th century tradition of filling empty egg shells with water has evolved into water games that include the throwing of water balloons.

Bolivia

La Diablada carnival, takes place in the city of Oruro in central Bolivia. It is celebrated in honor of the patron saint of the miners, *Vírgen de Socavon* (the Virgin of the Tunnels). Over 50 parade groups dance, sing and play music over a five kilometre-long course. Participants dress up as demons, devils, angels, Incas and Spanish conquerors. There are various kinds of dances such as caporales and tinkus.

The parade runs from morning until late at night, 18 hours a day, 3 days before Ash Wednesday. Meanwhile throughout the country celebrations are held involving traditional rhythms and water parties. In Santa Cruz de la Sierra, at the east side of the country, the tropical weather allows a Brazilian-type carnival, with agropuations of people called "Comparsas" dancing traditional songs in matching uniforms.

Brazil

The important part of the Brazilian Carnival takes place in the Rio Carnival, with *samba schools* parading in the Sambadrome ("sambódromo" in Portuguese). It's the largest carnival event in this country, considered to be the largest of the kind in the world.

Called "One of the biggest shows of the Earth", the festival attracts millions of tourists, both Brazilians and foreigners who come from everywhere to participate and enjoy the great show. *Samba Schools* are large, social entities with thousands of members and a theme for their song and parade each year. Tourists are allowed to participate, paying ($500–750) to buy a Samba costume and dance in the parade through the Sambadrome with one of the schools.

The price paid is used to buy the tourist's own costume and also the costumes of the people who do not have the money to afford it. *Blocos* are generally small informal groups also with a definite theme in their samba, usually satirical of the current political situation. But there are also a lot, about 30 of them in Rio de Janeiro, that are very big in number of participants, gathering hundreds of thousands of people. There are more than 200 *blocos* in Rio de Janeiro. *Bandas* are samba musical bands, usually formed by enthusiasts in the same neighborhood.

Colombia

There is documentary evidence that Carnival existed in Colombia in the 18th century and had already been a cause for concern for the colonial authorities, who censored the celebrations, especially in the main political centres such as Cartagena, Bogotá and Popayán.

The Carnival, therefore, continued its evolution and re-interpretation in the small and at that time unimportant towns where celebrations did not offend the ruling elites. The result was the uninterrupted celebration of Carnival festivals in Barranquilla, in other villages along the lower Magdalena River in northern Colombia, and in Pasto, Nariño in the south of the country. In modern times, there have been attempts to introduce Carnival in the capital, Bogotá, in the early 20th century, but it has always failed to gain the approval of authorities. The Bogotá Carnival has had to wait until the 21st century to be resurrected, this time by the authorities of the city.

Ecuador

In Ecuador, the celebrations have a history that begins before the arrival of Catholicism. It is known that the Huarangas Indians (from the Chimbos nation) used to celebrate the second moon of the year with a festival at which they threw flour, flowers and perfumed water. This once pagan tradition has since merged with the Catholic celebration of Carnaval.

A common feature of Ecuadorian Carnival is the *diablitos* (little devils) who play with water. As with snowball fights, the practice of throwing or dumping water on unsuspecting victims is especially revered by children and teenagers, and feared by some adults. Throwing water balloons, sometimes even eggs and flour both to friends and strangers passing by the street can be a lot of fun but can also raise the ire of unfamiliarised foreigners and even locals.

Although the government as well as school authorities forbid such games, it is still widely practiced throughout the country. Historians tell of a Bishop in 1867 who threatened the punishment of excommunication for the sin of playing Carnival games.

Different festivities are held in various regions of the country, where the locals wear disguises with colorful masks and dance to the rhythm of lively music. Usually, the celebrations begin with the election of the *Taita Carnaval* (Father Carnaval) who will head the festivities and lead the parades in each city.

French Guiana

The Carnival of French Guiana is a major aspect of the culture of that country. Although its roots are in the Creole culture, everyone participates – mainland French, Brazilians (Guiana has a frontier with Brazil) and Chinese as well as creoles.

Its duration is variable, determined by movable religious festivals: Carnival begins at Epiphany and ends on Ash Wednesday, and so typically lasts through most of January and February. During this period, from Friday evening until Monday morning the entire country throbs to the rhythm of the masked balls and street parades. Normal life slows almost to a stop.

Friday afternoons are the time for eating *galette des rois* (the cake of kings) and drinking champagne. The cake may be flavoured with frangipani, guava, or coconut.

On Sunday afternoons major parades are staged in the streets of Cayenne, Kourou, and Saint-Laurent du Maroni. Competing groups prepare for months. Dressed according to the agreed theme of the year, they strut along with carnival floats, drums, and brass bands.

Brazilian groups are also appreciated for their elaborate feathered and sequined costumes. However, they are not eligible for competition since the costumes do not change from one year to the next.

Certain mythical characters appear regularly in the parades:

- *Karolin*: A small person dressed in a magpie tail and top hat, riding on a shrew.
- *Les Nèg'marrons*: Groups of men dressed in red loincloths, bearing ripe tomatoes in their mouths and their bodies smeared with grease or molasses. These men deliberately try to come in contact with spectators, soiling their clothes.
- *Les makoumés*: Men in drag (out of the carnival context, *makoumé* is a pejorative term for a homosexual).
- *Soussouris* (the bat): a character dressed in a winged leotard from head to foot, usually black in colour. Traditionally malevolent, this character is liable to chase spectators and "sting" them.

Creole Tradition

A uniquely Creole tradition of this version of carnival is the so-called touloulous. These are women wearing highly decorative gowns, gloves, masks and headdresses which cover them completely so that they are not only unrecognisable, but the colour of their skin cannot even be determined. On Friday and Saturday nights of carnival, touloulou balls are held in so-called *universities*; in reality, large dance halls that only open in carnival time.

Touloulous get in free, and are even given condoms in the interest of the sexual health of the community. Men also attend the balls, but they have to pay admittance and they are not disguised. The touloulous pick their dance partners, who may not refuse the dance. Thus, the setup is designed to make it easy for a woman to create a temporary liaison with a man she fancies in total anonymity. Undisguised women are not welcome at the balls. By tradition, if one gets up to dance, the orchestra stops playing. Alcohol is served at bars – the disguised women also pick up men by whispering to them "touloulou thirsty", at which a round of drinks is expected, to be drunk through a straw so as not to unmask in the slightest.

In more modern times, Guyanais men have attempted to turn the tables by staging *soirées tololo*, in which it's the men who, in disguise, seek partners from undisguised women bystanders.

The final four days of carnival have a rigid tradition of celebration, and no work is done at all.

- Sunday: The Grand Parade, in which the competing groups show off their very best.
- Monday: Marriage burlesque, with men dressed as brides and women as grooms.
- Tuesday: Red Devil Day, with everyone wearing red or black.
- (Ash) Wednesday: Dress is black and white only, for the grand ceremony of burning the effigy of Vaval, the King of the Carnival.

Cajamarca

The town of Cajamarca is considered the capital of Peruvian carnival. Local residents of all ages as well as tourists dance around the *unhsa*, or *yunsa*, a tree adorned with ribbons, balloons, toys, fruits, bottles of liquor, and other prizes.

At a certain point the *Mayordomo* (governor of the feast) walks into the circle. The governor chooses a partner to go to the *unsha*, where they attempt to cut down the *unsha* by striking the tree three times with a machete. The machete is passed from couple to couple as each strikes the tree three times. When the unsha finally falls, the crowd rushes to grab the prizes. The person who successfully brings down the unsha becomes next year's governor of the feast.

Violence

The Peruvian carnival consists mostly of violent games that last all the month of February, extending to early March if Ash Wednesday falls on March, but rarely ending when it falls on February. Quoting the Lima police chief "The carnival is associated with criminal actions" (2007). It has even gone to major consequences.

The Peruvian carnival incorporates elements of violence and reflects the lately trends of urban violence in the Peruvian society after the internal conflict in Peru. Traditionally, Peruvian Andean festivities were held on this period every year because it's the rainy season. It was already violent during the 19th century, but the government managed to regulate it and during the early 20th century it followed the normal trends of partying and parading, while in the second half of the 20th century it has acquired the violent characteristics that it has today, to the point of being banned, first from the streets in 1958 and altogether in 1959 by the Prado government.

Uruguay

The Carnival in Uruguay is the longest of the world, with more than 80 days of celebration, generally occurring in January through mid March, with celebrations in Montevideo, the capital, being the largest and brightiest. The festival is performed in the European parade style with elements from Bantu and Angolan Benguela cultures imported with slaves in colonial times. The main attractions of Uruguayan Carnival include two colorful parades called *Desfile de Carnaval* (Carnival Parade) and *Desfile de Llamadas* (Calls Parade, a candombe-summoning parade).

During the eighty days of celebration, popular theaters called *tablados* are built in many places throughout the cities, especially in Montevideo. Traditionally formed by men and now starting to be open to women, the different Carnival groups called mainly Murgas, Lubolos or Parodistas perform a kind of popular opera at the *tablados*, singing and dancing songs that generally relate to social reality and political situation in the country. The 'Calls' groups, basically formed by drummers playing the tamboril, perform candombe rhythmic figures. Revelers also wear their festival clothing. Each group has its own theme. Women wearing elegant, bright dressed are called vedettes and provide the sensual touch to parades.

Venezuela

Carnival in Venezuela (2 days of festivals, 40 days before Easter) is a time when youth in many rural towns have water fights. Anybody and everybody that is out in the streets during the week of Carnival is subject to being soaked. Coastal town and provinces celebrate carnival much more fervently these days than any place in the country. Venezuela regard carnival about the same way they regard Christmas and Semana Santa (Holy Week; the week before Easter Sunday) when they take the opportunity to visit their families and enjoy this festive time with them.

PLACE IMAGE AND URBAN TOURISM

A place's image shapes the way citizens, visitors and businesses respond to it. Therefore, a place must manage its image. Unfortunately, most places in the world carry some negative associations that affect certain groups and interfere with the place's health. Place leaders need to figure out how to overcome the negatives, either by ignoring them, reversing them into positives or even by overwhelming them with other positives. This chapter will look at what determines a place's image, the challenge of strategic image management and specific tools for confronting negative image problems.

Crime in Chicago has been tracked by the Chicago Police Department's Bureau of Records since the beginning of the 20th century. Besides its gangland problems, Chicago saw a major rise in violent crime starting in the late 1960s. Murders in the city peaked first in 1974, with 970 murders when the city's population was over three million, resulting in a murder rate of around 29 per 100,000, and again in 1992, with 943 murders when the city had *fewer* than three million people, resulting in a murder rate of 34 per 100,000.

Following 1992, the murder count slowly decreased to 641 in 1999. In 2002, Chicago had fewer number of murders but a significantly higher murder rate than New York or Los Angeles.

In 1916, 198 homicides were recorded in Chicago, for a city of slightly over 2 million. This level of crime was not exceptional when compared to other American cities such as New York City, but it was much higher relative to European cities, such as London. Although three times the size, London recorded only 45 homicides in the same year. Specialists have developed numerous theories for the higher rates of violence in the US.

Like other major industrial cities in the US, Chicago had a major rise in violent crime starting in the late 1960s. Like most major American cities, Chicago has also experienced a decline in overall crime since the early 1990s. Murders in the city peaked first in 1974, with 970 murders when the city's population was over three million (resulting in a murder rate of around 29 per 100,000), and again in 1992, with 943 murders when the city had *fewer* than three million people, resulting in a murder rate of 34 per 100,000. Following 1992, the murder count slowly decreased to 705 by 1999. That year it still had the most murders of any big city in the U.S.

After adopting crime-fighting techniques in 2004 recommended by the Los Angeles and New York City Police Departments, Chicago recorded 448 homicides, the lowest total since 1965. This murder rate of 15.65 per 100,000 population is still above the U.S. average, an average which takes in many small towns and suburbs. This homicide rate is similar to that of Los Angeles in 2004 (13.4 per 100,000), and twice that of New York City (7.0 per 100,000). Chicago's homicide tally increased slightly in 2005 and 2006 to 450 and 467, respectively, though the overall crime rate in 2006 continued the downward trend that has taken place since the early 1990s, with 2.5% fewer violent crimes and 2.4% fewer property crimes compared to 2005.

According to the 2005 Homicide Report of the Chicago Police Department, the murder clearance rate (in terms of an arrest being made within two years of the homicide) has dropped from over 70% for 1991 to under 60% for 2003. Summer months have significantly higher murder rates, and over 70% of murders take place between 7PM and 5AM. The percentage of murder offenders between 14 and 16 years of age has declined from a 1994 high of approximately 15% to approximately 6% in 2005.

In 2005, 75% of murders involved a firearm, and 11% were the result of a stabbing. 41% of domestic murders were stabbings. 10% of murders in 2005 (39) were the result of an armed robbery, 9% were of undetermined cause, and at least 30% were gang altercations. Over 40% of victims and 60% of offenders were between the ages of 17 and 25. 85% of victims and 93% of offenders were male. 76% of victims were African American (77.4% of offenders were), 18.3% were Hispanic (17.3% of offenders), and 5.6% were white (5.3% of offenders). The African American murder victimization rate was approximately 34 per 100,000; the Hispanic rate was 11 per 100,000, and the white rate 3 per 100,000. Over 75% of victims and 88% of offenders had a prior arrest history. 11% of armed robbery victims were female, 50% of domestic victims were female, and 7% of gang-related victims were female. 31% of armed robbery victims were over 45 years old. 29% of domestic-related murders were committed by women. From 1991 to 2005, 19.2% of armed robbery murder victims were white, and only 4.3% of armed robbery murder offenders were white.

(2005) Victims of gang-related murders: 70% African American, 26% Hispanic, 3% white; 93% male. Offenders in gang-related murders: 76% African American, 20% Hispanic, 3% white; 99% male. Victims of domestic-related murders: 79% African American, 10% Hispanic, 11% white. Victims of armed robbery—related murders: 68% African American, 13% Hispanic, 19% white, 89% male. Offenders in armed robbery—related murders: 87% African American, 9% Hispanic, 4% white; 93% male.

Chicago was among the first U.S. cities to build an integrated emergency response center to coordinate the city's response to natural disasters, gang violence, and terrorist attacks. Built in 1995, the center is integrated with more than 2000 cameras, communications with all levels of city government, and a direct link to the National Counterterrorism Center. Police credited surveillance cameras with contributing to decreased crime in 2004.

Recently installed anti-crime cameras are capable of pinpointing gunshot sounds, calculating where the shots were fired, and pointing and zooming the cameras in the direction of the shots within a two-block radius. Since surveillance cameras have been placed in high-crime areas, some Chicagoans feel uneasy about being so closely watched, but others believe their streets are safer.[who?] The cameras have prompted some calls of discrimination since they have been placed in areas of gang activity and high gun violence that also are chiefly occupied by blacks and Latinos. Mayor Richard M. Daley is a member of the Mayors Against Illegal Guns Coalition, an organization formed in 2006 and co-chaired by New

York City mayor Michael Bloomberg and Boston mayor Thomas Menino.

Because the Chicago Police Department tallies data differently than police in other cities, the FBI often does not accept its crime statistics. Chicago police officers record all criminal sexual assaults, as opposed to only rape. They count aggravated battery together with the standard category of aggravated assault. As a result, Chicago is often omitted from studies such as Morgan Quitno's annual "Safest/Most Dangerous City" survey, which relies on FBI-collected data.

The Chicago Police Department developed to provide city residents with a tool to assist in problem-solving and combating crime and disorder in their neighborhoods. It is based upon the CLEAR (Citizen Law Enforcement Analysis and Reporting) system developed by the Department for use by its police officers. This web application enables citizens to search the Chicago Police Department's database of reported crime. Individuals will be able to see maps, graphs, and tables of reported crime. The database contains 90 days of information, which can be accessed in blocks of up to fourteen days. Data is refreshed daily. However, the most recent information is always seven days old.

Mogadishu is regarded as the most lawless and dangerous city on Earth. It is not safe for urban, leisure or tourism. If you are planning a visit for international aid work, etc, you will need expert advice and planning. Mogadishu is the official capital of Somalia. However, the internationally-recognized Transitional Federal Government (TFN) only controls a few square blocks; the rest is in the hands of Islamist and/or clan or warlord-affiliated militias.

In early 2006, the Union of Islamic courts removed a US-backed coalition of warlords from power and restored order to the volatile capital for some six months. On December 28, 2006, however, the Islamic regime fled the city to the south as Ethiopian-backed government troops re-took the capital without firing a shot in a surprising escalation of events.

However, the Ethiopian occupiers were widely despised and began withdrawing in 2007. Since then, various militias have been vying for control and most are opposed to the legitimate government. The fighting has created tens of thousands of fleeing refugees, has forced many non-government organizations (NGOs) to cease operations (such as providing food, shelter and medicine) and has brought Somalia's very existence as a country to breaking-point. The fact that even thousands of Somalis refuse to stay there should make the situation clear: the city is extremely dangerous.

The war film *Black Hawk Down*, in some ways, gives an understanding of the lawlessness and dangers that exist in Mogadishu and other parts of Somalia. However, the book Black Hawk Down by Mark Bowden gives more detail and a very accurate description of what Mogadishu was like back in 1993.

The Mogadishu airport was bombed in December 2006 by Ethiopia to keep the Islamic Fighters from receiving supplies. Jubba Airways serves Mogadishu from Dubai, Jeddah, Nairobi, Djibouti, as well as domestically from Hargeisa and Galkayo.

It is possible to drive into the city by truck, but this is considered a risky activity, unless you employ a group of local militia which are readily available for hire. Roads link the city with many Somali locales and with Kenya and Ethiopia. Armed guards, hired security forces, and experienced guides are all mandatory for a safe entry, and even then the risk of your being injured, killed or captured is extremely high.

Small cargo ships regularly leave from the Old Harbour of Mombasa for Mogadishu and sometimes Kismayo. Speak with the security officers at the gate of this tiny port and they will negotiate a fare with the captain. The journey will take 2-5 days, depending on conditions. The sea is rough in July-August, requiring lengthier travel.

Arriving by boat is risky, as there is the strong possibility of being attacked by pirates, though the port area is relatively secure.

It is perhaps the most dangerous city on the planet. Its citizens, if you can call them that absent any meaningful form of government, often opt for piracy given a dearth of viable alternatives to poverty or an early, unnatural death. Visitors are encouraged to stay away, as renting a militia to protect you is unlikely to top the odds in your favor to any compelling degree. From the minute you arrive at the airport, you are an attractive kidnap target; you are effectively the food on someone's table.

So, just why the hell would you travel to Mogadishu? This is the truest form of adventure travel. Forget about the hiking and climbing and wilderness trips that the so-called adventure guys rave about. That's all bullshit. They are designed for you to come home alive. Mogadishu, on the other hand? There are no safeguards, and you won't be asked to sign a release. Welcome to a world that's more than arm's reach from the calming presence of law.

Still intent on going to Somalia? Here are a few tips to keep in mind.

Safety ends when the wheels drop—Jubba Airways is the only commercial airline that services Mogadishu, and it claims an impeccable safety record. Once you get on the ground, however, the rules change — immediately. I kicked around taking a trip to Mogadishu last spring and spoke to the general manager of Jubba about arranging a same-day arrival and departure. He wouldn't take my money ... telling me the closest he'd bring me to Mogadishu was Hargeisa, Somaliland.

Get some security—Asking your Kung Fu-master buddy to hang with you on this trip is not enough. You need firepower, lots of it. Fortunately, there are militias that can be hired en route from the airport to the city. They are said to be generally unreliable, but at least you'll have something. Go into Mogadishu without protection, and you are in danger spot. There's no other way to put it.

Pick up some of your own heat—Since you won't be able to tote weapons to Somalia all that easily, you'll probably have to buy something when you get there. The Bakara Market can handle all your small arms needs. Pick up an AK-47 and enough ammo to last you a few days of intense fighting. Rocket-propelled grenades are probably overkill, since you'll be defending yourself from ground forces, not helicopters. And, don't forget to haggle — they love that.

Avoid the crowds—It will be easiest to move after a call to prayer, but you still won't be safe. Nonetheless, this is one of those rare cases in Mogadishu when things will get (slightly) easier for you. Don't be a dumbass: use it. In general, you'll want to steer clear of crowded spots, just because crowds mean more people who could kidnap you, and you probably don't want that.

Bring cash—Your plastic promise "everywhere you want to be," but it's working on the assumption that nobody would want to be in Mogadishu under any circumstances ... even with a battalion of Rangers behind you. The good news is that greenbacks still mean something in Mogadishu. So, you'll have some negotiating power. Just don't go flashing your wad around, or your trip will last a lot longer than you planned.

Check out the sights—There's more to Mogadishu than the Bakara Market. You could always go to the beach. But, you'll probably have more fun viewing the Arba-Runcun Mosque or the Mogadishu Cathedral. Both are close to the waterfront and the old city.

Mogadishu has had no effective government since 1991, which has left the transport network that was in place in disrepair. Roads are a muddy mess during rain, traffic lights do not work, and there are no enforced traffic laws or public transport. Roads may be blocked or closed with no notice by militiamen. Traffic drives on the right. Some reports say that to get through intersections near markets crowded with people, those wealthy enough to have vehicles fire machine guns into the air to clear a path. Safe travel through Mogadishu is only possible by convoy with heavily armed guides and guards, which actually can be hired quite easily. Even with guards, the likelihood of being injured, kidnapped, and/or killed is still very high, including potentially by said hirable guards.

HOW SAFE IS CARACAS?

Violent crime in Caracas is a major problem, and it has been getting steadily worse during the recent years: Caracas is now by some counts the world's most dangerous city, with 7,676 murders in 2009. In case you are robbed, simply hand over what is asked of you. For this reason, it is advisable to carry a "decoy" wallet with small bills (around $50). Most thieves carry guns and they will use them regardless of the consequences (there is a sense of immunity due to poor policing).

Stick to the tourist areas and dress like the average Venezuelans (jeans and short-sleeved shirt). The *barrios* (poor neighborhoods/shanty towns) are to be avoided. They are mostly built into the hills around the west side of Caracas, similar to the *favelas* in Brazil. These neighborhoods are extremely dangerous, but they are far from the main tourist areas.

Kidnapping is a major problem for upper-class Venezuelan, but is unlikely to be a concern for travelers. As with many other developing nations, petty theft is a problem. Ask hotel management to store your valuables when you leave your room and use a money belt for your passport/extra cash when traveling.

The police tends to be corrupt, including at the international airport. However, Venezuelans in general are friendly and helpful. Before traveling to Caracas, please go online and read carefully State Dept. travel advisory warnings about suspicious arrangements made between some Airport Staff and some Taxi drivers.

Use only taxis sent by your hotel, and only book at brand hotels that you are familiar with. Do not wear jewelery, carry a handbag, or move around with large amounts of cash. Some hotels suggest you DO NOT walk round the city at all.

Be aware that you cannot change cash at commercial banks, so carry any cash you may need. Only "cambios" can do cash transactions, and they may not be easily found.

STAY SAFE IN JOHANNESBURG

Be aware that Johannesburg has very high crime levels day and night. However, like many cities with a crime problem some places are quite safe while others can be quite dangerous, and with some places this may depend on whether it is day or night. Armed security (not necessarily the police) are not an uncommon sight in the city. Ask local people (e.g. hotel staff) what to do.

You should keep security constantly in mind and tourists must remain alert at all times, no matter where they are.

Shopping malls in Johannesburg are as safe as shopping malls anywhere else in the world, with pick-pocketing being the only (tiny) risk. Although the recent installation of surveillance cameras in the central business district has decreased daytime robbery and theft there, the area is largely deserted at night, during weekends, and on holidays; if visiting the CBD plan out where you are going to park and what you are going to visit beforehand, don't wander around aimlessly.

Northern suburbs care should be taken if walking around quiet back streets, but you should be fine walking from your guesthouse to a local restaurant / shopping mall - however distances can be large which makes driving / a taxi a better option. If you want to go jogging / go for a long walk then carry a map and minimal valuables, and make sure you are home before it gets dark.

Avoid travelling to areas such as Hillbrow or Berea at any time unless in a large group or with local guides. If travelling to townships, you should make sure that you go with an organised tour as crime is generally much higher in township areas, including Soweto and Alexandra. This warning, especially in the cases of Alexandra and Hillbrow, are not to be read as a paranoid or overly cautious warning - many locals, themselves, do not venture into these areas for safety reasons.

Alexandra Unlike most other dangerous areas in Johannesburg which would take some more effort or serious getting lost to accidentally get into, this very poor and most dangerous township deserves particular attention for the foreign visitor as it is next to the road you would drive on from the airport to Sandton and therefore easy to land up in if you get lost or take the wrong offramp. Do not **UNDER ANY CIRCUMSTANCES** take the London Road offramp from the N3 highway to get to Sandton (which you will see on the horizon and London Road may look like a shortcut even when reading a map or using GPS) as this road goes right through the heart of Alexandra and could lead to your speedy death (or at least being robbed of your car and everything of remote value, leaving you barefoot in your underwear on the pavement in the middle of a slum). To get to Sandton when coming from the airport, take **Marlboro Drive** from the N3 and drive straight until you reach the M1 highway (this is also called the Marlboro offramp). Don't turn south/left (coming from the N3) or right/south (coming from the M1/Sandton side) anywhere between the two freeways, including Louis Botha Avenue (which may be dangerous if you don't know the area). Alternatively if you don't want to risk getting this wrong, you can drive a few kilometers further (the N3 becomes the N1) and take **Rivonia Road** to the south, which will take you straight into central Sandton passing through only affluent areas for the entire length of this road.

Also when taking the Gautrain (which is very safe and nausiatingly well-guarded) between central Sandton and the airport, one of the stations it will stop at is **Marlboro Station**. This station is right on the edge of Alexandra and there is **ABSOLUTELY NO REASON WHATSOVER** (except dire emergency) why any foreigner would want to or need to exit at this station.

Night time It is also prudent to plan night-time journeys. If you must walk at night, make sure to remain in populated, well lit areas, walk confidently and with a purpose as if you know where you are going. Avoid giving the impression that you are lost and ask directions only from persons of authority (example: business owners) and not random people on the streets.

Safety whilst driving Carjacking is much less common than in the late 1990s but Johannesburg still has one of the highest rates in the world - but don't get paranoid and let it spoil your holiday. When you enter your car ensure that your doors are locked and windows are rolled up before starting your journey, night and day. If you have parked in a quiet area be particularly careful when going to and from your car as thieves often wait for victims to exit/ enter their vehicle. Do not leave any valuables on the seats as it is likely that your window will be smashed and your belongings grabbed. At night, do not stop at red traffic lights if you see people lingering there, as they may be up to no good. Slow down and go through the red traffic lights, if necessary paying the fine. At all times be vigilant, watch for vehicles following you or road blocks (stones, wood) on the roads. Many carjackings happen in the main highways such as R21 and R24 which link the O.R Tambo airport to the rest of the province. If faced with a suspicious/dangerous encounter turn around and drive to the nearest police station or well-lit populated area.

Public transport use is discouraged as frequent attacks occur on the crowded services. Depending on the area, the city's Metrobus service can be safe to ride, although it is often late and way too unreliably and confusing for a short-term foreign visitor to figure out. **Avoid** any public transport with out consulting your hosts. The Gautrain however is very secure.

Rape and sexual assault levels are exceptionally high and care should be taken due to the high HIV levels in Johannesburg. Females should avoid walking alone at all times and should try if possible to remain in large groups. If you want fitness, go to gym inside the hotel or shopping mall.

The best general advice is to try your best to look like a local and to avoid at all costs displaying any form of wealth, including ear rings as these have been ripped from unsuspecting tourist. Keep your cell phone hidden and avoid using it in public places. Avoid carrying backpacks, daypacks or purses. Use a cheap plastic bag, keep your values at the hotel and take only the amount of money you really need. Don't use a purse, but put coins or notes loose in your pockets.

If you fall victim to robbery, cooperate with your assailants, hand over your valuables, do not attempt to negotiate, do not look them in the eye and do not fight back.

Finally, keep things in perspective, J'burg does have a bad reputation for crime, but most of this is restricted to residents living in the townships. The overwhelming majority of visitors have a trouble-free stay.

Your Safety in Ciudad Juarez, Mexico

We cannot guarantee your safety in Juarez, Mexico, any more than we could guarantee your safety in Dallas, Texas, Atlanta, Georgia, Chicago, Illinois, or Tokyo, Japan. They are all big cities that undisputedly possess a criminal element. They are also all great cities full of good people and wonderful things to see and do. Use the same precautions you would use in any large metropolitan area.

All we seem to read regarding Ciudad Juárez in the American press, however, centers on crime. While these realities are tragic, especially that of young girls stricken down before their lives have even really begun, it should also be pointed out that this picture of Juárez *lacks balance*, which should be the first priority of any journalist. There is no shortage of serial killers and criminal behavior in any country, but coverage of other cities is more balanced. We get human interest stories, restaurant and nightclub reviews, stories about civic events, and interviews with the city's leadership. The *Time* and *Newsweek* reporters who come here, however, visit Juarez once or twice a year and publish stories which focus *exclusively* on crime.

They stay in 5-star hotels, aparently talk only to the police and newspaper editors about the crime here, and never seem to notice honest Mexican families enjoying lunch or dinner together. Yet the honest families these reporters choose to ignore are the true reality in this city. They are people such as those who live in my neighborhood. It's a very tranquil neighborhood where people actually know each other and bother to say hello. We don't know any drugs lords, and we don't dodge bullets when we walk to the store for a loaf of bread.

Yet the American press has stigmatized Ciudad Juárez as "The City of Death". Its sensational, unbalanced reporting has crippled tourism in the city, costing the local businesses millions of dollars each year. To smear an entire city in this manner, in my humble opinion, borders on being a crime against humanity. If *Time* or *Newsweek* were to publish nothing but stories about crime and murder in a U.S. city, they would surely face lawsuits to the tune of millions of dollars, simply because, once again, although factually true, such coverage lacks *balance*. So why is it okay, at the highest levels of journalism in the United States, to trash a great Mexican city like Ciudad Juárez? We should all be asking ourselves this question.

Unless you have come to corner a piece of the cocaine traffic, you have very little to worry about when visiting Juárez. Having been here on the ground for three years, ridden the buses, walked the streets, fallen in love, and even buried my dead here, I believe I know much, much more about Ciudad Juarez than the reporters from *Time* and *Newsweek* ever will, and I would not be urging you to visit if I thought you would be in danger.

The people in Ciudad Juarez are friendly, honest, and helpful to visitors. 99.9% of the people here are far too busy working 50-60 hours a week to feed their families to worry about who you are, where you are going, or what you are doing. You might find it a little off putting to have someone offering to sell you candy or roses on every corner, or a *parquero* wanting a quarter to help you back your car out of a deserted parking spot, but you have to remember that these people are out on the street 14 hours a day trying to make an honest living. You should probably salute them. Life is hard here for many people, and perhaps the real miracle is that, even in such difficult economic circumstances, more people *do not* turn to crime. The more you know about the people here, the more you realize that almost everything you have ever been told about the city, and Mexico in general, is simply not true. This web site was developed to bring you the truth.

There are a few things you *should* consider, however, when visiting Ciudad Juárez or any place in Mexico.

- Don't enter the country with so much as a spent shotgun shell or empty bullet casing rattling around in the trunk of your car or on your person. It is against the law to have anything relating to firearms in your possession, and this law is strictly enforced.
- Don't drive here without Mexican auto insurance. See the information about driving in Juárez, where I lay out the facts about bringing your car across the border as relates to insurance. If your insurance agent has told you that you are "covered", you'd best understand that being "covered" and being legal are two different things.
- Don't park anywhere questionable without asking if it's okay to park there. If you park in a restricted area, you may come back and find your license plates have been confiscated until you come into the station and pay a fine. You may very well be stopped on the way to the station because you do not have any license plates.
- You can get a ticket for no seat belts.
- If you get a ticket, the officer will take your license and take it to the station. It will stay there until you come to pay the fine.
- These policies are not as unreasonable as it may seem at first. Without them, most visitors would skip the country and never come back to own up to their responsibilities. The minute you cross the border you agree to abide by Mexican law, just as people agree to abide by U.S. law when they enter the United States. Respect the law, and you will have no problems. Generally, what is against the law in the United States is also illegal in Mexico.
- Do not have anything to do with drugs. Avoid anyone who uses drugs, offers to get drugs for you, or even mentions them. Mexican law is absolutely draconian regarding drugs, and it will be your burden to prove your innocence in the Mexican criminal justice system, not the state's burden to prove your

guilt. If the offense is related to drugs, you will be lucky if the American Consulate brings you a little toothbrush and a Sunday paper before wishing you the best of luck. It cannot do much to help you. You are in a foreign country.

- Avoid the area in el centro west of Avenida Juarez towards the south end of Avenida Juarez as you approach Ave. 16 de Septiembre. You will be accosted by drug addicts, street walkers, and cross-dressers. *Don't* confuse these people with the great people of Juarez, Mexico. Peg them as denizens of an impoverished, drug infested area similar to those found in L.A. or New York, and you've got the picture perfectly. I would not be surprised to see a vampire walking sideways up a wall in any of these places. Avoid this area of Juarez at all costs, especially at night.
- Stay on the beaten path until you get to know the city. All of the places in the Juarez Travel Guide are safe to visit.
- Don't get drunk in public. If you want to tie one on, get a hotel room and do it there. Modern Juárez is not a place to get in the mood to ride in hooting and hollering and shooting up the town. The days of Billy the Kid are long gone, and Juarez Police Department is around 24 hours a day to issue reminders of that fact.

The things you should really be worried about in Ciudad Juárez have very little do with being a victim of crime. That can happen anywhere. The things which worry you should have a lot more to do with your own behavior and reasons for coming to Mexico in the first place. If you are coming to spend an afternoon shopping, to have dinner, or spend your vacation enjoying the attractions here I cannot imagine you having any problems.

CULTURAL ANALYSIS AND URBAN TOURISM

The culture of China is one of the world's oldest and most complex cultures. The area in which the culture is dominant covers a large geographical region in eastern Asia with customs and traditions varying greatly between towns, cities and provinces.

Today there are 57 distinct recognized ethnic groups in China. In terms of letters however, the pre-eminent ethnic group is the Han Chinese. Throughout history, many groups have been assimilated into neighboring ethnicities or disappeared without a trace. At the same time, many within the Han identity have maintained distinct linguistic and regional cultural traditions. The term Zhonghua Minzu has been used to describe the notion of Chinese nationalism in general. Much of the traditional cultural identity within the community has to do with distinguishing the family name.

Regional

Traditional Chinese Culture covers large geographical territories, where each region is usually divided into distinct sub-cultures. Each region is often represented by three ancestral items. For example Guangdong is represented by chenpi, aged ginger and hay. Others include ancient cities like Lin'an (Hangzhou), which include tea leaf, bamboo shoot trunk and hickory nut.

Structure

Since the Three Sovereigns and Five Emperors period, some form of Chinese monarch has been the main ruler above all. Different periods of history have different names for the various positions within society. Conceptually each imperial or feudal period is similar, with the government and military officials ranking high in the hierarchy, and the rest of the population under regular Chinese law.

From the late Zhou Dynasty (1046–256 BCE) onwards, traditional Chinese society was organized into a hierarchic system of socio-economic classes known as the four occupations. However, this system did not cover all social groups while the distinctions between all groups became blurred ever since the commercialization of Chinese culture in the Song Dynasty (960–1279 CE). Ancient Chinese education also has a long history; ever since the Sui Dynasty (581–618 CE) educated candidates prepared for the Imperial examinations which drafted exam graduates into government as scholar-bureaucrats.

Trades and crafts were usually taught by a shifu. The female historian Ban Zhao wrote the Lessons for Women in the Han Dynasty and outlined the four virtues women must abide to, while scholars such as Zhu Xi and Cheng Yi would expand upon this. Chinese marriage and Taoist sexual practices are some of the customs and rituals found in society.

Values

Most social values are derived from Confucianism and Taoism. The subject of which school was the most influential is always debated as many concepts such as Neo-Confucianism, Buddhism and many others have come about. Reincarnation and other rebirth concept is a reminder of the connection between real-life and the after-life. In Chinese business culture, the concept of *guanxi*, indicating the primacy of relations over rules, has been well documented.

Language

The ancient written standard was Classical Chinese. It was used for thousands of years, but was mostly reserved for scholars and intellectuals. By the 20th century, millions of citizens, especially those outside of the imperial court were illiterate. Only after the May 4th Movement did the push for written vernacular Chinese begin. This allowed common citizens to read since it was modeled after the linguistics and phonology of the standard spoken language.

MYTHOLOGY AND SPIRITUALITY

Chinese religion was originally oriented to worshipping the supreme god Shang Di during the Xia and Shang dynasties, with the king and diviners acting as priests and using oracle bones. The Zhou dynasty oriented it to worshipping the broader concept of heaven. A large part of Chinese culture is based on the notion that a spiritual world exists. Countless methods of divination have helped answer questions, even serving as an alternate to medicine. Folklores have helped fill the gap for things that cannot be explained. There is often a blurred line between myth, religion and unexplained phenomenon.

While many deities are part of the tradition, some of the most recognized holy figures include Guan Yin, Jade Emperor and Buddha. Many of the stories have since evolved into traditional Chinese holidays. Other concepts have extended to outside of mythology into spiritual symbols such as Door god and the Imperial guardian lions. Along with the belief of the holy, there is also the evil. Practices such as Taoist exorcism fighting mogwai and jiang shi with peachwood swords are just some of the concepts passed down from generations. A few Chinese fortune telling rituals are still in use today after thousands of years of refinement.

Literature

Chinese literature began with record keeping and divination on Oracle Bones. The extensive collection of books that have been preserved since the Zhou Dynasty demonstrate just how advanced the intellectuals were at one time. Indeed, the era of the Zhou Dynasty is often looked to as the touchstone of Chinese cultural development. The Five Cardinal Points are the foundation for almost all major studies.

Concepts covered within the Chinese classic texts present a wide range of subjects including poetry, astrology, astronomy, calendar, constellations and many others. Some of the most important early texts include I Ching and Shujing within the Four Books and Five Classics. Many Chinese concepts such as Yin and Yang, Qi, Four Pillars of Destiny in relation to heaven and earth were all theorized in the dynastic periods.

Notable confucianists, taoists and scholars of all classes have made significant contributions to and from documenting history to authoring saintly concepts that seem hundred of years ahead of time. Many novels such as Four Great Classical Novels spawned countless fictional stories. By the end of the Qing Dynasty, Chinese culture would embark on a new era with written vernacular Chinese for the common citizens. Hu Shih and Lu Xun would be pioneers in modern literature.

Culture of United States

The culture of the United States of America is a Western culture, historically heavily influenced by European cultures. It has been developing since long before the United States became a country with its own unique social and cultural characteristics such as dialect, music, arts, social habits, cuisine, and folklore. Today the United States of America is an ethnically and racially diverse country as result of large-scale immigration from many different countries throughout its history .

Its chief early influences came from English and Irish settlers of colonial America. British culture, due to colonial ties with Britain that spread the English language, legal system and other cultural inheritances, had a formative influence. Other important influences came from other parts of western Europe, especially Germany, France, and Italy.

Original elements also play a strong role, such as the invention of Jeffersonian Democracy. Thomas Jefferson's *Notes on the State of Virginia* was perhaps the first influential domestic cultural critique by an American and a reactionary piece to the prevailing European consensus that America's domestic originality was degenerate. Prevalent ideas and ideals which evolved domestically such as national holidays, uniquely American sports, military tradition, and innovations in the arts and entertainment give a strong sense of national pride among the population as a whole.

American culture includes both conservative and liberal elements, military and scientific competitiveness, political structures, risk taking and free expression, materialist and moral elements. Despite certain consistent ideological principles (e.g. individualism, egalitarianism, and faith in freedom and democracy), American culture has a variety of expressions due to its geographical scale and demographic diversity. The flexibility of U.S. culture and its highly symbolic nature lead some researchers to categorize American culture as a *mythic* identity; others see it as American exceptionalism.

It also includes elements which evolved from Native Americans, and other ethnic subcultures; most prominently the culture of African American and different cultures from Latin America. Many cultural elements, especially popular culture have been exported across the globe through modern mass media where American culture is sometimes resented. A few[*which?*] of the cultural elements have remained rather exclusive to North America.

The United States has often been thought of as a melting pot, but recent developments tend towards cultural diversity, pluralism and the image of a salad bowl rather than a melting pot. Due to the extent of American culture there are many integrated but unique social subcultures within the United States. The cultural affiliations an individual in the United States may have commonly depend on social class, political orientation and a multitude of demographic characteristics such as religious background, occupation and ethnic group membership.

Although the United States has no official language at the federal level, 30 states have passed legislation making English the official language and it is considered to be the *de facto* national language. According to the 2000 U.S. Census, more than 97% of Americans can speak English well, and for 81% it is the only language spoken at home. There are more than 300 languages besides English which can claim native speakers in the United States—some of which are spoken by the indigenous peoples (about 150 living languages) and others which were imported by immigrants.

Spanish has official status in the commonwealth of Puerto Rico and the state of New Mexico; Spanish is the primary spoken language in Puerto Rico and various smaller linguistic enclaves.

According to the 2000 census, there are nearly 30 million native speakers of Spanish in the United States. Bilingual speakers may use both English and Spanish reasonably well but code-switch according to their dialog partner or context. Some refer to this phenomenon as Spanglish.

Indigenous languages of the United States include the Native American languages, which are spoken on the country's numerous Indian reservations and Native American cultural events such as pow wows; Hawaiian, which has official status in the state of Hawaii; Chamorro, which has official status in the commonwealths of Guam and the Northern Mariana Islands; Carolinian, which has official status in the commonwealth of the Northern Mariana Islands; and Samoan, which has official status in the commonwealth of American Samoa. American Sign Language, used mainly by the deaf, is also native to the country.

The national dialect is known as American English. There are four major regional dialects in the United States: northeastern, south, inland north, and midwestern. The Midwestern accent (considered the "standard accent" in the United States, and analogous in some respects to the received pronunciation elsewhere in the English-speaking world) extends from what were once the "Middle Colonies" across the Midwest to the Pacific states.

Native language statistics for the United States

The following information is an estimation as actual statistics constantly vary.

According to the CIA, the following is the percentage of total population's native languages in the United States:

- English (82.1%)
- Spanish (10.7%)
- Other Indo-European languages (3.8%)
- Other Asian or Pacific Islander languages (2.7%)
- Other languages (0.7%)

Religion

Among developed countries, the U.S. is one of the most religious (primarily Christian) in terms of its demographics.

According to a 2002 study by the Pew Global Attitudes Project, the U.S. was the only developed nation in the survey where a majority of citizens reported that religion played a "very important" role in their lives, an attitude similar to that found in its neighbors in Latin America. Today, governments at the national, state, and local levels are secular institution, with what is often called the "separation of church and state" prevailing.

Several of the original Thirteen Colonies were established by English and Irish settlers who wished to practice their own religion without discrimination or persecution: Pennsylvania was established by Quakers, Maryland by Roman Catholics and the Massachusetts Bay Colony by Puritans. The first bible printed in a European language in the Colonies was by German immigrant Christopher Sauer. Nine of the thirteen colonies had official public religions. Yet by the time of the Philadelphia Convention of 1787, the United States became one of the first countries in the world to codify freedom of religion into law, although this originally applied only to the federal government, and not to state governments or their political subdivisions.

Modeling the provisions concerning religion within the Virginia Statute for Religious Freedom, the framers of the United States Constitution rejected any religious test for office, and the First Amendment specifically denied the central government any power to enact any law respecting either an establishment of religion, or prohibiting its free exercise. In following decades, the animating spirit behind the constitution's Establishment Clause led to the disestablishment of the official religions within the member states.

The framers were mainly influenced by secular, Enlightenment ideals, but they also considered the pragmatic concerns of minority religious groups who did not want to be under the power or influence of a state religion that did not represent them. Thomas Jefferson, author of the Declaration of Independence said "The priest has been hostile to liberty. He is always in alliance with the despot."

Religious Statistics for the United States

It should be noted the following information is an estimation as actual statistics constantly vary.

According to the CIA, the following is the percentage of followers of different religions in the United States:

- Christian: (80.2%)
  - o Protestant (51.3%)
  - o Roman Catholic (23.9%)
  - o Mormon (1.7%)
  - o Other Christian (1.6%)
- Jewish (1.7%)
- Buddhist (0.7%)
- Muslim (0.6%)
- Other/Unspecified (2.5%)
- Unaffiliated (12.1%)
- None (4%)

Other religions include neo-pagan, most prominently Wicca. In more recent surveys, approximately 16% of American citizens identified as atheist, agnostic, or having no religion.

Education

Education in the United States is provided mainly by government, with control and funding coming from three levels: federal, state, and local. School attendance is mandatory and nearly universal at the elementary and high school levels often known outside the United States as the primary and secondary levels.

Students have the options of having their education held in public schools, private schools, or home school. In most public and private schools, education is divided into three levels: elementary school, junior high school (also often called middle school), and high school. In almost all schools at these levels, children are divided by age groups into grades. Post-secondary education, better known as "college" or "university" in the United States, is generally governed separately from the elementary and high school system.

In the year 2000, there were 76.6 million students enrolled in schools from kindergarten through graduate schools. Of these, 72 percent aged 12 to 17 were judged academically "on track" for their age (enrolled in school at or above grade level). Of those enrolled in compulsory education, 5.2 million (10.4 percent) were attending private schools. Among the country's adult population, over 85 percent have completed high school and 27 percent have received a bachelor's degree or higher.

Race and Ancestry

Race in the United States is based on physical characteristics and skin color and has played an essential part in shaping American society even before the nation's conception. Until the civil rights movement of the 1960s, racial minorities in the United States faced discrimination and social as well as economic marginalization. Today, the U.S. Department of Commerce's Bureau of the Census recognizes four races, Native American or American Indian, African American, Asian and White (European American).

According to the U.S. government, Hispanic Americans do not constitute a race, but rather an ethnic group. During the 2000 U.S. Census Whites made up 75.1% of the population with those being Hispanic or Latino constituting the nation's prevalent minority with 12.5% of the population. African Americans made up 12.3% of the total population, 3.6% were Asian American and 0.7% were Native American.

Approximately 62% of White Americans today are either wholly or partly of English, Welsh, Irish, or Scottish ancestry. Approximately 86% of White Americans are of northwestern European descent, and 14% are of southern and eastern European ancestry. Until the Thirteenth Amendment to the United States Constitution was ratified on December 6th 1865 the United States was a slave society. While the northern states had outlawed slavery in their territory in the late 18th and early 19th century their industrial economies relied on the raw materials produced by slave labor. Following the Reconstruction period in the 1870s, Southern states initialized an apartheid regulated by Jim Crow laws that provided for legal segregation.

Lynching occurred throughout the U.S. until the 1930s, continuing well into the civil rights movement in the South. Asian Americans were also marginalized during much of U.S. history. Between 1882 and 1943 the United States government instituted the Chinese Exclusion Act which prohibited Chinese immigrants from entering the nation. During the second world war roughly 120,000 Japanese Americans, 62% of whom were U.S. citizens, were imprisoned in Japanese internment camps.

Hispanic Americans also faced segregation and other types of discrimination; they were regularly subject to second class citizen status, in practice if not by law. Largely as a result of being de jure or de facto excluded and marginalized from so-called mainstream society, racial minorities in the United States developed their own unique sub-cultures. During the 1920s for example, Harlem, New York became home to the Harlem Renaissance. Music styles such as Jazz, Blues and Rap, Rock and roll as well as numerous folk-songs such as Blue Tail Fly (Jimmy Crack Corn) originated within the realms of African American culture. Chinatowns can be found in many cities across the nation and Asian cuisine has become a common staple in America.

The Hispanic community has also had a dramatic impact on American culture. Today, Catholics are the largest religious denomination in the United States and out-number Protestants in the South-west and California. Mariachi music and Mexican cuisine are commonly found throughout the Southwest, with some Latin dishes such burritos and tacos found anywhere in the nation. Economic discrepancies and de-facto segregation, however, continue and is a prominent feature of mundane life in the United States.

While Asian Americans have prospered and have a median household income and educational attainment far exceeding that of Whites, the same cannot be said for the other racial minorities. African Americans, Hispanics and Native Americans have considerably lower income and education than do White Americans. In 2005 the median household income of Whites was 62.5% higher than that of African American, nearly one-quarter of whom live below the poverty line. Furthermore 46.9% of homicide victims in the United States are African American indicating the many severe socio-economic problems African Americans and minorities in general continue to face in the twenty-first century.

Some aspects of American culture codify racism. For example, the prevailing idea in American culture, perpetuated by the media, has been that that black features are less attractive or desirable than white features. The idea that blackness was ugly was highly damaging to the psyche of African Americans, manifesting itself as internalized racism. The Black is beautiful cultural movement sought to dispel this notion.

In the years after September 11th, discrimination against Arabs and Muslims in the U.S. has increased significantly. The American-Arab Anti-Discrimination Committee (ADC) reported an increase in hate speech, cases of airline discrimination, hate crimes, police misconduct and racial profiling. The USA PATRIOT Act, signed into effect by President Bush on October 26, 2001, has also raised concerns for violating civil liberties. Section 412 of the act provides the government with "sweeping new powers to detain immigrants and other foreign nationals indefinitely with little or no due process at the discretion of the Attorney General." Other sections also allow the government to conduct secret searches, seizures, and surveillance, and to freely interpret the definition of "terrorist activities".

Literature

The right to freedom of expression in the American constitution can be traced to German immigrant John Peter Zenger and his legal fight to make truthful publications in the Colonies a protected legal right, ultimately paving the way for the protected rights of American authors.

In the eighteenth and early nineteenth centuries, American art and literature took most of its cues from Europe. During its early history, America was a series of British colonies on the eastern coast of the present-day United States. Therefore, its literary tradition begins as linked to the broader tradition of English literature. However, unique American characteristics and the breadth of its production usually now cause it to be considered a separate path and tradition.

Writers such as Nathaniel Hawthorne, Edgar Allan Poe, and Henry David Thoreau established a distinctive American literary voice by the middle of the nineteenth century. Mark Twain and poet Walt Whitman were major figures in the century's second half; Emily Dickinson, virtually unknown during her lifetime, would be recognized as America's other essential poet. Eleven U.S. citizens have won the Nobel Prize in Literature, most recently Toni Morrison in 1993. Ernest Hemingway, the 1954 Nobel laureate, is often named as one of the most influential writers of the twentieth century.

A work seen as capturing fundamental aspects of the national experience and character—such as Herman Melville's *Moby-Dick*

(1851), Twain's *The Adventures of Huckleberry Finn* (1885), and F. Scott Fitzgerald's *The Great Gatsby* (1925)—may be dubbed the "Great American Novel". Popular literary genres such as the Western and hardboiled crime fiction were developed in the United States.

The cuisine of the United States is extremely diverse, owing to the vastness of the continent, the relatively large population (1/3 of a billion people) and the number of native and immigrant influences. Mainstream American culinary arts are similar to those in other Western countries. Wheat is the primary cereal grain. Traditional American cuisine uses ingredients such as turkey, white-tailed deer venison, potatoes, sweet potatoes, corn, squash, and maple syrup, indigenous foods employed by American Indians and early European settlers. Slow-cooked pork and beef barbecue, crab cakes, potato chips, cotton candy and chocolate chip cookies are distinctively American styles.

The types of food served at home vary greatly and depend upon the region of the country and the family's own cultural heritage. Recent immigrants tend to eat food similar to that of their country of origin, and Americanized versions of these cultural foods, such as American Chinese cuisine or Italian-American cuisine often eventually appear; an example is Vietnamese cuisine, Korean cuisine and Thai cuisine. German cuisine has a profound impact on American cuisine, especially mid-western cuisine, with potatoes, noodles, roasts, stews and cakes/pastries being the most iconic ingredients in both cuisines. Dishes such as the hamburger, pot roast, baked ham and hot dogs are examples of American dishes derived from German cuisine.

Different regions of the United States have their own cuisine and styles of cooking. The state of Louisiana, for example, is known for its Cajun and Creole cooking. Cajun and Creole cooking are influenced by French, Acadian, and Haitian cooking, although the dishes themselves are original and unique. Examples include Crawfish Etouffee, Red Beans and Rice, Seafood or Chicken Gumbo, Jambalaya, and Boudin. Italian, German, Hungarian and Chinese influences, traditional Native American, Caribbean, Mexican and Greek dishes have also diffused into the general American repertoire. It is not uncommon for a "middle class" family from "middle America" to eat, for example, restaurant pizza, home-made pizza, enchiladas con carne, chicken paprikas, beef stroganof and bratwurst with sauerkraut for dinner throughout a single week.

Soul food, developed by African slaves, is popular around the South and among many African Americans elsewhere. Syncretic cuisines such as Louisiana creole, Cajun, Pennsylvania Dutch, and Tex-Mex are regionally important. Iconic American dishes such as apple pie, fried chicken, pizza, hamburgers, and hot dogs derive from the recipes of various immigrants and domestic innovations. So-called French fries, Mexican dishes such as burritos and tacos, and pasta dishes freely adapted from Italian sources are consumed.

Americans generally prefer coffee to tea, with more than half the adult population drinking at least one cup a day. Marketing by U.S. industries is largely responsible for making orange juice and milk (now often fat-reduced) ubiquitous breakfast beverages. During the 1980s and 1990s, Americans' caloric intake rose 24%; frequent dining at fast food outlets is associated with what health officials call the American "obesity epidemic." Highly sweetened soft drinks are popular; sugared beverages account for 9% of the average American's daily caloric intake.

Social Class and Work

Though most Americans today identify themselves as middle class, American society and its culture are considerably more fragmented.[38] Social class, generally described as a combination of educational attainment, income and occupational prestige, is one of the greatest cultural influences in America. Nearly all cultural aspects of mundane interactions and consumer behavior in the U.S. are guided by a person's location within the country's social structure.

Distinct lifestyles, consumption patterns and values are associated with different classes. Early sociologist-economist Thorstein Veblen, for example, noted that those at the very top of the social ladder engage in conspicuous leisure as well as conspicuous consumption. Upper middle class persons commonly identify education and being cultured as prime values. Persons in this particular social class tend to speak in a more direct manner that projects authority, knowledge and thus credibility. They often tend to engage in the consumption of so-called mass luxuries, such as designer label clothing. A strong preference for natural materials and organic foods as well as a strong health consciousness tend to be prominent features of the upper middle class. Middle class individuals in general value expanding one's horizon, partially because they are more educated and can afford greater leisure and travels. Working class individuals take great pride in doing what they consider to be "real work," and keep very close-knit kin networks that serve as a safeguard against frequent economic instability.[38]

Working class Americans as well as many of those in the middle class may also face occupation alienation. In contrast to upper middle class professionals who are mostly hired to conceptualize, supervise and share their thoughts, many Americans enjoy only little autonomy or creative latitude in the workplace. As a result white collar professionals tend to be significantly more satisfied with their work. More recently those in the center of the income strata, who may still identify as middle class, have faced increasing economic insecurity, supporting the idea of a working class majority.

In the United States occupation is one of the prime factors of social class and is closely linked to an individual's identity. The average work week in the U.S. for those employed full-time was 42.9 hours long with 30% of the population working more than 40 hours a week. It should be noted, however, that many of those in the top two earning quintiles often worked more than 50 hours a week. The Average American worker earned $16.64 an hour in the first two quarters of 2006. Overall Americans worked more than their counterparts in other developed post-industrial nations. While the average worker in Denmark enjoyed 30 days of vacation annually, the average American only had 16 annual vacation days. In 2000 the average American worked 1,978 hours per year, 500 hours more than the average German, yet 100 hours less than the average Czech. Overall the U.S. labor force was the most productive in the world (overall, not by hour worked), largely due to its workers working more than those in any other post-industrial country (excluding South Korea). Americans generally hold working and being productive in high regard; being busy as and working extensively may also serve as the means to obtain esteem.

Housing

Immediately after World War II, Americans began living in increasing numbers in the suburbs, belts around major cities with higher density than rural areas, but much lower than urban areas. This move has been attributed to many factors such as the automobile, the availability of large tracts of land, the convenience of more and longer paved roads, the increasing violence in urban centers (see white flight), and the cheapness of housing. These new single-family houses were usually one or two stories tall, and often were part of large contracts of homes built by a single developer.

The resulting low-density development has been given the pejorative label "urban sprawl." This is changing, however. "White flight" is reversing, with many Yuppies and upper-middle-class, empty nest Baby Boomers returning to urban living, usually in condominiums, such as in New York City's Lower East Side, and Chicago's South Loop. The result has been the displacement of many poorer, inner-city residents. (see gentrification). American cities with housing prices near the national median have also been losing the middle income neighborhoods, those with median income between 80% and 120% of the metropolitan area's median household income.

Here, the more affluent members of the middle class, who are also often referred to as being professional or upper middle class, have left in search of larger homes in more exclusive suburbs. This trend is largely attributed to the so called "Middle class squeeze," which has caused a starker distinction between the statistical middle class and the more privileged members of the middle class. In more expensive areas such as California, however, another trend has been taking place where an influx of more affluent middle class households has displaced those in the actual middle of society and converted former middle-middle class neighborhoods into upper middle class neighborhoods.

The population of rural areas has been declining over time as more and more people migrate to cities for work and entertainment. The great exodus from the farms came in the 1940s; in recent years fewer than 2% of the population lives on farms (though others live in the countryside and commute to work). Electricity and telephone, and sometimes cable and Internet services are available to all but the most remote regions. As in the cities, children attend school up to and including high school and only help with farming during the summer months or after school.

About half of Americans now live in what is known as the suburbs. The suburban nuclear family has been identified as part of the "American dream": a married couple with children owning a house in the suburbs. This archetype is reinforced by mass media, religious practices, and government policies and is based on traditions from Anglo-Saxon cultures. One of the biggest differences in suburban living as compared to urban living is the housing occupied by the families. The suburbs are filled with single-family homes separated from retail districts, industrial areas, and sometimes even public schools. However, many American suburbs are incorporating these districts on smaller scales, attracting more people to these communities.

Housing in urban areas may include more apartments and semi-attached homes than in the suburbs or small towns. Aside from housing, the major difference from suburban living is the density and diversity of many different subcultures, as well as retail and manufacturing buildings mixed with housing in urban areas. Urban residents are also more likely to travel by mass transit, and children are more likely to walk or bicycle rather than being driven by their parents.

Americans, by and large, are often fascinated by new technology and new gadgets. There are many within the United States that share the attitude that through technology, many of the evils in the society can be solved. Many of the new technological innovations in the modern world were either first invented in the United States and/or first widely adopted by Americans. Examples include: the lightbulb, the airplane, the transistor, nuclear power, the personal computer, video games and online shopping, as well as the development of the Internet. By comparison with Japan, however, only a small fraction of electronic devices make it to sale in the U.S., and household items such as toilets are rarely festooned with remotes and electronic buttons as they are in some parts of Asia.

Automobiles play a great role in American culture, whether it is in the mundane lives of private individuals or in the areas of arts and entertainment. The rise of suburbs and the need for workers to commute to cities brought about the popularization of automobiles. In 2001, 90% of Americans drove to work in cars.

Lower energy and land costs favor the production of relatively large, powerful cars. The culture in the 1950s and 1960s often catered to the automobile with motels and drive-in restaurants. Americans tend to view obtaining a driver's license as a rite of passage. Outside of a relative few urban areas, it is considered a necessity for most Americans to own and drive cars. New York City is the only locality in the United States where more than half of all households do not own a car.

Gender Relations

Couples often meet through religious institutions, work, school, or friends. "Dating services," services that are geared to assist people in finding partners, are popular both on and offline. The trend over the past few decades has been for more and more couples deciding to cohabit before, or instead of, getting married. The 2000 Census reported 9.7 million different-sex partners living together and about 1.3 million same-sex partners living together. These cohabitation arrangements have not been the subject of many laws regulating them, though some states now have domestic partner statutes and judge-made palimony doctrines that confer some legal support for unmarried couples.

Adolescent sex is common; most Americans first have intercourse in their teens. The current data suggests that by the time a person turns 18, slightly more than half of females and nearly two-thirds of males will have had intercourse. More than half of sexually active teens have had sexual partners they are dating. Risky sexual behaviors that involve "anything intercourse related" are "rampant" among teenagers. Teen pregnancies in the United States decreased 28% between 1990 and 2000 from 117 pregnancies per every 1,000 teens to 84 per 1,000. The U.S. is rated, based on 2002 numbers, 84 out of 170 countries based on teenage fertility rate, according to the World Health Organization.

Marriage and Divorce

Marriage laws are established by individual states. Same-sex marriage is currently legal in Massachusetts, Iowa, Vermont, Maine, New Hampshire, and Connecticut. New Jersey, California, Oregon, Washington D.C., Washington, and Nevada allow same-sex couples access to most state-level marriage benefits with civil unions or domestic partnerships; Hawaii, Maryland and Colorado offer some benefits to couples in domestic partnerships. New York recognizes out-of-state same-sex marriages but does not perform them.

In many states, it is illegal to cross state lines to obtain a marriage that would be illegal in the home state. The typical wedding involves a couple proclaiming their commitment to one another in front of their close relatives and friends, often presided over by a religious figure such as a minister, priest, or rabbi, depending upon the faith of the couple. In traditional Christian ceremonies, the bride's father will "give away" (hand off) the bride to the groom. Secular weddings are also common, often presided over by a judge, Justice of the Peace, or other municipal official.

Divorce is the province of state governments, so divorce law varies from state to state. Prior to the 1970s, divorcing spouses had to allege that the other spouse was guilty of a crime or sin like abandonment or adultery; when spouses simply could not get along, lawyers were forced to manufacture "uncontested" divorces. The no-fault divorce revolution began in 1969 in California; South Dakota was the last state to allow no-fault divorce, in 1985. No-fault divorce on the grounds of "irreconcilable differences" is now available in all states. However, many states have recently required separation periods prior to a formal divorce decree.

State law provides for child support where children are involved, and sometimes for alimony. "Married adults now divorce two-and-a-half times as often as adults did 20 years ago and four times as often as they did 50 years ago... between 40% and 60% of *new* marriages will eventually end in divorce. The probability within... the first five years is 20%, and the probability of its ending within the first 10 years is 33%... Perhaps 25% of children ages 16 and under live with a stepparent." The median length for a marriage in the U.S. today is 11 years with 90% of all divorces being settled out of court.

Gender Roles

Since the 1970s, traditional gender roles of male and female have been increasingly challenged by both legal and social means. Today, there are far fewer roles that are legally restricted by one's sex. The military remains a notable exception, where women may not be put into direct combat by law. Asymmetrical warfare, however, has put women into situations which are direct combat operations in all but name.

Most social roles are not gender-restricted by law, though there are still cultural inhibitions surrounding certain roles. More and more women have entered the workplace, and in the year 2000 made up 46.6% of the labor force, up from 18.3% in 1900. Most men, however, have not taken up the traditional full-time homemaker role; likewise, few men have taken traditionally feminine jobs such as receptionist or nurse (although nursing was traditionally a male role before the American Civil War).

Death Rituals

It is customary for Americans to hold a wake in a funeral home within a couple days of the death of a loved one. The body of the deceased may be embalmed and dressed in fine clothing if there will be an open-casket viewing. Traditional Jewish and Muslim practice include a ritual bath and no embalming. Friends, relatives and acquaintances gather, often from distant parts of the country, to "pay their last respects" to the deceased. Flowers are brought to the coffin and sometimes eulogies, elegies, personal anecdotes or group prayers are recited. Otherwise, the attendees sit, stand or kneel in quiet contemplation or prayer. Kissing the corpse on the forehead is typical among Italian Americans and others. Condolences are also offered to the widow or widower and other close relatives.

A funeral may be held immediately afterwards or the next day. The funeral ceremony varies according to religion and culture. American Catholics typically hold a funeral mass in a church, which sometimes takes the form of a Requiem mass. Jewish Americans may hold a service in a synagogue or temple. Pallbearers carry the coffin of the deceased to the hearse, which then proceeds in a procession to the place of final repose, usually a cemetery. The unique Jazz funeral of New Orleans features joyous and raucous music and dancing during the procession.

Mount Auburn Cemetery (founded in 1831) is known as "America's first garden cemetery." American cemeteries created since are distinctive for their park-like setting. Rows of graves are covered by lawns and are interspersed with trees and flowers.

Headstones, mausoleums, statuary or simple plaques typically mark off the individual graves. Cremation is another common practice in the United States, though it is frowned upon by various religions. The ashes of the deceased are usually placed in an urn, which may be kept in a private house, or they are interred. Sometimes the ashes are released into the atmosphere. The "sprinkling" or "scattering" of the ashes may be part of an informal ceremony, often taking place at a scenic natural feature (a cliff, lake or mountain) that was favored by the deceased.

A so-called death industry has developed in the United States that has replaced earlier, more informal traditions. Before the popularity of funeral homes, a wake would be held in an ordinary, private house. Often the most elegant room was reserved for this purpose.

Today, family arrangements in the United States reflect the diverse and dynamic nature of contemporary American society. Although for a relatively brief period of time in the 20th century most families adhered to the nuclear family concept (two-married adults with a biological child), single-parent families, childless/childfree couples, and fused families now constitute the majority of families.

Most Americans will marry and get divorced at least once during their life; thus, most individuals will live in a variety of family arrangements. A person may grow up in a single-parent family, go on to marry and live in childless couple arrangement, then get divorced, live as a single for a couple of years, re-marry, have children and live in a nuclear family arrangement.

"The nuclear family... is the idealized version of what most people think when they think of "family..." The old definition of what a family is... the nuclear family- no longer seems adequate to cover the wide diversity of household arrangements we see today, according to many social scientists (Edwards 1991; Stacey 1996). Thus has arisen the term *postmodern family*, which is meant to describe the great variability in family forms, including single-parent families and child-free couples.

Other changes to the landscape of American family arrangements include dual-income earner households and delayed independence among American youths. Whereas most families in the 1950s and 1960s relied on one income earner, most commonly the husband, the vast majority of family households now have two-income earners.

Another change is the increasing age at which young Americans leave their parental home. Traditionally, a person past "college age" who lived with their parent(s) was viewed negatively, but today it is not uncommon for children to live with their parents until their mid-twenties. This trend can be mostly attributed to rising living costs that far exceed those in decades past. Thus, many young adults now remain with their parents well past their mid-20s. This topic was a cover article of TIME magazine in 2005.

Regional Variations

Semi-distinct cultural regions of the United States include New England, the Mid-Atlantic States, the Southern United States, the Midwestern United States, the Southwest United States, the Western United States and the Pacific Northwest. The western coast of the continental U.S. consisting of California, Oregon, and the state of Washington is also sometimes referred to as the Left Coast, indicating its left-leaning political orientation and tendency towards liberal norms, folkways and values.

Strong cultural differences have a long history in the U.S. with the southern slave society in the antebellum period serving as a prime example. Not only social, but also economic tensions between the Northern and Southern states were so severe that they eventually caused the South to declare itself an independent nation, the Confederate States of America; thus provoking the American civil war. One example of regional variations is the attitude towards the discussion of sex, often sexual discussions would have less restrictions in the Northeastern United States, but yet is seen as taboo in the Southern United States.

In his 1989 book, "Albion's Seed" (ISBN 0195069056), David Hackett Fischer makes a strong case for the theory that the United States is made up today of four distinct regional cultures. The book's focus is on the folkways of four groups of settlers from the British Isles that emigrated from distinct regions of Britain and Ireland to the British American colonies during the 17th and 18th centuries. Fischer's thesis is that the culture and folkways of each of these groups persisted, albeit with some modification over time, providing the basis for the four modern regional cultures of the United States.

According to Fischer, the foundation of American culture was formed from four mass migrations from four different regions of the British Isles by four distinct socio-religious groups. New England's earliest settlement period occurred between 1629 and 1640 when Puritans, mostly from East Anglia in England, settled there, forming the New England regional culture. The next mass migration was of southern English cavaliers and their Irish and Scottish domestic servants to the Chesapeake Bay region between 1640 and 1675. This facilitated the development of the Southern American culture.

Then, between 1675 and 1725, thousands of Irish, English and German Quakers, led by William Penn, settled in the Delaware Valley. This settlement resulted in the formation of what is today considered the "General American" culture, although, according to Fischer, it is really just a regional American culture, even if it does today encompass most of the U.S. from the mid-Atlantic states to the Pacific Coast. Finally, Irish, Scottish and English settlers from the borderlands of Britain and Ireland migrated to Appalachia between 1717 and 1775. They formed the regional culture of the Upland South, which has since spread west to such areas as West Texas and parts of the U.S. Southwest.

Fischer suggests that the U.S. today is not a country with one General American culture and three or more regional sub-cultures. He asserts that the country is composed of just regional cultures, and that understanding that helps one to understand many things about modern American life. Fischer also makes the point that the development of these regional cultures derived not only from where exactly the settlers first came, but when they came. Fischer asserts that during different periods to time, a population of people will have very distinct beliefs, fears, hopes and prejudices, and that various groups of settlers brought these feelings to the New World where they more or less froze in time in America, even if they eventually changed in their place of origin.

Drugs, Alcohol and Smoking

American attitudes towards drugs and alcoholic beverages have evolved considerably throughout the country's history. In the 19th century, alcohol was readily available and consumed, and no laws restricted the use of other drugs. Attitudes on drug addiction started to change, resulting in the Harrison Act which eventually became proscriptive.

A movement to ban alcoholic beverages, called the Temperance movement, emerged in the late 19th century. Several American Protestant religious groups, as well as women's groups such as the Women's Christian Temperance Union, supported the movement. In 1919, Prohibitionists succeeded in amending the Constitution to prohibit the sale of alcohol. Although the Prohibition period did result in lowering alcohol consumption overall, banning alcohol outright proved to be unworkable, as the previously legitimate distillery industry was replaced by criminal gangs which trafficked in alcohol. Prohibition was repealed in 1931. States and localities retained the right to remain "dry", and to this day, a handful still do.

During the Vietnam War era, attitudes swung well away from prohibition. Commentators noted that an 18 year old could be drafted to war but could not buy a beer. Most states lowered the legal drinking age to 18.

Since 1980, the trend has been toward greater restrictions on alcohol and drug use. The focus this time, however, has been to criminalize behaviors associated with alcohol, rather than attempt to prohibit consumption outright. New York was the first state to enact tough drunk-driving laws in 1980; since then all other states have followed suit. A "Just Say No to Drugs" movement replaced the more libertine ethos of the 1960s.

Scientific

There is a fondness for scientific advancement and technological innovation in American culture. Some of these efforts are centered in Silicon Valley and Cambridge, Massachusetts. Other strong scientific areas include nuclear research, space (NASA), military research, and biotech. Respect for scientific advancement still ranks high in the U.S. and the element of competitiveness is exercised as early as in elementary school. American culture has also made significant gains through the immigration of accomplished scientists. For example, numerous members of the European intelligentsia emigrated during World War II to escape Fascist persecution. At the time, the U.S. was one of the few safe countries to flee to.

Visual Arts

In the late eighteenth and early nineteenth centuries, American artists primarily painted landscapes and portraits in a realistic style.

A parallel development taking shape in rural America was the American craft movement, which began as a reaction to the Industrial Revolution. Developments in modern art in Europe came to America from exhibitions in New York City such as the Armory Show in 1913. After World War II, New York emerged as a center of the art world. Painting in the United States today covers a vast range of styles.

Architecture

Architecture in the United States is regionally diverse and has been shaped by many external forces, not only English. U.S. architecture can therefore be said to be eclectic, something unsurprising in such a multicultural society. In the absence of a single large-scale architectural influence from indigenous peoples such as those in Mexico or Peru, generations of designers have incorporated influences from around the world. Currently, the overriding theme of American Architecture is modernity: an example of which are the skyscrapers of the 20th century.

Early Neoclassicism accompanied the Founding Father's idealization of European Enlightenment, making it the predominant architectural style for public buildings and large manors. However, in recent years, the suburbanization and mass migration to the Sun Belt has allowed architecture to reflect a Mediterranean style as well.

Sculpture

The history of sculpture in the United States reflects the country's 18th century foundation in Roman republican civic values as well as Protestant Christianity. Perhaps the most iconic American sculpture is the Mount Rushmore National Memorial, an 18m high relief of four U.S. Presidents' faces carved into the granite face of Mount Rushmore.

Popular Culture

American popular culture has expressed itself through a number of media, including movies, music, sports and cultural icons like Mickey Mouse. Americans have adapted elements of other cultures, such as pizza, hamburgers, and hibachi.

Fashion

Apart from professional business attire, fashion in the United States is eclectic and predominantly informal. While Americans' diverse cultural roots are reflected in their clothing, particularly those of recent immigrants, cowboy hats and boots and leather motorcycle jackets are emblematic of specifically American styles. Blue jeans were popularized as work clothes in the 1850s by merchant Levi Strauss, a German immigrant in San Francisco, and adopted by many American teenagers a century later.

They are worn in every state by people of all ages and social classes. Along with mass-marketed informal wear in general, blue jeans are arguably U.S. culture's primary contribution to global fashion. The country is also home to the headquarters of many leading designer labels such as Ralph Lauren and Calvin Klein. Labels such as Abercrombie & Fitch and Eckō cater to various niche markets.

Theater

Theater of the United States is based in the Western tradition. Today, it is heavily interlaced with American literature, film, television, and music, and it is not uncommon for a single story to appear in all forms. Regions with significant music scenes often have strong theater and comedy traditions as well. Musical theater may be the most popular form: it is certainly the most colorful, and choreographed motions pioneered on stage have found their way onto movie and television screens.

Broadway in New York City is generally considered the pinnacle of commercial U.S. theater, though this art form appears all across the country. Off-Broadway and off-off-Broadway diversify the theater experience in New York. New York's Theater District is also the largest in the country with Cleveland's being the second largest. Another city of particular note is Chicago, which boasts the most diverse and dynamic theater scene in the country. Regional or resident theaters in the United States are professional theater companies outside of New York City that produce their own seasons. Often tiny rural communities are able to awe audiences with extravagant productions.

Television

Television is one of the major mass media of the United States. Ninety-seven percent of American households have at least one television set and the majority of households have more than three.The U.S. can be said to be the homeland of modern network television.

Music

American music can be heard all over the world. Live music is especially popular with bands and solo artists. American popular music also contains many styles of music that developed in the United States and were popular music when they came up (or still are). Examples are hip-hop, House Music, Techno Music, Dance, swing, jazz, blues, country, R&B, funk, Rock & Roll, Rock, Metal, pop and various others.

Films

American films are very popular, including icons like *Star Wars*, *The Godfather*, *Rocky*, *Jaws*, *The Terminator*, and *The Matrix*. American movie actors and actresses are recognized such as Robert Redford, James Stewart, Al Pacino, Charlton Heston, Brad Pitt, Grace Kelly, George Clooney, Will Smith, Meryl Streep, Robert De Niro, James Cagney, Denzel Washington, Marlon Brando, Johnny Depp and Clint Eastwood. Outside the U.S., American cinema is usually referred to in a generalizing manner as Hollywood.

Dance

There is great variety in dance in the United States, it is the home of the Lindy Hop and its derivative Rock and Roll, and modern square dance (associated with the United States of America due to its historic development in that country—nineteen U.S. states have designated it as their official state dance) and one of the major centers for modern dance. There is a variety of social dance and concert or performance dance forms with also a range of traditions of Native American dances.

Social Groups

As the United States is a diverse nation, it is home to numerous organization and social groups and individuals may derive their group affiliated identity from a variety of sources. Many Americans, especially white collar professionals belong to professional organizations such as the APA, ASA or ATFLC, although books like Bowling Alone indicate that Americans affiliate with these sorts of groups less often than they did in the 1950s and 1960s. Today, Americans derive a great deal of their identity through their work and professional affiliation, especially among individuals higher on the economic ladder.

Recently professional identification has led to many clerical and low-level employees giving their occupations new, more respectable titles, such as "Sanitation service engineer" instead of "Janitor." Additionally many Americans belong to non-profit organizations and religious establishments and may volunteer their services to such organizations. The Rotary Club, the Knights of Columbus or even the SPCA are examples of such non-profit and mostly volunteer run organizations. Ethnicity plays another important role in providing some Americans with group identity, especially among those who recently immigrated.

Many American cities are home to ethnic enclaves such as a Chinatown and Little Italies remain in some cities. Local patriotism may be also provide group identity. For example, a person may be particularly proud to be from California or New York City, and may display clothing from local sports team. Political lobbies such as the AARP not only provide individuals with a sentiment of intra-group allegiance but also increase their political representation in the nation's political system. Combined, profession, ethnicity, religious, and other group affiliations have provided Americans with a multitude of options from which to derive their group based identity.

Firearms

In sharp contrast to most other developed nations, firearms laws in the United States are permissive and private gun ownership is common, with about 40% of households containing at least one firearm. In fact, there are more privately owned firearms in the United States than in any other nation, both per capita and in total.

Rates of gun ownership vary greatly by region and by state, with gun ownership tending to be most common in Alaska, the Mountain States and the South and least common in Hawaii, the island territories and the Northeast megalopolis.

Hunting, plinking and target shooting are popular pastimes, although ownership of firearms purely for utilitarian purposes such as self-defense is common as well. Ownership of handguns, while not uncommon, is less common than ownership of long guns. Gun ownership is much more prevalent among men than women, with men being approximately four times more likely to report owning guns than women.

Other Aspects

America is one of a few countries that does not primarily use the metric system; though many products are dual-labelled, the United States customary units system is dominant. Capital punishment is used in the U.S. for capital crimes. Other developed nations using the death penalty include Singapore, Japan, and South Korea. Some states do not employ this penalty and it is infrequently used in most others.

THE METROPOLIS AND TOURISM

Although there is no clear definition or classification of what a metropolis constitutes, it is a term that is generally used to represent a large city or urban area. It can be from one million people to five or more. Big cities belonging to a larger urban agglomeration, but which are not the core of that agglomeration, are not generally considered a metropolis but a part of it. A metropolis is usually a significant economic, political and cultural center for some country or region, and an important hub for regional or international connections and communications. The plural of the word is most commonly *metropolises*, though *metropolis* is sometimes used as well.

With the historical meaning, it refers to the city or state of origin of a colony as of ancient Greece, a city regarded as a center of a specified activity, or a large important city. In the past, *metropolis* was the designation for a city or state of origin of a colony. Many large cities founded by ancient civilizations have been considered important world metropolises of their times due to their large populations and importance. Some of these ancient metropolises survived until the modern days and are among the world's oldest continuously inhabited cities.

MODERN USAGE

The word comes from the Greek word meter meaning "mother" and *pólis* meaning "city"/"town", which is how the Greek colonies of antiquity referred to their original cities, with whom they retained cultic and political-cultural connections. The word was used in post-classical Latin for the chief city of a province, the seat of the government and, in particular, ecclesiastically for the seat or see of a metropolitan bishop to whom suffragan bishops were responsible. This usage equates the province with the diocese or episcopal see.

In modern usage the word has come to refer to a metropolitan area, a set of adjacent and interconnected cities clustered around a major urban center. In this sense *metropolitan* usually means "spanning the whole metropolis" (as in "metropolitan administration"); or "proper of a metropolis" (as in "metropolitan life", and opposed to "provincial" or "rural").

Global Cities

The concept of a Global city (or a World city) means a city that has a direct and tangible effect on global affairs through socioeconomic means. The term has become increasingly familiar, because of the rise of globalization (i.e., global finance, communications, and travel). An attempt to define and categorize world cities by financial criteria was made by the Globalization and World Cities Study Group & Network (GaWC), based primarily at Loughborough University in England.

The study ranked cities based on their provision of "advanced producer services" such as accountancy, advertising, finance and law. The Inventory identifies three levels of world cities and several sub-ranks.

A metropolis is not necessarily a global city—or, being one, it could not be among the top-ranking—due to its standards of living, development, and infrastructures.

Local Definitions by Country

Bangladesh

In the People's Republic of Bangladesh, there are seven metropolitan areas Dhaka, Chittagong, Rajshahi, Khulna, Sylhet, Barisal and Rangpur. Lands are highly priced and residents are considered to have a better urban lifestyle. Special police departments are entitled for the metropolitan cities as well as there are city corporations for which mayors are being elected for five years regime. Most of these cities have population density of 35,000/sq mile or more. Dhaka is considered as a mega city because of its population crossed 10 million.

Canada

Statistics Canada defines a census metropolitan area as one or more adjacent municipalities situated around a major urban core where the urban core has a population of at least 100,000.

India

In the Republic of India, declared metropolitan cities are Mumbai, Delhi, Chennai, Kolkata, Bangalore and Hyderabad. Residents of these cities are also entitled to a higher house-rent allowance. The Census Commission defines the qualification for metropolitan city as population more than 4 million, so Pune, and Ahmedabad are qualified to be declared as metropolitan cities.

Italy

With the 2001 reform of the Title V of the Constitution of Italy, the Italian republic has provided for the institution of *Aree Metropolitane*. *Aree Metropolitane* will be instituted at least for the major conurbations of Rome, Milan, Turin and Naples, but, as of January 2009, it is yet unclear whether the *Aree Metropolitane* will replace Provinces, or just be added to the older administrative subdivisions.

Japan

The Japanese legal term is commonly translated as "metropolis". Structured like a prefecture instead of a normal city, there is only one *to* in Japan, namely Tokyo. As of 2008[update], Japan has 11 other cities with populations greater than one million.

Pakistan

In Pakistan declared metropolitan cities are Karachi and Lahore.

Philippines

With an estimated population of 16.3 Mio. Metro Manila is the most populous metropolitan area in the Philippines and the 11th in the world. Metro Manila is the largest and richest metropolis in Southeast Asia in terms of GDP. Including Metro Manila, the Philippines has twelve metropolitan areas as defined by the National Economic and Development Authority (NEDA). Metro Angeles, Metro Bacolod, Metro Baguio, Metro Batangas, Metro Cagayan de Oro, Metro Cebu, Metro Dagupan, Metro Davao, Metro Iloilo-Guimaras, Metro Naga, Metro Olongapo.

Poland

The *Union of Polish Metropolises* (Polish: *Unia Metropolii Polskich*), established in 1990, is an organization uniting the largest cities in country. Presently twelve cities are members of the organization, of which 11 have more than a quarter million inhabitants. The largest metropolis in Poland, if ranked solely by the number of inhabitants, is Upper Silesian Metropolis with 2 million inhabitants (five million inhabitants in the Silesian metropolitan area), followed by Warsaw, with 1.7 million inhabitants in city proper, and 2.7 million in Warsaw metropolitan area. Upper Silesian Metropolis is an initiative of recent years, attempt to unite large conurbation/urban area into one official urban organism.

United Kingdom

Various conurbations in the United Kingdom are considered to be metropolitan areas (see Metropolitan county). The term *Metropolis* itself is rarely used. London is archaically referred to as "the Metropolis", which is only retained by the London police force, the Metropolitan Police Service. (The chief officer of the Met is formally known as the Commissioner of Police of the Metropolis.)

United States

In the United States an incorporated area or group of areas having a population more than 50,000 is required to have a metropolitan planning organization in order to facilitate major infrastructure projects and to ensure financial solvency. Thus, a population of 50,000 or greater has been used as a de facto standard in the United States to define a metropolis. A similar definition is used by the United States Census Bureau. They define a metropolitan statistical area as *at least one urbanized area of 50,000 or more inhabitants.*

Metropolis as a Mainland Area

In France, Portugal and Spain, *metropolis* (*métropole* (Fr.) / *metrópole* (Port.) / *metrópoli* (Spa.)) designates the mainland part of a country near or on the European continent; in the case of France, this would mean France without its overseas departments; for Portugal and Spain during the Spanish Empire and Portuguese Empire period, it used to be common to designate Portugal or Spain except its colonies (the *Ultramar*). In France *metropolis* is also used to refer to large agglomerations.

Megacity

A megacity is usually defined as a metropolitan area with a total population in excess of 10 million people. Some definitions also set a minimum level for population density (at least 2,000 persons/square km). A megacity can be a single metropolitan area or two or more metropolitan areas that converge. The terms conurbation, metropolis and metroplex are also applied to the latter. The terms *megapolis* and *megalopolis* are sometimes used synonymously with *megacity.* As of 2011, there are 21 megacities in existence – with conurbations such as Mumbai, Tokyo, New York City, and Mexico City having populations in excess of 10 million inhabitants.

Tokyo is the World's largest megacity

History

In 1800, only 3% of the world's population lived in cities, a figure that has risen to 47% by the end of the twentieth century. In

1950, there were 83 cities with populations exceeding one million; by 2007, this number had risen to 468. If the trend continues, the world's urban population will double every 38 years. The UN forecasts that today's urban population of 3.2 billion will rise to nearly 5 billion by 2030, when three out of five people will live in cities.

This increase will be most dramatic on the least-urbanized continents, Asia and Africa. Surveys and projections indicate that all urban growth over the next 25 years will be in developing countries. One billion people, one-sixth of the world's population, now live in shanty towns. In many poor countries overpopulated slums exhibit high rates of disease due to unsanitary conditions, malnutrition, and lack of basic health care. By 2030, over 2 billion people in the world will be living in slums. Over 90% of the urban population of Ethiopia, Malawi and Uganda, three of the world's most rural countries, already live in slums.

By 2025, according to the *Far Eastern Economic Review*, Asia alone will have at least 10 megacities, including Mumbai (33 million), Shanghai (27 million), Karachi, Pakistan (26.5 million), Dhaka, Bangladesh (26 million) and Jakarta, Indonesia (24.9 million people). Lagos, Nigeria has grown from 300,000 in 1950 to an estimated 12.5 million today, and the Nigerian government estimates that the city will have expanded to 25 million residents by 2015.

Largest Cities

Growth

For almost a thousand years, Rome was the largest, wealthiest, and most politically important city in Europe. and its population passed a million people by the end of the 1st century BC. Rome's population started dropping in 402 AD when Flavius Honorius moved the government to Ravenna and Rome's population declined to a mere 20,000 during the Early Middle Ages, reducing the sprawling city to groups of inhabited buildings interspersed among large areas of ruins and vegetation.

Baghdad was likely the largest city in the world from shortly after its foundation in 762 AD until the 930s, with some estimates putting its population at over one million.

Chinese capital cities Chang'an, Kaifeng also experienced huge population booms during prosperous empires. According to the census in the year 742 recorded in the *New Book of Tang*, 362,921 families with 1,960,188 persons were counted in Jingzhao Fu (¬NFQœ^), the metropolitan area including small cities in the vicinity.

The medieval settlement surrounding Angkor, the one-time capital of the Khmer Empire which flourished between the 9th and 15th centuries, could have supported a population of up to one million people.

In 1950, New York City was the only urban area with a population of over 10 million. Geographers had identified 25 such areas as of October 2005, as compared with 19 megacities in 2004 and only nine in 1985. This increase has happened as the world's population moves towards the high (75–85%) urbanization levels of North America and Western Europe. The 1990 census marked the first time the majority of US citizens lived in cities with over 1 million inhabitants.

In the 2000s, the largest megacity is the Greater Tokyo Area. The population of this urban agglomeration includes areas such as Yokohama and Kawasaki, and is estimated to be between 35 and 36 million. This variation in estimates can be accounted for by different definitions of what the area encompasses. While the prefectures of Tokyo, Chiba, Kanagawa, and Saitama are commonly included in statistical information, the Japan Statistics Bureau only includes the area within 50 kilometers of the Tokyo Metropolitan Government Offices in Shinjuku, thus arriving at a smaller population estimate. A characteristic issue of megacities is the difficulty in defining their outer limits and accurately estimating the populations.

Major Challenges

Slums

According to the United Nations, the proportion of urban dwellers living in slums decreased from 47 percent to 37 percent in the developing world between 1990 and 2005. However, due to rising population, the absolute number of slum dwellers is rising. The majority of these come from the fringes of urban margins, located in legal and illegal settlements with insufficient housing and sanitation.

This has been caused by massive migration, both internal and transnational, into cities, which has caused growth rates of urban populations and spatial concentrations not seen before in history. These issues raise problems in the political, social, and economic arenas. Slum dwellers often have minimal or no access to education, healthcare, or the urban economy.

Homelessness

Megacities often have significant numbers of homeless people. The actual legal definition of homelessness varies from country to country, or among different entities or institutions in the same country or region.

Traffic Congestion

Traffic congestion is a condition on road networks that occurs as use increases, and is characterized by slower speeds, longer trip times, and increased vehicular queueing.

Urban Sprawl

Urban sprawl, also known as suburban sprawl, is a multifaceted concept, which includes the spreading outwards of a city and its suburbs to its outskirts to low-density, auto-dependent development on rural land, with associated design features that encourage car dependency. As a result, some critics argue that sprawl has certain disadvantages, including, longer transport distances to work, high car dependence, inadequate facilities e.g.: health, cultural. etc. and higher per-person infrastructure costs. Discussions and debates about sprawl are often obfuscated by the ambiguity associated with the phrase. For example, some commentators measure sprawl only with the average number of residential units per acre in a given area. But others associate it with decentralization (spread of population without a well-defined center), discontinuity (leapfrog development), segregation of uses, etc.

Gentrification

Gentrification and urban gentrification denote the socio-cultural changes in an area resulting from wealthier people buying housing property in a less prosperous community. Consequent to gentrification, the average income increases and average family size decreases in the community, which may result in the informal economic eviction of the lower-income residents, because of increased rents, house prices, and property taxes. This type of population change reduces industrial land use when it is redeveloped for commerce and housing. In addition, new businesses, catering to a more affluent base of consumers, tend to move into formerly blighted areas, further increasing the appeal to more affluent migrants and decreasing the accessibility to less wealthy natives.

Environmental Problems

Air Pollution

Air pollution is the introduction of chemicals, particulate matter, or biological materials that cause harm or discomfort to humans or other living organisms, or damages the natural environment, into the atmosphere. Many urban areas have significant problems with smog, a type of air pollution derived from vehicular emission from internal combustion engines and industrial fumes that react in the atmosphere with sunlight to form secondary pollutants that also combine with the primary emissions to form photochemical smog.

Smog is also caused by large amounts of coal burning, which creates a mixture of smoke and sulfur dioxide. World coal consumption was about 6,743,786,000 short tons in 2006 and is expected to increase 48% to 9.98 billion short tons by 2030. China produced 2.38 billion tons in 2006. India produced about 447.3 million tons in 2006. 68.7% of China's electricity comes from coal. The USA consumes about 14% of the world total, using 90% of it for generation of electricity.

Urban Sprawl

Urban sprawl, also known as suburban sprawl, is a multifaceted concept, which includes the spreading outwards of a city and its suburbs to its outskirts to low-density and auto-dependent development on rural land, high segregation of uses (e.g. stores and residential), and various design features that encourage car dependency. As a result, many urban planners, government officials, and social scientists contend that sprawl has a number of disadvantages, including:

- High car dependence
- Inadequate facilities, e.g.: cultural, emergency, health, and so forth
- Low public support for sprawl
- High per-person infrastructure costs
- Inefficient street layouts
- Inflated costs for public transportation
- Lost time and productivity for commuting
- High levels of racial and socioeconomic segregation
- Low diversity of housing and business types
- High rates of obesity due to less walking and biking
- Less space for conservation and parks
- High per-capita use of energy, land, and water
- Perceived low aesthetic value

Notwithstanding these disadvantages, some government officials and private business employers contend that sprawl has certain advantages, such as more single family residences on larger lots, lower land prices, and higher profits for businesses due to the lack of laws limiting urban sprawl.

Discussions and debates about sprawl are often obfuscated by the ambiguity associated with the phrase. "The aim of creating sustainable and compact cities is inhibited by urban sprawl as development is uncontrolled." (K.H Sebonego) For example, some commentators measure sprawl only with the average number of residential units per acre in a given area. But others associate it with decentralization (spread of population without a well-defined center), discontinuity (leapfrog development, as defined below), segregation of uses, etc.

Urban economists have entered the debate relatively recently. They tend to examine urban sprawl as the aggregate extent of urban land use or as the average urban land use density. It has been shown that urban sprawl can increase the aggregate urban land use and lower the average land use density while at the same time lowering average commuting travel times and increasing discretionary mobility.

The term urban sprawl generally has negative connotations due to the health, environmental and cultural issues associated with the phrase. Residents of sprawling neighborhoods tend to emit more pollution per person and suffer more traffic fatalities. Sprawl is controversial, with supporters claiming that consumers prefer lower density neighborhoods and that sprawl does not necessarily increase traffic. Sprawl is characterized by several land use patterns which usually occur in unison:

Single-use Zoning

This refers to a situation where commercial, residential, institutional and industrial areas are separated from one another. Consequently, large tracts of land are devoted to a single use and are segregated from one another by open space, infrastructure, or other barriers. As a result, the places where people live, work, shop, and recreate are far from one another, usually to the extent that walking, transit use and bicycling are impractical, so all these activities generally require an automobile.

Low-density Zoning

Sprawl consumes much more land per-capita than traditional urban developments because zoning laws generally require that new developments are of low density. The exact definition of "low density" is arguable, but a common example is that of single family homes on large lots, with four or fewer units per net acre. Buildings usually have fewer stories and are spaced farther apart, separated by lawns, landscaping, roads or parking lots. Lot sizes are larger, and because more automobiles are used much more land is designated for parking. The impact of low density development in many communities is that developed or "urbanized" land is increasing at a faster rate than the population.

Overall density is often lowered by "leap-frog development". This term refers to the relationship, or lack thereof, between subdivisions. Such developments are typically separated by large green belts, i.e. tracts of undeveloped land, resulting in an average density far lower even than the low density described in the previous paragraph. This is a 20th and 21st century phenomenon generated by the current custom of requiring a developer to provide subdivision infrastructure as a condition of development (DeGrove and Turner, 1991).

Usually, the developer is required to set aside a certain percentage of the developed land for public use, including roads, parks and schools. In the past, when a local government built all the streets in a given location, the town could expand without interruption and with a coherent circulation system, because it had condemnation power. Private developers generally do not have such power (although they can sometimes find local governments willing to help), and often choose to develop on the tracts that happen to be for sale at the time they want to build, rather than pay extra or wait for a more appropriate location.

Car-dependent Communities

Areas of urban sprawl are also characterized as highly dependent on automobiles for transportation, a condition known as automobile dependency. Most activities, such as shopping and commuting to work, require the use of a car as a result of both the area's isolation from the city and the isolation the area's residential zones have from its industrial and commercial zones.

Walking and other methods of transit are not practical; therefore, many of these areas have few or no sidewalks. In many suburban communities, stores and activities that are in close proximity "as the crow flies" require automobiles, because the different areas are separated by fences, walls, and drainage ditches. Some critics argue that excessive parking requirements exacerbate car dependency.

Job Sprawl and Spatial Mismatch

Job Sprawl is another land use symptom of urban sprawl and car-dependent communities. It is defined as low-density, geographically spread-out patterns of employment, where the majority of jobs in a given metropolitan area are located outside of the main city's Central Business District (CBD), and increasingly in the suburban periphery.

It is often the result of urban disinvestment, the geographic freedom of employment location allowed by predominantly car-dependent commuting patterns of many American suburbs, and many companies' desire to locate in low-density areas that are often more affordable and offer potential for expansion.

Spatial mismatch is related to job sprawl and economic Environmental Justice. Spatial Mismatch is defined as the situation where poor urban, predominantly minority citizens are left without easy access to entry-level jobs, as a result of increasing job sprawl and limited transportation options to facilitate a reverse commute to the suburbs.

Job sprawl has been documented and measured in various ways. It has been shown to be a growing trend in America's metropolitan areas.{cn} The Brookings Institution has published multiple articles on the topic. In 2005, author Michael Stoll defined job sprawl simply as jobs located more than 5-mile (8.0 km) radius from the CBD, and measured the concept based on year 2000 U.S. Census data. Other ways of measuring the concept with more detailed rings around the CBD include a 2001 article by Edward Glaeser and Elizabeth Kneebone's 2009 article, which show that sprawling urban peripheries are gaining employment while areas closer to the CBD are losing jobs.

These two authors used three geographic rings limited to a 35-mile (56 km) radius around the CBD: 3 miles (4.8 km) or less, 3 to 10 miles (16 km), and 10 to 35 miles (56 km). Kneebone's study showed the following nationwide breakdown for the largest metropolitan areas in 2006: 21.3% of jobs located in the inner ring, 33.6% of jobs in the 3-10 mile ring, and 45.1% in the 10-35 mile ring. This compares to the year 1998 - 23.3%, 34.2%, and 42.5% in those respective rings. The study shows CBD employment share shrinking, and job growth focused in the suburban and exurban outer metropolitan rings.

In terms of measurement, spatial mismatch can be thought of as the percentage of people who would have to move in order to be distributed in the same way as jobs. Stoll's research shows that a substantially higher percentage of African Americans (53.5%) experience spatial mismatch than European Americans (35.6%). On average, more than half of African American citizens would need to move to accomplish similar distribution to jobs. Latinos (45.8%) experience spatial mismatch as well, though to a lesser extent than African Americans.

Developments Characteristic of Sprawl

Housing Subdivisions

Housing subdivisions are large tracts of land consisting entirely of newly-built residences. Prominent New Urbanist architectural firm Duany Plater-Zyberk & Company claim that housing subdivisions "are sometimes called villages, towns, and neighborhoods by their developers, which is misleading since those terms denote places which are not exclusively residential." They are also referred to as developments.

Subdivisions often incorporate curved roads and cul-de-sacs. Such subdivisions may offer only a few places to enter and exit the development, causing traffic to use high volume collector streets. All trips, no matter how short, must enter the collector road in a suburban system. (Duany Plater-Zyberk 5, 34)

Strip Malls

Shopping centers are locations consisting of retail space. In the U.S. and Canada, these vary from strip malls which refer to collections of buildings sharing a common parking lot, usually built on a high-capacity roadway with commercial functions (i.e., a "strip"). Similar developments in the UK are called Retail Parks. Strip malls/retail parks contain a wide variety of retail and non-retail functions that also cater to daily use (e.g. video rental, takeout food, laundry services, hairdresser). Strip malls consisting mostly of big box stores or category killers are sometimes called "power centers" (U.S.).

These developments tend to be low-density; the buildings are single-story and there is ample space for parking and access for delivery vehicles. This character is reflected in the spacious landscaping of the parking lots and walkways and clear signage of the retail establishments. Some strip malls are undergoing a transformation into Lifestyle centers; entailing investments in common areas and facilities (plazas, cafes) and shifting tenancy from daily goods to recreational shopping. European countries such as France, Belgium and Germany have implemented size restrictions for superstores found in strip malls in an effort to limit sprawl (Davies 1995).

Shopping Malls

Another prominent form of retail development in areas characterized by "sprawl" is the shopping mall. Unlike the strip mall, this is usually composed of a single building surrounded by a parking lot which contains multiple shops, usually "anchored" by one or more department stores (Gruen and Smith 1960). The function and size is also distinct from the strip mall. The focus is almost exclusively on recreational shopping rather than daily goods. Shopping malls also tend to serve a wider (regional) public and require higher-order infrastructure such as highway access and can have floorspaces in excess of a million square feet (ca. 100,000 m²).

Shopping malls are often detrimental to downtown shopping centers of nearby cities since the shopping malls acts as a surrogate for the city center (Crawford 1992). Some downtowns have responded to this challenge by building shopping centers of their own (Frieden and Sagelyn 1989; consider also Toronto Eaton Centre (1977), Ottawa's Rideau Centre, Boston's Shops at Prudential Center, and Providence's Providence Place).

In the 1970s, the Ontario government created the Ontario Downtown Renewal Programme, which helped finance the building of several downtown malls across Ontario (such as the aforementioned Eaton Centre). The program was created to reverse the tide of small business leaving downtowns for larger sites surrounding the city.

Fast Food Chains

Fast food chains are common in suburban areas. They are often built early in areas with low property values where the population is expected to boom and where large traffic is predicted, and set a precedent for future development. Eric Schlosser, in his book Fast Food Nation, argues that fast food chains accelerate suburban sprawl and help set its tone with their expansive parking lots, flashy signs, and plastic architecture (65). Duany Plater Zyberk & Company believe that this reinforces a destructive pattern of growth in an endless quest to move away from the sprawl that only results in creating more of it (Duany Plater-Zyberk 26).

Examples

According to the National Resources Inventory (NRI), about 8,900 square kilometers (2.2 million acres) of land in the United

States was developed between 1992 and 2002. Presently, the NRI classifies approximately 100,000 more square kilometers (40,000 square miles) (an area approximately the size of Kentucky) as developed than the Census Bureau classifies as urban.

The difference in the NRI classification is that it includes rural development, which by definition cannot be considered to be "urban" sprawl. Currently, according to the 2000 Census, approximately 2.6 percent of the U.S. land area is urban. Approximately 0.8 percent of the nation's land is in the 37 urbanized areas with more than 1,000,000 population. In 2002, these 37 urbanized areas supported around 40% of the total American population.

Nonetheless, some urban areas have expanded geographically even while losing population. But it was not just urbanized areas in the U.S. that lost population and sprawled substantially. According to data in "Cities and Automobile Dependence" by Kenworthy and Laube (1999), urbanized area population losses occurred while there was an expansion of sprawl between 1970 and 1990 in Brussels, Belgium; Copenhagen, Denmark; Frankfurt, Hamburg, and Munich, Germany; and Zurich, Switzerland, albeit without the wholesale dismantling of public transit systems that occurred in the United States.

At the same time, the urban cores of these and nearly all other major cities in the United States, Western Europe, and Japan that did not annex new territory experienced the related phenomena of falling household size and, particularly in the U.S., "white flight", sustaining population losses. This trend has slowed somewhat in recent years, as more people have regained an interest in urban living.

Los Angeles was one of the world's first low density urbanized areas, resulting from its large geographic metropolitan area. Due to the threat of earthquakes, the city couldn't build upward so it built outward. This in turn, caused wide automobile ownership from residents so they could effectively traverse the large region. However, Los Angeles has become more dense over the past half-century, principally due to small lot zoning and a high demand for housing due to population growth.

The city of Los Angeles has increased its density rate up to approximately 7,000 people per square mile in the year 2000, however that is still substantially less than New York City's 27,000 average, San Francisco's 17,000 average, and Chicago's 12,000 average. Land consumption per resident in 2000 was 0.11-acre (450 m2), which made the entire Los Angeles metropolitan area the most densely populated urbanized area in the United States. It should be pointed out, however, that average density is not the only measure of sprawl; some urbanists argue that the city's car-dependent, decentralized form is itself a type of "sprawl" development.

Urban sprawl is not limited to developed countries, and may be more prevalent in developing countries. For example, there is considerable land consumed by urban sprawl in Mexico City, in Beijing, in Antananarivo (the capital of Madagascar), in Johannesburg, and in eastern parts of South Africa.

Smart Growth and the Compact City

The term 'smart growth' has been particularly used in North America. The terms 'compact city' or 'urban intensification' are often used to describe similar concepts, in Europe and particularly the UK where it has influenced Government policy and planning practice in recent years.

The first urban growth boundary in the U.S. was in Fayette County, Kentucky in 1958. Fifteen years later, the state of Oregon enacted a law in 1973 limiting the area urban areas could occupy, through urban growth boundaries. As a result, Portland, the state's largest urban area, has become a leader in smart growth policies that seek to make urban areas more compact (they are called urban consolidation policies).

After the creation of this boundary, the population density of the urbanized area increased somewhat (from 1,135 in 1970 to 1,290 per km² in 2000) USA Urbanized Areas 1950-1990 USA Urbanized Areas 2000. While the growth boundary has not been tight enough to vastly increase density, the consensus is that the growth boundaries have protected great amounts of wild areas and farmland around the metro area.

Many parts of the San Francisco Bay Area have also adopted urban growth boundaries; 25 of its cities and 5 of its counties have urban growth boundaries. Many of these were adopted with the support and advocacy of Greenbelt Alliance, a non-profit land conservation and urban planning organization.

In other areas, the design principles of District Regionalism and New Urbanism have been employed to combat urban sprawl.

While cities such as Los Angeles are well known for sprawling suburbs, policies and public opinion are changing. Transit-oriented development, in which higher-density mixed-use areas are permitted or encouraged near transit stops is encouraging more compact development in certain areas-particularly those with light and heavy heavy rail transit systems.

Bicycling-oriented Development (BOD)

Bicycles are the preferred means of travel in many countries. Also, bicycles are permitted in public transit. Businesses in areas of some towns where bicycle use is high are thriving. Bicycles and transit are contributing in two important ways toward the success of businesses:

- First is that on average the people living the closest to these business districts have more money to spend locally because they don't spend as much on their cars.
- Second, because these people rely more on bicycling, walking and transit than on driving, they tend to focus more of their commerce on locally-owned neighborhood businesses that are convenient for them to reach.

Sustainable Urban Design

Walkability is a measure of how friendly an area is to walking. Walkability has many health, environmental, and economic benefits. However, evaluating walkability is challenging because it requires the consideration of many subjective factors. Factors influencing walkability include the presence or absence and quality of footpaths, sidewalks or other pedestrian right-of-ways, traffic and road conditions, land use patterns, building accessibility, and safety, among others. Walkability is an important concept in sustainable urban design.

A heavy reliance on automobiles increases traffic throughout the city as well as automobile crashes, pedestrian injuries, and air pollution. Motor vehicle crashes are the leading cause of death for

Americans between the ages of five and twenty-four and is the leading accident-related cause for all age groups. Residents of more sprawling areas are at greater risk of dying in a car crash.

Urbanized neighborhoods and subdivisions.

Criticism

Arguments opposing urban sprawl run the gamut from the more concrete effects such as health and environmental issues to more abstract consequences involving neighborhood vitality.

Health and Environmental Impact

Urban sprawl is associated with a number of negative environmental and public health outcomes, with the primary result being increased dependence on automobiles.

However, this is mitigated significantly with nearby development of shopping and recreation areas. Also, many people prefer to live close to their place of business which is increasingly centered less around urban areas.

Increased Obesity

The American Journal of Public Health and the American Journal of Health Promotion, have both stated that there is a significant connection between sprawl, obesity, and hypertension. Many urbanists argue that this is due to less walking in sprawl-type developments. Living in a car centered culture forces inhabitants to drive everywhere, thus walking far less than their urban (and generally healthier) counterparts.

Decrease in social capital

Urban sprawl may be partly responsible for the decline in social capital in the United States. Compact neighborhoods can foster casual social interactions among neighbors, while sprawl creates barriers. Sprawl tends to replace public spaces with private spaces such as fenced-in backyards.

Decrease in Land and Water Quantity and Quality

Due to the larger area consumed by sprawling suburbs compared to urban neighborhoods, more farmland and wildlife habitats are displaced per resident. As forest cover is cleared and covered with impervious surfaces (concrete and asphalt) in the suburbs, rainfall is less effectively absorbed into the ground water aquifers. This threatens both the quality and quantity of water supplies. Sprawl increases water pollution as rain water picks up gasoline, motor oil, heavy metals, and other pollutants in runoff from parking lots and roads. Sprawl fragments the land which increases the risk of invasive species spreading into the remaining forest.

Increased Infrastructure Costs

Living in larger, more spread out spaces generally makes public services more expensive. Since car usage becomes endemic and public transport often becomes significantly more expensive, city planners are forced to build large highway and parking infrastructure, which in turn decreases taxable land and revenue, and decreases the desirability of the area adjacent to such structures. Providing services such as water, sewers, and electricity is also more expensive per household in less dense areas.

Increased Personal Transportation Costs

Residents of low-density areas spend a higher proportion of their income on transportation than residents of high density areas. The RAC estimates that the average cost of operating a car in the UK is £5,000 a year, most of which stems from financing costs and depreciation. In comparison, a yearly underground ticket for a suburban commuter in London (where the average wage is higher than the national average) costs £1,000-1,500, which, because of subsidies do not cover financing for the rail or depreciation of the infrastructure. In the Euro-15, rail transit requires $69 billion euros in subsidies while road transportation nets $107 billion euros in additional taxes.

Neighborhood Quality

Critics of sprawl maintain that quality of life is eroded by lifestyles promoted by sprawl promotes. Duany and Plater-Zyberk believe that in traditional neighborhoods the nearness of the workplace to retail and restaurant space that provides cafes and convenience stores with daytime customers is an essential component to the successful balance of urban life.

Furthermore, they state that the closeness of the workplace to homes also gives people the option of walking or riding a bicycle to work or school and that without this kind of interaction between the different components of life the urban pattern quickly falls apart. (Duany Plater-Zyberk 6, 28). James Howard Kunstler has argued that poor aesthetics in suburban environments make them "places not worth caring about", and that they lack a sense of history and identity.

White Flight

Some blame suburbs for what they see as a homogeneity of society and culture, leading to sprawling suburban developments of people with similar race, background and socioeconomic status. They claim that segregated and stratified development was institutionalized in the early 1950s and 1960s with the financial industries' then-legal process of redlining neighborhoods to prevent certain people from entering and residing in affluent districts.

Sprawl may have a negative impact on public schools as finances have been pulled out of city cores and diverted to wealthier suburbs. They argue that the residential and social segregation of whites from blacks in the United States creates a socialization process that limits whites' chances for developing meaningful relationships with blacks and other minorities, and that the segregation experienced by whites from blacks fosters segregated lifestyles and can lead to positive views about themselves and negative views about blacks.

Groups that Oppose Sprawl

The American Institute of Architects and the American Planning Association recommend against sprawl and instead endorses smart, mixed-use development, including buildings in close proximity to one another that cut down on automobile use, save energy, and promote walkable, healthy, well-designed neighborhoods. The Sierra Club, the San Francisco Bay Area's Greenbelt Alliance, and other environmental organizations oppose sprawl and support investment in existing communities. NumbersUSA, a national organization advocating immigration reduction, also opposes urban sprawl, and its executive director, Roy Beck, specializes in the study of this issue.

Response

American public policy analyst Randal O'Toole of the Cato Institute, a libertarian think tank, has argued that sprawl, thanks to the automobile, gave rise to affordable suburban neighborhoods for middle class and lower class individuals, including non-whites. He notes that efforts to combat sprawl often result in subsidizing development in wealthier and whiter neighborhoods while condemning and demolishing poorer minority neighborhoods.

Consumer Preference for Sprawl

Peter Gordon, a professor of planning and economics at the University of Southern California's School of Urban Planning and Development, argues that many households in the United States, Canada, and Australia, especially middle and upper class families, have shown a preference for the suburban lifestyle. Reasons cited include a preference towards lower-density development (for lower ambient noise and increased privacy), better schools, less crime, and a generally slower lifestyle than the urban one. Those in favor of the current pro low-density land use policies also argue that this sort of living situation is an issue of personal choice and economic means. One suburban Detroit politician defends low-density development as the preferred lifestyle choice of his constituents, calling it "...the American Dream unfolding before your eyes."

Urban Sprawl and Automobile Dependency

Whether urban sprawl does increase problems of automobile dependency and whether conversely, policies of smart growth can reduce them have been fiercely contested issues over several decades. An influential study in 1989 by Peter Newman and Jeff Kenworthy compared 32 cities across North America, Australia, Europe and Asia. The study has been criticised for its methodology but the main finding that denser cities, particularly in Asia, have lower car use than sprawling cities, particularly in North America, has been largely accepted although the relationship is clearer at the extremes across continents than it is within countries where conditions are more similar.

Within cities, studies from across many countries (mainly in the developed world) have shown that denser urban areas with greater mixture of land use and better public transport tend to have lower car use than less dense suburban and ex-urban residential areas. This usually holds true even after controlling for socio-economic factors such as differences in household composition and income. This does not necessarily imply that suburban sprawl causes high car use, however.

One confounding factor, which has been the subject of many studies, is residential self-selection: people who prefer to drive tend to move towards low density suburbs, whereas people who prefer to walk, cycle or use transit tend to move towards higher density urban areas, better served by public transport. Some studies have found that, when self-selection is controlled for, the built environment has no significant effect on travel behaviour. More recent studies using more sophisticated methodologies have generally refuted these findings: density, land use and public transport accessibility can influence travel behaviour, although social and economic factors, particularly household income, usually exert a stronger influence.

The Paradox of Intensification

Reviewing the evidence on urban intensification, smart growth and their effects on travel behaviour Melia et al. (2011) found support for the arguments of both supporters and opponents of smart growth measures to counteract urban sprawl. Planning policies which increase population densities in urban areas do tend to reduce car use, but the effect is a weak one, so doubling the population density of a particular area will not halve the frequency or distance of car use.

Debate Over Traffic and Commute Times

Those not opposed to low density development argue that traffic intensities tend to be less, traffic speeds faster and, as a result, ambient air pollution is lower. (See demographia's report.) Kansas City, Missouri is often cited as an example of ideal low-density development, with congestion below the mean and home prices below comparable Midwestern cities. Wendell Cox and Randal O'Toole are the leading figures supporting lower density development.

Longitudinal (time-lapse) studies of commute times in major metropolitan areas in the United States have shown that commute times decreased for the period 1969 to 1995 even though the geographic size of the city increased.

Risk of Increased Housing Prices

There is also some concern that Portland-style anti-sprawl policies will increase housing prices. Some research suggests Oregon has had the largest housing affordability loss in the nation, but other research shows that Portland's price increases are comparable to other Western cities.

In Australia, it is claimed by some that housing affordability has hit "crisis levels" due to "urban consolidation" policies implemented by state governments. In Sydney, the ratio of the price of a house relative to income is 9:1. The issue was being debated between the major political parties in the lead up to the Australian federal election.

Freedom

There are some sociologists such as Durkheim who suggest there is a link between population density and the number of rules that must be imposed. The theory goes that as people are moved closer together geographically their actions are more likely to noticeably impact others around them. This potential impact requires the creation of additional social or legal rules to prevent conflict. A simple example would be as houses become closer together the acceptable maximum volume of music decreases, as it becomes intrusive to other residents.

Crowding and Increased Aggression

Numerous studies link increased population density with increased aggression. Some people believe that increased population density encourages crime and anti-social behavior. It is argued that human beings, while social animals, need significant amounts of social space or they become agitated and aggressive. However, the relationship between higher densities and increased social pathology has been largely discredited

Sprawl does not Cause Obesity

University of Toronto economics professor Matthew Turner argues that there is no evidence that sprawl affects obesity; instead that previous findings of a positive relationship most likely reflect a failure to control properly for the fact the individuals who are more likely to be obese choose to live in more sprawling neighborhoods.

James Robins, a professor of epidemiology in the Harvard School of Public Health, has read news reports of the sprawl research, concluding "This seems so far from what people would take as strong scientific evidence or a direct causal link."

Active Transportation Network

One solution to the dilemma posed by the ubiquitous expansion of suburban sprawl is the potential for the development of the active transportation network. Cities such as Seattle where the 42 mi (62 km) Burke-Gilman multi-use trail has been in use for over 30 years have seen a significant number of commuters utilize the network for long distance travel both with human-powered and increasingly with electric-assist mobility aids (e-bikes).

The dual benefits of exercise and mobility may contribute to a mitigation of the negative effects of sprawl in areas where the active transportation network is adequately developed. The opportunity to load bicycles onto public transit allows such a network to function even during inclement weather and provides a new hope for those metropolitan areas where available rights-of-way and greenbelt lands still exist for the development of the active transportation network.

URBAN TOURISM AND URBAN CHANGE

Urbanization, urbanisation or urban drift is the physical growth of urban areas as a result of global change. Urbanization is also defined by the United Nations as movement of people from rural to urban areas with population growth equating to urban migration. The United Nations projected that half of the world's population would live in urban areas at the end of 2008.

Urbanization is closely linked to modernization, industrialization, and the sociological process of rationalization. Urbanization can describe a specific condition at a set time, ie. the proportion of total population or area in cities or towns, or the term can describe the increase of this proportion over time. So the term urbanization can represent the level of urban relative to overall population, or it can represent the rate at which the urban proportion is increasing.

As more and more people leave villages and farms to live in cities, urban growth results. The rapid growth of cities like Chicago in the late 19th century and Mumbai a century later can be attributed largely to rural-urban migration. This kind of growth is especially commonplace in developing countries.

The rapid urbanization of the world's population over the twentieth century is described in the 2005 Revision of the UN World Urbanization Prospects report. The global proportion of urban population rose dramatically from 13% (220 million) in 1900, to 29% (732 million) in 1950, to 49% (3.2 billion) in 2005. The same report projected that the figure is likely to rise to 60% (4.9 billion) by 2030.

However, French economist Philippe Bocquier, writing in THE FUTURIST magazine, has calculated that "the proportion of the world population living in cities and towns in the year 2030 would be roughly 50%, substantially less than the 60% forecast by the United Nations (UN), because the messiness of rapid urbanization is unsustainable. Both Bocquier and the UN see more people flocking to cities, but Bocquier sees many of them likely to leave upon discovering that there's no work for them and no place to live."

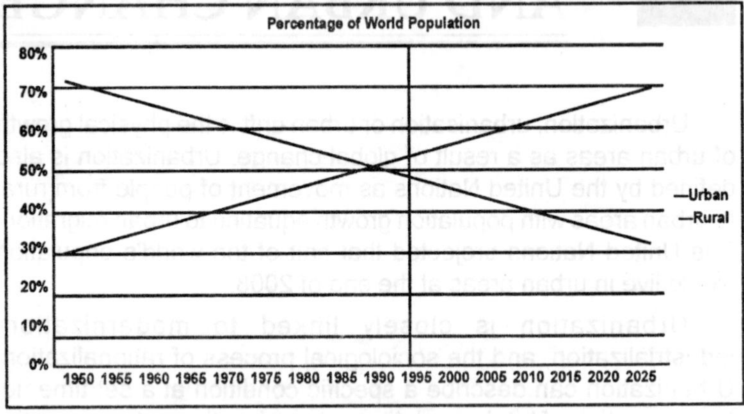

Percentage of World Population: Urban vs. Rural.

According to the UN State of the World Population 2007 report, sometime in the middle of 2007, the majority of people worldwide will be living in towns or cities, for the first time in history; this is referred to as the arrival of the "Urban Millennium" or the 'tipping point'. In regard to future trends, it is estimated 93% of urban growth will occur in developing nations, with 80% of urban growth occurring in Asia and Africa.

Urbanization rates vary between countries. The United States and United Kingdom have a far higher urbanization level than China, India, Swaziland or Niger, but a far slower annual urbanization rate, since much less of the population is living in a rural area.

- Urbanization in the United States never reached the Rocky Mountains in locations such as Jackson Hole, Wyoming;

Telluride, Colorado; Taos, New Mexico; Douglas County, Colorado and Aspen, Colorado. The state of Vermont has also been affected, as has the coast of Florida, the Birmingham-Jefferson County, AL area, the Pacific Northwest and the barrier islands of North Carolina.

- In the United Kingdom, two major examples of new urbanization can be seen in Swindon, Wiltshire and Milton Keynes, Buckinghamshire. These two towns show some of the quickest growth rates in Europe.

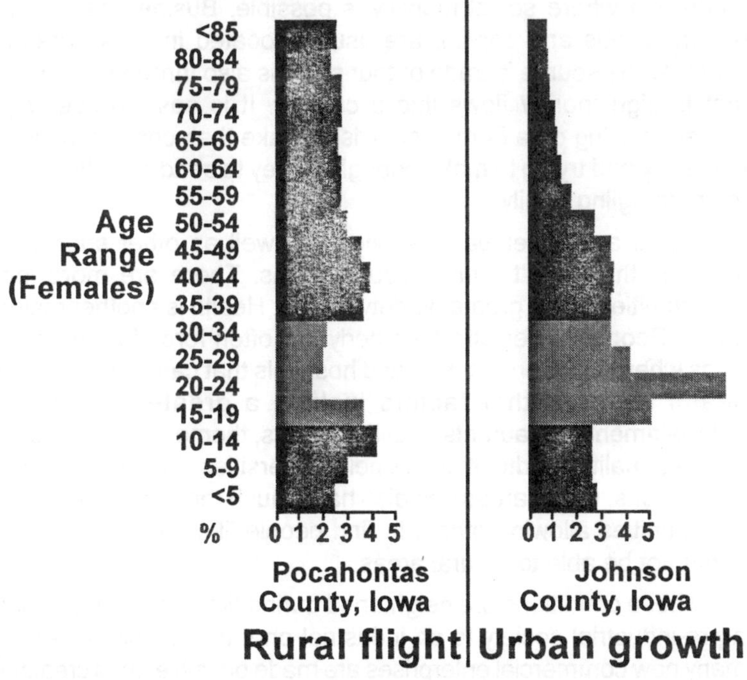

Urbanization occurs naturally from individual and corporate efforts to reduce time and expense in commuting and transportation while improving opportunities for jobs, education, housing, and transportation. Living in cities permits individuals and families to take advantage of the opportunities of proximity, diversity, and marketplace competition.

People move into cities to seek economic opportunities. A major contributing factor is known as "rural flight". In rural areas, often on small family farms, it is difficult to improve one's standard of living beyond basic sustenance. Farm living is dependent on unpredictable environmental conditions, and in times of drought, flood or pestilence, survival becomes extremely problematic. In modern times, industrialization of agriculture has negatively affected the economy of small and middle-sized farms and strongly reduced the size of the rural labour market.

Cities, in contrast, are known to be places where money, services and wealth are centralized. Cities are where fortunes are made and where social mobility is possible. Businesses, which generate jobs and capital, are usually located in urban areas. Whether the source is trade or tourism, it is also through the cities that foreign money flows into a country. It is easy to see why someone living on a farm might wish to take their chance moving to the city and trying to make enough money to send back home to their struggling family.

There are better basic services as well as other specialist services that aren't found in rural areas. There are more job opportunities and a greater variety of jobs. Health is another major factor. People, especially the elderly are often forced to move to cities where there are doctors and hospitals that can cater for their health needs. Other factors include a greater variety of entertainment (restaurants, movie theaters, theme parks, etc) and a better quality of education, namely universities. Due to their high populations, urban areas can also have much more diverse social communities allowing others to find people like them when they might not be able to in rural areas.

These conditions are heightened during times of change from a pre-industrial society to an industrial one. It is at this time that many new commercial enterprises are made possible, thus creating new jobs in cities. It is also a result of industrialization that farms become more mechanized, putting many labourers out of work. This is currently occurring fastest in India.

Economic Effects

One of the last houses of the old Russian village of Lukeryino, most of which has been demolished over the last 30 years to make way for 9-story apartment buildings in the growing city of Kstovo, such as the one in the background

In recent years, urbanization of rural areas has increased. As agriculture, more traditional local services, and small-scale industry give way to modern industry the urban and related commerce with the city drawing on the resources of an ever-widening area for its own sustenance and goods to be traded or processed into manufactures.

Research in urban ecology finds that larger cities provide more specialized goods and services to the local market and surrounding areas, function as a transportation and wholesale hub for smaller places, and accumulate more capital, financial service provision, and an educated labor force, as well as often concentrating administrative functions for the area in which they lie. This relation among places of different sizes is called the urban hierarchy.

As cities develop, effects can include a dramatic increase in costs, often pricing the local working class out of the market, including such functionaries as employees of the local municipalities. For example, Eric Hobsbawm's book *The age of the revolution: 1789–1848* (published 1962 and 2005) chapter 11, stated "Urban development in our period [1789–1848] was a gigantic process of class segregation, which pushed the new labouring poor into great morasses of misery outside the centres of government and business and the newly specialised residential areas of the bourgeoisie. The almost universal European division into a 'good' west end and a 'poor' east end of large cities developed in this period."

This is likely due the prevailing south-west wind which carries coal smoke and other airborne pollutants downwind, making the western edges of towns preferable to the eastern ones. Similar problems now affect the developing world, rising inequality resulting from rapid urbanisation trends. The drive for rapid urban growth and often efficiency can lead to less equitable urban development, think tanks such as the Overseas Development Institute have even proposed policies that encourage labour intensive growth as a means of absorbing the influx of low skilled and unskilled labour .

Urbanization is often viewed as a negative trend, but can in fact, be perceived simply as a natural occurrence from individual and corporate efforts to reduce expense in commuting and transportation while improving opportunities for jobs, education, housing, and transportation. Living in cities permits individuals and families to take advantage of the opportunities of proximity, diversity, and marketplace competition.

Environmental Effects

The urban heat island has become a growing concern and is increasing over the years. The urban heat island is formed when industrial and urban areas are developed and heat becomes more abundant. In rural areas, a large part of the incoming solar energy is used to evaporate water from vegetation and soil. In cities, where less vegetation and exposed soil exists, the majority of the sun's energy is absorbed by urban structures and asphalt.

Hence, during warm daylight hours, less evaporative cooling in cities allows surface temperatures to rise higher than in rural areas. Additional city heat is given off by vehicles and factories, as well as by industrial and domestic heating and cooling units. This effect causes the city to become 2 to 10° F (1 to 6° C) warmer than surrounding landscapes.. Impacts also include reducing soil moisture and intensification of carbon dioxide emissions.

In his book *Whole Earth Discipline*, Stewart Brand argues that the effects of urbanization are on the overall positive for the environment. Firstly, the birth rate of new urban dwellers falls immediately to replacement rate, and keeps falling. This can prevent overpopulation in the future. Secondly, it puts a stop to destructive subsistence farming techniques, like slash and burn agriculture. Finally, it minimizes land use by humans, leaving more for nature.

Changing Forms

Different forms of urbanization can be classified depending on the style of architecture and planning methods as well as historic growth of areas.In cities of the developed world, urbanization traditionally exhibited a concentration of human activities and settlements around the downtown area, the so-called *in-migration*. In-migration refers to migration from former colonies and similar places. The fact that many immigrants settle in impoverished city centres led to the notion of the "peripheralization of the core", which simply describes that people who used to be at the periphery of the former empires now live right in the centre.

Recent developments, such as inner-city redevelopment schemes, mean that new arrivals in cities no longer necessarily settle in the centre. In some developed regions, the reverse effect, originally called counter urbanisation has occurred, with cities losing population to rural areas, and is particularly common for richer families. This has been possible because of improved communications, and has been caused by factors such as the fear of crime and poor urban environments. Later termed *"white flight"*, the effect is not restricted to cities with a high ethnic minority population.

When the residential area shifts outward, this is called suburbanization. A number of researchers and writers suggest that suburbanization has gone so far to form new points of concentration outside the downtown both in developed and developing countries such as India. This networked, poly-centric form of concentration is considered by some an emerging pattern of urbanization. It is called variously exurbia, edge city (Garreau, 1991), network city (Batten, 1995), or postmodern city (Dear, 2000). Los Angeles is the best-known example of this type of urbanization.

Rural migrants are attracted by the possibilities that cities can offer, but often settle in shanty towns and experience extreme poverty. In the 1980s, this was attempted to be tackled with the urban bias theory which was promoted by Michael Lipton who wrote: "...the most important class conflict in the poor countries of the world today is not between labour and capital. Nor is it between foreign and national interests. It is between rural classes and urban classes. The rural sector contains most of the poverty and most of the low-cost sources of potential advance; but the urban sector contains most of the articulateness, organization and power.

So the urban classes have been able to win most of the rounds of the struggle with the countryside..." . Most of the urban poor in developing countries able to find work can spend their lives in insecure, poorly paid jobs. According to research by the Overseas Development Institute pro-poor urbanisation will require labour intensive growth, supported by labour protection, flexible land use regulation and investments in basic services.'

Urbanization can be planned urbanization or organic. Planned urbanization, ie: planned community or the garden city movement, is based on an advance plan, which can be prepared for military, aesthetic, economic or urban design reasons. Examples can be seen in many ancient cities; although with exploration came the collision of nations, which meant that many invaded cities took on the desired planned characteristics of their occupiers.

Many ancient organic cities experienced redevelopment for military and economic purposes, new roads carved through the cities, and new parcels of land were cordoned off serving various planned purposes giving cities distinctive geometric designs.

UN agencies prefer to see urban infrastructure installed before urbanization occurs. Landscape planners are responsible for landscape infrastructure (public parks, sustainable urban drainage systems, greenways etc) which can be planned before urbanization takes place, or afterward to revitalize an area and create greater livability within a region. Concepts of control of the urban expansion are considered in the American Institute of Planners.

Counter Urbanization

Counter urbanisation is a demographic and social process whereby people move from urban areas to rural areas. It first took place as a reaction to inner-city deprivation and overcrowding. Initial study of counter urbanisation was carried out by human geographer Brian Berry. More recent research has documented the social and political drivers of counter urbanisation, and the impacts of the same, in developing countries, which are currently undergoing processes of mass-urbanisation, such as China.

Process

The process involves the moving of the population away from urban areas such as towns and cities to a new town, a new estate, a commuter town or a village. The first two of these destinations were often encouraged by government schemes whereas the latter two were generally the choice of more middle class, socially mobile persons from their own prerogative. With the improvement of innercity transport infrastructure, and more sustainable public transport, people no-longer have to live close to their work, and so can easily commute each day.

Factors of Moving

Many factors can come in to account when someone decides to move from an urban area to a rural area including; housing density, housing prices, pollution levels (health afflictions), crime levels, peaceful retirement, and a wish to improve quality of life. Developments in rural electrification and rural Internet bring to rural areas some of the amenities of urbanity; thus eliminating one of the obstacles preventing some people from moving to a more rural setting.

Sustainable Tourism

Sustainable tourism is an industry committed to making a low impact on the environment and local culture, while helping to generate future employment for local people. The aim of sustainable tourism is to ensure that development brings a positive experience for the local people, tourism companies and the tourists themselves, but sustainable tourism is not the same as ecotourism.

Global economists forecast continuing international tourism growth, ranging between 3 and 6 percent annually, depending on the location. As one of the world's largest and fastest growing industries, this continuous growth will place great stress on remaining biologically diverse habitats and indigenous cultures, which are often used to support mass tourism. Tourists who promote sustainable tourism are sensitive to these dangers and seek to protect tourist destinations, and to protect tourism as an industry.

Sustainable tourists can reduce the impact of tourism in many ways, including:

- informing themselves of the culture, politics, and economy of the communities visited
- anticipating and respecting local cultures, expectations and assumptions
- contributing to intercultural understanding and tolerance
- supporting the integrity of local cultures by favoring businesses which conserve cultural heritage and traditional values
- supporting local economies by purchasing local goods and participating with small, local businesses
- conserving resources by seeking out businesses that are environmentally conscious, and by using the least possible amount of non-renewable resources

Increasingly, destinations and tourism operations are endorsing and following "responsible tourism" as a pathway towards sustainable tourism. Responsible tourism and sustainable tourism have an identical goal, that of sustainable development. The pillars of responsible tourism are therefore the same as those of sustainable tourism - environmental integrity, social justice and economic development.

The major difference between the two is that, in responsible tourism, individuals, organisations and businesses are asked to take responsibility for their actions and the impacts of their actions. This shift in emphasis has taken place because some stakeholders feel that insufficient progress towards realising sustainable tourism has been made since the Earth Summit in Rio.

This is partly because everyone has been expecting others to behave in a sustainable manner. The emphasis on responsibility in responsible tourism means that everyone involved in tourism - government, product owners and operators, transport operators, community services, NGO's and CBO's, tourists, local communities, industry associations - are responsible for achieving the goals of responsible tourism.

Responsible Tourism

Responsible Tourism can be regarded as a behaviour. It is more than a form of tourism as it represents an approach to engaging with tourism, be that as a tourist, a business, locals at a destination or any other tourism stakeholder. It emphasises that all stakeholders are responsible for the kind of tourism they develop or engage in. Whilst different groups will see responsibility in different ways, the shared understanding is that responsible tourism should entail an improvement in tourism. Tourism should become 'better' as a result of the responsible tourism approach.

Within the notion of betterment resides the acknowledgement that conflicting interests need to be balanced. However, the objective is to create better places for people to live in and to visit. Importantly, there is no blueprint for responsible tourism: what is deemed responsible may differ depending on places and cultures. Responsible Tourism is an aspiration that can be realised in different ways in different originating markets and in the diverse destinations of the world (Goodwin, 2002).

Focusing in particular on businesses, according to the Cape Town Declaration on Responsible Tourism, it will have the following characteristics:

- minimises negative economic, environmental, and social impacts
- generates greater economic benefits for local people and enhances the well-being of host communities, improves working conditions and access to the industry
- involves local people in decisions that affect their lives and life chances
- makes positive contributions to the conservation of natural and cultural heritage, to the maintenance of the world's diversity
- provides more enjoyable experiences for tourists through more meaningful connections with local people, and a greater understanding of local cultural, social and environmental issues
- provides access for physically challenged people and
- is culturally sensitive, engenders respect between tourists and hosts, and builds local pride and confidence.

Sustainable tourism is where tourists can enjoy their holiday and at the same time respect the culture of people and also respect the environment. It also means that local people (such as the Masaai) get a fair say about tourism and also receive some money from the profit which the game reserve make. The environment is being damaged quite a lot by tourists and part of Sustainable tourism is to make sure that the damaging does not carry on.

There are many private companies who are working into embracing the principles and aspects of Responsible Tourism, some for the purpose of Corporate Social Responsibility activities, and others such WorldHotel-Link, which was originally a project of the International Finance Corporation, have built their entire business model around responsible tourism, local capacity building and increasing market access for small and medium tourism enterprises.

Responsible Hospitality

As with the view of Responsible Tourism, Responsible Hospitality is essentially about creating better places for people to live in, and better places for people to visit. This does not mean all forms of hospitality are also forms of tourism although hospitality is the largest sector of the tourism industry. As such we should not be surprised at overlaps between Responsible Hospitality and Responsible Tourism. In the instance where place of permanent residence is also the place where the hospitality service is consumed, if for example a meal is consumed in a local restaurant, this does not obviate the requirement to improve the place of residence. As such, the essence of Responsible Hospitality is not contingent upon touristic forms of hospitality.

While Friedman (1962) famously argued that, admittedly within legal parameters, the sole responsibility of business was to generate profit for shareholders the idea that businesses' responsibility extends beyond this has existed for decades and is most frequently encountered in the concept of corporate social responsibility (Carroll, 1999). There are numerous ways businesses can and do engage in activities that are not intended to benefit shareholders and management, at least not in the short term. However, often acts of corporate social responsibility are undertaken because of the perceived benefit to business. Usually in hospitality this relates to the cost reductions associated with improved energy efficiency (Pizam, 2009) but may also relate to, for example, the rise in ethical consumerism and the view that being seen to be a responsible business is beneficial to revenue growth.

As per the Cape Town Declaration on Responsible Tourism (see www.icrtourism.org), Responsible Hospitality is culturally sensitive. Instead of then calling for the unachievable, Responsible Hospitality simply makes the case for more responsible forms of hospitality, hospitality that benefits locals first, and visitors second. Certainly, all forms of hospitality can be improved and managed so that negative impacts are minimised whilst striving for a maximisation of positive impacts.

Carroll, A. (1999). Corporate Social Responsibility. Business & Society, 38(3), 268-295.

Friedman, M. (1962). Capitalism and Freedom. Chicago: University of Chicago Press.

Pizam, A. (2009). Editorial: Green hotels: A fad, ploy or fact of life? International Journal of Hospitality Management, 28(1), 1.

Coastal Tourism

Many coastal areas are experiencing particular pressure from growth in lifestyles and growing numbers of tourists. Coastal environments are limited in extent consisting of only a narrow strip along the edge of the ocean. Coastal areas are often the first environments to experience the detrimental impacts of tourism. A detailed study of the impact on coastal areas, with reference to western India can be an example.

The inevitable change is on the horizon as holiday destinations put more effort into sustainable tourism. Planning and management controls can reduce the impact on coastal environments and ensure that investment into tourism products supports sustainable coastal tourism.

Some Conceptual Models in Coastal Tourism

Some of the recent studies have led to some interesting conceptual models applicable for coastal tourism. The 'inverted funnel model' and the 'embedded model' can be good metaphors for understanding the interplay of different stake-holders like government, local community, tourists and business community in developing tourist destinations.

Community-based Management

There has been the promotion of sustainable tourism practices surrounding the management of tourist locations by locals or more concisely, the community.

This form of tourism is based on the premise that the people living next to a resource are the ones best suited to protecting it. This means that the tourism activities and businesses are developed and operated by local community members, and certainly with their consent and support.

Sustainable tourism typically involves the conservation of resources that are capitalized upon for tourism purposes, such as coral reefs and pristine forests. Locals run the businesses and are responsible for promoting the conservation messages to protect their environment.

Community-based sustainable tourism (CBST) associates the success of the sustainability of the ecotourism location to the management practices of the communities who are directly or indirectly dependent on the location for their livelihoods.

A salient feature of CBST is that local knowledge is usually utilised alongside wide general frameworks of ecotourism business models. This allows the participation of locals at the management level and typically allows a more intimate understanding of the environment. The use of local knowledge also means an easier entry level into a tourism industry for locals whose jobs or livelihoods are affected by the use of their environment as tourism locations. The involvement of locals restores the ownership of the environment to the local community and allows an alternative sustainable form of development for communities and their environments that are typically unable to support other forms of development.. However, recent research has found that economic linkages generated by CBST may only be sporadic, and that the linkages with agriculture are negatively affected by seasonality and by the small scale of the cultivated areas. This means that CBST may only have small-scale positive effects for these communities.

Non-governmental Organizations

Non-governmental organizations are one of the stakeholders in advocating sustainable tourism. Their roles can range from spearheading sustainable tourism practices to simply doing research. University research teams and scientists can be tapped to aid in the process of planning. Such solicitation of research can be observed in the planning of Cat Ba National Park in Vietnam.

Dive resort operators in Bunaken National Park, Indonesia, play a crucial role but developing exclusive zones for diving and fishing respectively, such that both tourists and locals can benefit from the venture

Large conventions, meetings and other major organized events drive the travel, tourism and hospitality industry. Cities and convention centers compete to attract such commerce, commerce which has heavy impacts on resource use and the environment. Major sporting events, such as the Olympic Games, present special problems regarding environmental burdens and degradation. But burdens imposed by the regular convention industry can be vastly more significant.

Green conventions and events are a new but growing sector and marketing point within the convention and hospitality industry. More environmentally aware organizations, corporations and government agencies are now seeking more sustainable event practices, greener hotels, restaurants and convention venues, and more energy efficient or climate neutral travel and ground transportation.

Additionally, some convention centers have begun to take direct action in reducing the impact of the conventions they host. One example is the Moscone Center in San Francisco, California, which has a very aggressive recycling program, a large solar power system, and other programs aimed at reducing impact and increasing efficiency.

Tourists

With the advent of the internet, some traditional conventions are being replaced with virtual conventions, where the attendees remain in their home physical location and "attend" the convention by use of a web-based interface programmed for the task. This sort of "virtual" meeting eliminates all of the impacts associated with travel, accommodation, food wastage, and other necessary impacts of traditional, physical conventions.

Travel over long distances requires a large amount of time and/or energy. Generally this involves burning fossil fuels, a largely unsustainable practice and one that contributes to climate change, via CO2 emissions.

Air travel is perhaps the worst offender in this regard, contributing to between 2 and 3% of global carbon emissions . Given a business-as-usual approach, this could be expected to rise to 5% by 2015 and 10% by 2050. Car travel is the next worst offender.

Mass transport is the most climate friendly method of travel, and generally the rule is "the bigger the better" - compared to cars, buses are relatively more sustainable, and trains and ships are even more so. Human energy and renewable energy are the most efficient, and hence, sustainable. Travel by bicycle, solar powered car, or sailing boat produces no carbon emissions (although the embodied energy in these vehicles generally comes at the expense of carbon emission).

Humane Tourism

Humane tourism is part of the movement of responsible tourism. The idea is to empower local communities through travel related businesses around the world, first and foremost in developing countries. The idea of humane travel or humane tourism is to connect travelers from Europe, North America, Australia and New Zealand seeking new adventures and authentic experiences directly, to local businesses in the specific locations they wish to visit - thus, giving economic advantages to local businesses and giving travelers authentic and truly unique travel experiences. Humane travel or humane tourism focuses on the people, the local community. The idea is to enable travelers to experience the world through the eyes of its local people while contributing directly to those people, ensuring that tourist dollars benefit the local community directly.

Humane tourism is about giving opportunity to the local people, empower them, enable them to enjoy the fruits of tourism directly. The Internet is changing tourism. More and more travelers are planning their travels and vacations via the net. The Internet enables people to cut off commissions. The traveler can search for new destinations to visit, talk or read about other people experience, and buy the services directly. The Internet platform can encourage local people to start new businesses and that already existing small businesses will begin to promote themselves through the net and receive the economic advantages of this directly in their communities. The world is now in a new tourism age, with globalization and the Internet playing a key role.

The new travelers have traveled the world, they have seen the classic sites. Staying at a Western hotel is not attractive enough, and they are excited by the prospect of experiencing the authentic local way of life: to go fishing with a local fisherman, to eat the fish with his family, to sleep in a typical village house. These tourists or travellers, are happy to know that while doing so they promote the economic wellbeing of those same people they spend time with.

Humane tourism is part of Responsible tourism. The concept of Responsible Tourism originated in the work of Jost Krippendorf in The Holiday Makers (1987) called for "rebellious tourists and rebellious locals" to create new forms of tourism. His vision was "to develop and promote new forms of tourism, which will bring the greatest possible benefit to all the participants - travellers, the host population and the tourist business, without causing intolerable ecological and social damage." As one can see he already talked, back in the 80s about benefits for the host population and used the term human tourism. Humane travel focuses on that host local population.

The South African national tourism policy (1996) used the term "responsible tourism" and mentioned the wellbeing of the local community as a main factor.

The Cape Town Declaration on Responsible Tourism in Destinations, agreed in 2002, that Responsible Tourism is about "making better places for people to live in and better places for people to visit." The decleration focused on "places" but did nention the local population.

From the Rio summit or earth summit on 1992 until the UN Commission on Sustainable Development in 1999, the main focus of the tourism industry was the earth, the planet, the places, "green" or "eco" tourism. Now there is a trend to include the local population. This trend or branch of responsible tourism is called humane tourism or humane travel.

MANAGING URBAN TOURISM

Hospitality management is the academic study of the hospitality industry. A degree in Hospitality management is often conferred from either a university college dedicated to the studies of hospitality management or a business school with a department in hospitality management studies. Degrees in hospitality management may also be referred to as hotel management, hotel and tourism management, or hotel administration. Degrees conferred in this academic field include Bachelors of Arts, Bachelors of Business Administration, Bachelors of Science, Masters of Science, MBA, and Doctorate of Philosophy.

Hospitality management studies provides a focus on management of hospitality operations including hotels, restaurants, cruise ships, amusement parks, destination marketing organizations, convention centers, country clubs, and related industries.

In America, Hospitality and Tourism Management curriculum follow similar core subject applications to that of a business degree but with a focus on hospitality management. Core subject areas include accounting, administration, finance, information systems, marketing, human resource management, public relations, strategy, quantitative methods, and sectoral studies in the various areas of hospitality business. Cornell University, University of Nevada, Las Vegas (UNLV), and University of Central Florida (UCF) are considered the top Hospitality Management undergraduate colleges in America. One of the newest graduate degree programs in hospitality management is offered by The George Washington University School of Business in Washington, D.C..

In addition to the core coursework above, degree-specific coursework normally includes:

- Restaurant Management (Examples: Management of Food and Beverage Operations, Food Science, Food Selection and Preparation, Food and Beverage Cost Control)
- Lodging Operations (Examples: Lodging Management, Hotel Operations, Resort Timeshare Management, Reservation Sales and Marketing, Hospitality Physical Plant)
- Global Tourism (Examples: Tourism Management, Airline Industry, Sustainable Tourism, Hospitality and Research Methods)
- Attractions Management (Examples: Theme Park Management, Entertainment Arts)
- Event Management (Examples: Event Industry, Catering Management, Hospitality Marketing Management)
- Food Preparation (Examples: Basic Food Preparation, Food Sanitation, Beer and Wine Labs)

Many hospitality programs require concurrent field experience within the industry in the form of internships or co-operative placements.

GRADUATE PLACEMENT

Several large hospitality corporations such as Marriott, Hilton Worldwide, IHG, Hyatt, Sasi park, Wyndham, beeran international Parks and Resorts, and various management companies offer internship programs as well as management training programs and direct placements for students majoring in Hospitality and Tourism Management. Similar to other business fields, management training programs and direct placement opportunities are highly competitive.

HUMAN RESOURCE MANAGEMENT

Human resource management (HRM) is the strategic and coherent approach to the management of an organization's most valued assets - the people working there who individually and collectively contribute to the achievement of the objectives of the business. The terms "human resource management" and "human resources" (HR) have largely replaced the term "personnel management" as a description of the processes involved in managing people in organizations. In simple words, HRM means employing people, developing their capacities, utilizing, maintaining and compensating their services in tune with the job and organizational requirement.

Its features include:

- Organizational management
- Personnel administration
- Manpower management
- Industrial management

But these traditional expressions are becoming less common for the theoretical discipline. Sometimes even employee and industrial relations are confusingly listed as synonyms, although these normally refer to the relationship between management and workers and the behavior of workers in companies.

The theoretical discipline is based primarily on the assumption that employees are individuals with varying goals and needs, and as such should not be thought of as basic business resources, such as trucks and filing cabinets. The field takes a positive view of workers, assuming that virtually all wish to contribute to the enterprise productively, and that the main obstacles to their endeavors are lack of knowledge, insufficient training, and failures of process.

Human Resource Management(HRM) is seen by practitioners in the field as a more innovative view of workplace management than the traditional approach. Its techniques force the managers of an enterprise to express their goals with specificity so that they can be understood and undertaken by the workforce, and to provide the resources needed for them to successfully accomplish their assignments. As such, HRM techniques, when properly practiced, are expressive of the goals and operating practices of the enterprise overall. HRM is also seen by many to have a key role in risk reduction within organisations.

Synonyms such as personnel management are often used in a more restricted sense to describe activities that are necessary in the recruiting of a workforce, providing its members with payroll and benefits, and administrating their work-life needs. So if we move to actual definitions, Torrington and Hall (1987) define personnel management as being:

"a series of activities which: first enable working people and their employing organisations to agree about the objectives and nature of their working relationship and, secondly, ensures that the agreement is fulfilled" (p. 49).

While Miller (1987) suggests that HRM relates to:

".......those decisions and actions which concern the management of employees at all levels in the business and which are related to the implementation of strategies directed towards creating and sustaining competitive advantage" (p. 352).

Academic Theory

Research in the area of HRM has much to contribute to the organisational practice of HRM. For the last 20 years, empirical work has paid particular attention to the link between the practice of HRM and organisational performance, evident in improved employee commitment, lower levels of absenteeism and turnover, higher levels of skills and therefore higher productivity, enhanced quality and efficiency . This area of work is sometimes referred to as 'Strategic HRM' or SHRM.

Within SHRM three strands of work can be observed: Best practice, Best Fit and the Resource Based View (RBV).

The notion of best practice - sometimes called 'high commitment' HRM - proposes that the adoption of certain best practices in HRM will result in better organisational performance. Perhaps the most popular work in this area is that of Pfeffer who argued that there were seven best practices for achieving competitive advantage through people and 'building profits by putting people first'.

These practices included: providing employment security, selective hiring, extensive training, sharing information, self-managed teams, high pay based on company performance and the reduction of status differentials. However, there is a huge number of studies which provide evidence of best practices, usually implemented in coherent bundles, and therefore it is difficult to draw generalised conclusions about which is the 'best' way (For a comparison of different sets of best practices see Becker and Gerhart, 1996

Best fit, or the contingency approach to HRM, argues that HRM improves performance where there is a close vertical fit between the HRM practices and the company's strategy. This link ensures close coherence between the HR people processes and policies and the external market or business strategy. There are a range of theories about the nature of this vertical integration. For example, a set of 'lifecycle' models argue that HR policies and practices can be mapped onto the stage of an organisation's development or lifecycle.

Competitive advantage models take Porter's (1985) ideas about strategic choice and map a range of HR practices onto the organisation's choice of competitive strategy. Finally 'configurational models' provide a more sophisticated approach which advocates a close examination of the organisation's strategy in order to determine the appropriate HR policies and practices. However, this approach assumes that the strategy of the organisation can be identified - many organisations exist in a state of flux and development.

The Resource Based View (RBV), argued by some to be at the foundation of modern HRM , focusses on the internal resources of the organisation and how they contribute to competitive advantage. The uniqueness of these resources is preferred to homogeneity and HRM has a central role in developing human resources that are valuable, rare, difficult to copy or substitute and that are effectively organised.

Overall, the theory of HRM argues that the goal of human resource management is to help an organization to meet strategic goals by attracting, and maintaining employees and also to manage them effectively. The key word here perhaps is "fit", i.e. a HRM approach seeks to ensure a fit between the management of an organisation's employees, and the overall strategic direction of the company (Miller, 1989).

The basic premise of the academic theory of HRM is that humans are not machines, therefore we need to have an interdisciplinary examination of people in the workplace. Fields such as psychology, industrial relations, industrial engineering, sociology, economics, and critical theories: postmodernism, post-structuralism play a major role. Many colleges and universities offer bachelor and master degrees in Human Resources Management or in Human Resources and Industrial Relations.

One widely used scheme to describe the role of HRM, developed by Dave Ulrich, defines 4 fields for the HRM function:

- Strategic business partner
- Change Agent
- Employee champion
- Administration Expert

Business Practice

Human resources management involves several processes. Together they are supposed to achieve the above mentioned goal. These processes can be performed in an HR department, but some tasks can also be outsourced or performed by line-managers or other departments. When effectively integrated they provide significant economic benefit to the company.

- Workforce planning
- Recruitment (sometimes separated into attraction and selection)
- Induction, Orientation and Onboarding
- Skills management
- Training and development
- Personnel administration
- Compensation in wage or salary
- Time management
- Travel management (sometimes assigned to accounting rather than HRM)
- Payroll (sometimes assigned to accounting rather than HRM)
- Employee benefits administration

- Personnel cost planning
- Performance appraisal
- Labor relations

HRM strategy

An HRM strategy pertains to the means as to how to implement the specific functions of Human Resourse Management. An organization's HR function may possess recruitment and selection policies, disciplinary procedures, reward/recognition policies, an HR plan, or learning and development policies, however all of these functional areas of HRM need to be aligned and correlated, in order to correspond with the overall business strategy. An HRM strategy thus is an overall plan, concerning the implementation of specific HRM functional areas.

An HRM strategy typically consists of the following factors:-

- "Best fit" and "best practice" - meaning that there is correlation between the HRM strategy and the overall corporate strategy. As HRM as a field seeks to manage human resources in order to achieve properly organizational goals, an organization's HRM strategy seeks to accomplish such management by applying a firm's personnel needs with the goals/objectives of the organisation. As an example, a firm selling cars could have a corporate strategy of increasing car sales by 10% over a five year period. Accordingly, the HRM strategy would seek to facilitate how exactly to manage personnel in order to achieve the 10% figure. Specific HRM functions, such as recruitment and selection, reward/recognition, an HR plan, or learning and development policies, would be tailored to achieve the corporate objectives.
- Close co-operation (at least in theory) between HR and the top/senior management, in the development of the corporate strategy. Theoretically, a senior HR representative should be present when an organization's corporate objectives are devised. This is so, since it is a firm's personnel who actually construct a good, or provide a service. The personnel's proper management is vital in the firm being successful, or even existing as a going concern. Thus, HR can be seen as one of

the critical departments within the functional area of an organization.

- Continual monitoring of the strategy, via employee feedback, surveys, etc.

The implementation of an HR strategy is not always required, and may depend on a number of factors, namely the size of the firm, the organizational culture within the firm or the industry that the firm operates in and also the people in the firm.

An HRM strategy can be divided, in general, into two facets - the people strategy and the HR functional strategy. The people strategy pertains to the point listed in the first paragraph, namely the careful correlation of HRM policies/actions to attain the goals laid down in the corporate strategy. The HR functional strategy relates to the policies employed within the HR functional area itself, regarding the management of persons internal to it, to ensure its own departmental goals are met.

Careers and Education

Several universities offer programs of study pertaining to HRM and broader fields. Cornell University created the world's first school for college-level study in HRM (ILR School). University of Illinois at Urbana-Champaign also now has a school dedicated to the study of HRM, while several business schools also house a center or department dedicated to such studies; e.g., University of Wisconsin-Madison, University of Minnesota, Michigan State University, Ohio State University, Roosevelt University,and Purdue University.

There are both generalist and specialist HRM jobs. There are careers involved with employment, recruitment and placement and these are usually conducted by interviewers, EEO (Equal Employment Opportunity) specialists or college recruiters. Training and development specialism is often conducted by trainers and orientation specialists. Compensation and benefits tasks are handled by compensation analysts, salary administrators, and benefits administrators.

Professional Organizations

Professional organizations in HRM include the Society for Human Resource Management, the Australian Human Resources

Institute (AHRI), the Chartered Institute of Personnel and Development (CIPD), the International Public Management Association for HR (IPMA-HR), Management Association of Nepal (MAN) and the International Personnel Management Association of Canada (IPMA-Canada), Human Capital Institute. National Human Resource Development Network in India.

Variety of Activities

The Human Resources Management (HRM) function includes a variety of activities, and key among them is deciding the staffing needs of an organization and whether to use independent contractors or hire employees to fill these needs, recruiting and training the best employees, ensuring they are high performers, dealing with performance issues, and ensuring your personnel and management practices conform to various regulations. Activities also include managing your approach to employee benefits and compensation, employee records and personnel policies. Usually small businesses (for-profit or nonprofit) have to carry out these activities themselves because they can't yet afford part- or full-time help. However, they should always ensure that employees have-and are aware of-personnel policies which conform to current regulations. These policies are often in the form of employee manuals, which all employees have.

Note that some people distinguish a difference between HRM (a major management activity) and HRD (Human Resource Development, a profession). Those people might include HRM in HRD, explaining that HRD includes the broader range of activities to develop personnel inside of organizations, including, e.g., career development, training, organization development, etc.

There is a long-standing argument about where HR-related functions should be organized into large organizations, e.g., "should HR be in the Organization Development department or the other way around?"

The HRM function and HRD profession have undergone major changes over the past 20-30 years. Many years ago, large organizations looked to the "Personnel Department," mostly to manage the paperwork around hiring and paying people. More recently, organizations consider the "HR Department" as playing an important role in staffing, training and helping to manage people so that people and the organization are performing at maximum capability in a highly fulfilling manner.

Marketing

Marketing is the process of performing market research, selling products and/or services to customers and promoting them via advertising to further enhance sales. It generates the strategy that underlies sales techniques, business communication, and business developments. It is an integrated process through which companies build strong customer relationships and create value for their customers and for themselves.

Marketing is used to identify the customer, to satisfy the customer, and to keep the customer. With the customer as the focus of its activities, it can be concluded that marketing management is one of the major components of business management. Marketing evolved to meet the stasis in developing new markets caused by mature markets and overcapacities in the last 2-3 centuries. The adoption of marketing strategies requires businesses to shift their focus from production to the perceived needs and wants of their customers as the means of staying profitable.

The term marketing concept holds that achieving organizational goals depends on knowing the needs and wants of target markets and delivering the desired satisfactions. It proposes that in order to satisfy its organizational objectives, an organization should anticipate the needs and wants of consumers and satisfy these more effectively than competitors.

Marketing is defined by the American Marketing Association (AMA) as "the activity, set of institutions, and processes for creating, communicating, delivering, and exchanging offerings that have value for customers, clients, partners, and society at large. Marketing is a product or service selling related overall activities. The term developed from an original meaning which referred literally to going to a market to buy or sell goods or services. Seen from a systems point of view, sales process engineering marketing is "a set of processes that are interconnected and interdependent with other functions, whose methods can be improved using a variety of relatively new approaches."

The Chartered Institute of Marketing defines marketing as "the management process responsible for identifying, anticipating and satisfying customer requirements profitably." A different concept is the value-based marketing which states the role of marketing to contribute to increasing shareholder value. In this context, marketing is defined as "the management process that seeks to maximise returns to shareholders by developing relationships with valued customers and creating a competitive advantage."

Marketing practice tended to be seen as a creative industry in the past, which included advertising, distribution and selling. However, because the academic study of marketing makes extensive use of social sciences, psychology, sociology, mathematics, economics, anthropology and neuroscience, the profession is now widely recognized as a science, allowing numerous universities to offer Master-of-Science (MSc) programmes. The overall process starts with marketing research and goes through market segmentation, business planning and execution, ending with pre- and post-sales promotional activities. It is also related to many of the creative arts. The marketing literature is also adept at re-inventing itself and its vocabulary according to the times and the culture.

Evolution of Marketing

An orientation, in the marketing context, related to a perception or attitude a firm holds towards its product or service, essentially concerning consumers and end-users. Throughout history, marketing has changed considerably in time with consumer tastes.

Earlier Approaches

The marketing orientation evolved from earlier orientations, namely, the production orientation, the product orientation and the selling orientation.

Orientation	Profit driver	Western European timeframe	Description
Production	Production methods	until the 1950s	A firm focusing on a production orientation specializes in producing as much as possible of a given product or service. Thus, this signifies a firm exploiting economies of scale until the minimum efficient scale is reached. A production orientation may be deployed when a high demand for a product or service exists, coupled with a good certainty that consumer tastes will not rapidly alter (similar to the sales orientation).
Product	Quality of the product	until the 1960s	A firm employing a product orientation is chiefly concerned with the quality of its own product. A firm would also assume that as long as its product was of a high standard, people would buy and consume the product.
Selling	Selling methods	1950s and 1960s	A firm using a sales orientation focuses primarily on the selling/promotion of a particular product, and not determining new consumer desires as such. Consequently, this entails simply selling an already existing product, and using promotion techniques to attain the highest sales possible.
Marketing	Needs and wants of customers	1970 to present day	Such an orientation may suit scenarios in which a firm holds dead stock, or otherwise sells a product that is in high demand, with little likelihood of changes in consumer tastes diminishing demand. The **'marketing orientation'** is perhaps the most common orientation used in contemporary marketing. It involves a firm essentially basing its marketing plans around the marketing concept, and thus supplying products to suit new consumer tastes. As an example, a firm would employ market research to gauge consumer desires, use R&D to develop a product attuned to the revealed information, and then utilize promotion techniques to ensure persons know the product exists.

Contemporary Approaches

Recent approaches in marketing include relationship marketing with focus on the customer, business marketing or industrial marketing with focus on an organization or institution and social marketing with focus on benefits to society. New forms of marketing also use the internet and are therefore called internet marketing or more generally e-marketing, online marketing, search engine marketing, desktop advertising or affiliate marketing.

It attempts to perfect the segmentation strategy used in traditional marketing. It targets its audience more precisely, and is sometimes called personalized marketing or one-to-one marketing. Internet marketing is sometimes considered to be broad in scope, because it not only refers to marketing on the Internet, but also includes marketing done via e-mail and wireless media.

Orientation	Profit driver	Western European timeframe	Description
Relationship marketing / **Relationship management**[10]	Building and keeping good customer relations	1960s to present day	Emphasis is placed on the whole relationship between suppliers and customers. The aim is to provide the best possible customer service and build customer loyalty.
Business marketing / Industrial marketing	Building and keeping relationships between organizations	1980s to present day	In this context, marketing takes place between businesses or organizations. The product focus lies on industrial goods or capital goods rather than consumer products or end products. Different forms of marketing activities, such as promotion, advertising and communication to the customer are used.
Social marketing[10]	Benefit to society	1990s to present day	Similar characteristics as marketing orientation but with the added proviso that there will be a curtailment of any harmful activities to society, in either product, production, or selling methods.
Branding	Brand value	2000s to present day	In this context, "branding" is the main company philosophy and marketing is considered an instrument of branding philosophy.

Customer Orientation

A firm in the market economy survives by producing goods that persons are willing and able to buy. Consequently, ascertaining consumer demand is vital for a firm's future viability and even existence as a going concern. Many companies today have a customer focus (or market orientation). This implies that the company focuses its activities and products on consumer demands. Generally, there are three ways of doing this: the customer-driven approach, the market change identification approach and the product innovation approach.

In the consumer-driven approach, consumer wants are the drivers of all strategic marketing decisions. No strategy is pursued until it passes the test of consumer research. Every aspect of a market offering, including the nature of the product itself, is driven by the needs of potential consumers. The starting point is always the consumer. The rationale for this approach is that there is no reason to spend R&D funds developing products that people will not buy. History attests to many products that were commercial failures in spite of being technological breakthroughs.

A formal approach to this customer-focused marketing is known as SIVA (Solution, Information, Value, Access). This system is basically the four Ps renamed and reworded to provide a customer focus. The SIVA Model provides a demand/customer-centric alternative to the well-known 4Ps supply side model (product, price, placement, promotion) of marketing management.

Product	→	Solution
Price	→	Value
Place	→	Access
Promotion	→	Information

If any of the 4Ps were problematic or were not in the marketing factor of the business, the business could be in trouble and so other companies may appear in the surroundings of the company, so the consumer demand on its products will decrease.

Organizational Orientation

In this sense, a firm's marketing department is often seen as of prime importance within the functional level of an organization. Information from an organization's marketing department would be used to guide the actions of other departments within the firm. As an example, a marketing department could ascertain (via marketing research) that consumers desired a new type of product, or a new usage for an existing product. With this in mind, the marketing department would inform the R&D department to create a prototype of a product/service based on consumers' new desires.

The production department would then start to manufacture the product, while the marketing department would focus on the promotion, distribution, pricing, etc. of the product. Additionally, a firm's finance department would be consulted, with respect to securing appropriate funding for the development, production and promotion of the product. Inter-departmental conflicts may occur, should a firm adhere to the marketing orientation. Production may oppose the installation, support and servicing of new capital stock, which may be needed to manufacture a new product. Finance may oppose the required capital expenditure, since it could undermine a healthy cash flow for the organization.

Herd Behavior

Herd behavior in marketing is used to explain the dependencies of customers' mutual behavior. The Economist reported a recent conference in Rome on the subject of the simulation of adaptive human behavior. It shared mechanisms to increase impulse buying and get people "to buy more by playing on the herd instinct." The basic idea is that people will buy more of products that are seen to be popular, and several feedback mechanisms to get product popularity information to consumers are mentioned, including smart card technology and the use of Radio Frequency Identification Tag technology. A "swarm-moves" model was introduced by a Florida Institute of Technology researcher, which is appealing to supermarkets because it can "increase sales without the need to give people discounts."

Other recent studies on the "power of social influence" include an "artificial music market in which some 19,000 people downloaded previously unknown songs" (Columbia University, New York); a Japanese chain of convenience stores which orders its products based on "sales data from department stores and research companies;" a Massachusetts company exploiting knowledge of social networking to improve sales; and online retailers who are increasingly informing consumers about "which products are popular with like-minded consumers" (e.g., Amazon, eBay).

Further orientations

- An emerging area of study and practice concerns internal marketing, or how employees are trained and managed to deliver the brand in a way that positively impacts the acquisition and retention of customers, see also employer branding.
- Diffusion of innovations research explores how and why people adopt new products, services, and ideas.
- With consumers' eroding attention span and willingness to give time to advertising messages, marketers are turning to forms

of permission marketing such as branded content, custom media and reality marketing.

Marketing Research

Marketing research involves conducting research to support marketing activities, and the statistical interpretation of data into information. This information is then used by managers to plan marketing activities, gauge the nature of a firm's marketing environment and attain information from suppliers. Marketing researchers use statistical methods such as quantitative research, qualitative research, hypothesis tests, Chi-squared tests, linear regression, correlations, frequency distributions, poisson distributions, binomial distributions, etc. to interpret their findings and convert data into information.

The marketing research process spans a number of stages, including the definition of a problem, development of a research plan, collection and interpretation of data and disseminating information formally in the form of a report. The task of marketing research is to provide management with relevant, accurate, reliable, valid, and current information.

A distinction should be made between marketing research and market research. Market research pertains to research in a given market. As an example, a firm may conduct research in a target market, after selecting a suitable market segment. In contrast, marketing research relates to all research conducted within marketing. Thus, market research is a subset of marketing research.

Market segmentation pertains to the division of a market of consumers into persons with similar needs and wants. For instance, Kellogg's cereals, Frosties are marketed to children. Crunchy Nut Cornflakes are marketed to adults. Both goods denote two products which are marketed to two distinct groups of persons, both with similar needs, traits, and wants.

Market segmentation allows for a better allocation of a firm's finite resources. A firm only possesses a certain amount of resources. Accordingly, it must make choices (and incur the related costs) in servicing specific groups of consumers. In this way, the diversified tastes of contemporary Western consumers can be served better. With growing diversity in the tastes of modern consumers, firms are taking note of the benefit of servicing a multiplicity of new markets. Market segmentation can be defined in terms of the STP acronym, meaning Segment, Target and Position.

Types of Marketing Research

Marketing research, as a sub-set aspect of marketing activities, can be divided into the following parts:

- Primary research (also known as field research), which involves the conduction and compilation of research for a specific purpose.
- Secondary research (also referred to as desk research), initially conducted for one purpose, but often used to support another purpose or end goal.

By these definitions, an example of primary research would be market research conducted into health foods, which is used solely to ascertain the needs/wants of the target market for health foods. Secondary research in this case would be research pertaining to health foods, but used by a firm wishing to develop an unrelated product.

Primary research is often expensive to prepare, collect and interpret from data to information. Nevertheless, while secondary research is relatively inexpensive, it often can become outdated and outmoded, given that it is used for a purpose other than the one for which it was intended. Primary research can also be broken down into quantitative research and qualitative research, which, as the terms suggest, pertain to numerical and non-numerical research methods and techniques, respectively. The appropriateness of each mode of research depends on whether data can be quantified (quantitative research), or whether subjective, non-numeric or abstract concepts are required to be studied (qualitative research).

There also exist additional modes of marketing research, which are:

- Exploratory research, pertaining to research that investigates an assumption.

- Descriptive research, which, as the term suggests, describes "what is".
- Predictive research, meaning research conducted to predict a future occurrence.
- Conclusive research, for the purpose of deriving a conclusion via a research process.

Marketing Planning

The marketing planning process involves forging a plan for a firm's marketing activities. A marketing plan can also pertain to a specific product, as well as to an organization's overall marketing strategy. Generally speaking, an organization's marketing planning process is derived from its overall business strategy.

Thus, when top management are devising the firm's strategic direction or mission, the intended marketing activities are incorporated into this plan. There are several levels of marketing objectives within an organization. The senior management of a firm would formulate a general business strategy for a firm. However, this general business strategy would be interpreted and implemented in different contexts throughout the firm.

Marketing Strategy

The field of marketing strategy encompasses the strategy involved in the management of a given product. A given firm may hold numerous products in the marketplace, spanning numerous and sometimes wholly unrelated industries. Accordingly, a plan is required in order to effectively manage such products. Evidently, a company needs to weigh up and ascertain how to utilize its finite resources. For example, a start-up car manufacturing firm would face little success should it attempt to rival Toyota, Ford, Nissan, Chevrolet, or any other large global car maker. Moreover, a product may be reaching the end of its life-cycle. Thus, the issue of divest, or a ceasing of production, may be made. Each scenario requires a unique marketing strategy. Listed below are some prominent marketing strategy models.

Marketing Specializations

With the rapidly emerging force of globalization, the distinction between marketing within a firm's home country and marketing within external markets is disappearing very quickly. With this in mind, firms need to reorient their marketing strategies to meet the challenges of the global marketplace, in addition to sustaining their competitiveness within home markets.

Buying Behaviour

A marketing firm must ascertain the nature of customers' buying behavior if it is to market its product properly. In order to entice and persuade a consumer to buy a product, marketers try to determine the behavioral process of how a given product is purchased. Buying behavior is usually split into two prime strands, whether selling to the consumer, known as business-to-consumer (B2C), or to another business, known as business-to-business (B2B).

B2C Buying Behaviour

This mode of behaviour concerns consumers and their purchase of a given product. For example, if one imagines a pair of sneakers, the desire for a pair of sneakers would be followed by an information search on available types/brands. This may include perusing media outlets, but most commonly consists of information gathered from family and friends. If the information search is insufficient, the consumer may search for alternative means to satisfy the need/want.

In this case, this may mean buying leather shoes, sandals, etc. The purchase decision is then made, in which the consumer actually buys the product. Following this stage, a post-purchase evaluation is often conducted, comprising an appraisal of the value/utility brought by the purchase of the sneakers. If the value/utility is high, then a repeat purchase may be made. This could then develop into consumer loyalty to the firm producing the sneakers.

B2B Buying Behaviour

Relates to organizational/industrial buying behavior. "B2B" stands for Business to Business. B2B marketing involves one business marketing a product or service to another business. B2C and B2B behavior are not precise terms, as similarities and differences exist, with some key differences listed below:

In a straight re-buy, the fourth, fifth and sixth stages are omitted. In a modified re-buy scenario, the fifth and sixth stages are precluded. In a new buy, all stages are conducted.

Use of Technologies

Marketing management can also rely on various technologies within the scope of its marketing efforts. Computer-based information systems can be employed, aiding in better processing and storage of data. Marketing researchers can use such systems to devise better methods of converting data into information, and for the creation of enhanced data gathering methods. Information technology can aid in enhancing an MKIS' software and hardware components, and improve a company's marketing decision-making process.

In recent years, the netbook personal computer has gained significant market share among laptops, largely due to its more user-friendly size and portability. Information technology typically progresses at a fast rate, leading to marketing managers being cognizant of the latest technological developments. Moreover, the launch of smartphones into the cellphone market is commonly derived from a demand among consumers for more technologically advanced products. A firm can lose out to competitors should it ignore technological innovations in its industry.

Technological advancements can lessen barriers between countries and regions. Using the World Wide Web, firms can quickly dispatch information from one country to another without much restriction. Prior to the mass usage of the Internet, such transfers of information would have taken longer to send, especially if done via snail mail, telex, etc.

Services Marketing

Services marketing relates to the marketing of services, as opposed to tangible products. A service (as opposed to a good) is typically defined as follows:

- The use of it is inseparable from its purchase (i.e., a service is used and consumed simultaneously)
- It does not possess material form, and thus cannot be touched, seen, heard, tasted, or smelled.

- The use of a service is inherently subjective, meaning that several persons experiencing a service would each experience it uniquely.

For example, a train ride can be deemed a service. If one buys a train ticket, the use of the train is typically experienced concurrently with the purchase of the ticket. Although the train is a physical object, one is not paying for the permanent ownership of the tangible components of the train.

Services (compared with goods) can also be viewed as a spectrum. Not all products are pure goods, nor are all pure services. An example would be a restaurant, where a waiter's service is intangible, but the food is tangible.

Consumer Behaviour

Consumer behaviour is the study of when, why, how, and where people do or do not buy a product. It blends elements from psychology, sociology, social anthropology and economics. It attempts to understand the buyer decision making process, both individually and in groups. It studies characteristics of individual consumers such as demographics and behavioural variables in an attempt to understand people's wants. It also tries to assess influences on the consumer from groups such as family, friends, reference groups, and society in general.

Customer behaviour study is based on consumer buying behaviour, with the customer playing the three distinct roles of user, payer and buyer. Relationship marketing is an influential asset for customer behaviour analysis as it has a keen interest in the re-discovery of the true meaning of marketing through the re-affirmation of the importance of the customer or buyer. A greater importance is also placed on consumer retention, customer relationship management, personalisation, customisation and one-to-one marketing. Social functions can be categorized into social choice and welfare functions.

Each method for vote counting is assumed as social function but if Arrow's possibility theorem is used for a social function, social welfare function is achieved. Some specifications of the social functions are decisiveness, neutrality, anonymity, monotonicity, unanimity, homogeneity and weak and strong Pareto optimality.

No social choice function meets these requirements in an ordinal scale simultaneously. The most important characteristic of a social function is identification of the interactive effect of alternatives and creating a logical relation with the ranks. Marketing provides services in order to satisfy customers. With that in mind, the productive system is considered from its beginning at the production level, to the end of the cycle, the consumer (Kioumarsi et al., 2009).

Black Box Model

ENVIRONMENTAL FACTORS		BUYER'S BLACK BOX		
Marketing Stimuli	**Environmental Stimuli**	**Buyer Characteristics**	**Decision Process**	**BUYER'S RESPONSE**
Product Price Place Promotion	Economic Technological Political Cultural Demographic Natural	Attitudes Motivation Perceptions Personality Lifestyle Knowledge	Problem recognition Information search Alternative evaluation Purchase decision Post-purchase behaviour	Product choice Brand choice Dealer choice Purchase timing Purchase amount

The black box model shows the interaction of stimuli, consumer characteristics, decision process and consumer responses. It can be distinguished between interpersonal stimuli (between people) or intrapersonal stimuli (within people). The black box model is related to the black box theory of behaviourism, where the focus is not set on the processes inside a consumer, but the relation between the stimuli and the response of the consumer.

The marketing stimuli are planned and processed by the companies, whereas the environmental stimulus are given by social factors, based on the economical, political and cultural circumstances of a society. The buyers black box contains the buyer characteristics and the decision process, which determines the buyers response.

The black box model considers the buyers response as a result of a conscious, rational decision process, in which it is assumed that the buyer has recognized the problem. However, in reality many decisions are not made in awareness of a determined problem by the consumer.

Information Search

Once the consumer has recognised a problem, they search for information on products and services that can solve that problem. Belch and Belch (2007) explain that consumers undertake both an internal (memory) and an external search.

Sources of information include:

- Personal sources .
- Commercial sources
- Public sources
- Personal experience

The relevant internal psychological process that is associated with information search is perception. Perception is defined as "the process by which an individual receives, selects, organises, and interprets information to create a meaningful picture of the world".

The selective perception process

Stage Description

- Selective exposure consumers select which promotional messages they will expose themselves to.
- Selective attention consumers select which promotional messages they will pay attention to.
- Selective comprehension consumer interpret messages in line with their beliefs, attitudes, motives and experiences.
- Selective retention consumers remember messages that are more meaningful or important to them.

The implications of this process help develop an effective promotional strategy, and select which sources of information are more effective for the brand.

Information Evaluation

At this time the consumer compares the brands and products that are in their evoked set. How can the marketing organization increase the likelihood that their brand is part of the consumer's evoked (consideration) set? Consumers evaluate alternatives in terms of the functional and psychological benefits that they offer. The marketing organization needs to understand what benefits consumers are seeking and therefore which attributes are most important in terms of making a decision.

Purchase Decision

Once the alternatives have been evaluated, the consumer is ready to make a purchase decision. Sometimes purchase intention does not result in an actual purchase. The marketing organization must facilitate the consumer to act on their purchase intention. The organisation can use variety of techniques to achieve this. The provision of credit or payment terms may encourage purchase, or a sales promotion such as the opportunity to receive a premium or enter a competition may provide an incentive to buy now. The relevant internal psychological process that is associated with purchase decision is integration.Once the integration is achieved, the organisation can influence the purchase decisions much more easily.

Post-purchase Evaluation

The EKB model was further developed by Rice (1993) which suggested there should be a feedback loop, Foxall (2005) further suggests the importance of the post purchase evaluation and that the post purchase evaluation is key due to its influences on future purchase patterns.

Internal Influences

Consumer behaviour is influenced by: demographics, psychographics (lifestyle), personality, motivation, knowledge, attitudes, beliefs, and feelings. Consumer behaviour concern with consumer need consumer actions in the direction of satisfying needs leads to his behaviour of every individuals depend on thinking.

TRAVEL ACTIVITIES IN URBAN TOURISM

Whether you look at them as the most expensive photographs you've ever taken, or the least expensive souvenirs you've ever purchased... whether you "take snapshots" or "create images"... travel photography is one of the most popular activities for those who travel.

The single most important choice to make is what kind of camera to purchase and/or bring along. There's no single "best" camera - or even kind of camera - for travel photography. The kind of pictures you want to take, how much flexibity or ease-of-use you want, your budget, and even how much you want to carry all factor into it.

Regardless of media type, cameras tend to fall into three categories of ease-of-use and features; an increase of one tends to decrease the other:

Consumer cameras tend to be cheapest, smallest, and easiest to use. These fit your pocket, are light, and can be taken almost everywhere. Most ordinary travelers will be happiest with these. One increasingly common subset of this type is the built-in camera on many phones, which are best reserved for very casual low-volume use.

Professional cameras have the most features (e.g. interchangeable lenses, various exposure control methods) but you pay for it in complexity, size, and expense. If you're serious enough about photography to own one of these, you probably aren't reading this introduction to travel photography.

"Prosumer" cameras fall between the two in most respects, and are best for serious amateurs who feel limited by the capabilities of consumer-grade cameras, and are willing put up with some bulk, complexity, and expense to get the kinds of pictures they want to be able to take.

How your camera records images - digitally or on film - is probably the biggest choice in selecting a camera today. Fortunately, either of them is a good, viable choice for most people. It used to be that a film camera only got you prints you could pass around, and a digital camera only got you files you could use on a computer. If you wanted them in the other format you had to scan them or print them yourself. But photo processors increasingly offer the option of getting files on a CD from your film negatives, or high-quality prints from your digital files.

DIGITAL CAMERAS

The price of digital cameras has fallen significantly, and the quality of the images they capture has increased, to the point that they're rapidly replacing film cameras in many travelers' luggage. They usually have the advantage of allowing instant review of the shots taken and deleting/repeating those that went wrong. Digital storage can hold far more pictures in a smaller amount of space; you may be able to take thousands of photos without reloading. The storage cards can also be reused from one trip to the next, and you save the cost of buying and developing film.

However, digital cameras still tend to be more expensive than film cameras with comparable features, and high-end digital cameras with interchangeable lenses still command a price premium over 35mm SLRs. They demand much more power (requiring frequent battery recharges or replacing expensive disposable batteries) than film cameras.

The various storage media (SD, Memory Stick, Compact Flash etc.) all work pretty much the same; all that really matters is the capacity of the cards you buy. Longer trips will require more memory, unless you bring along a laptop or another way to backup your pictures and clear your memory card. These days, many cameras are sold with a small memory card, and you will almost certainly need to buy a larger one before leaving on your travels. You could also consider buying additional memory cards for additional space and to avoid putting all your eggs in one basket.

Digital cameras usually have different quality modes available which use more/less storage space for each picture. They sometimes have confusing names like SHQ, HQ, and SQ1, and different resolutions (how many pixels). Experiment ahead of time to figure out what quality setting you want to use. Keep in mind that you don't need multi-megapixel images to fill a computer screen or make a pocket-sized print, and you'll be able to fit a lot more photos on the same card with lower settings. Don't use the in-camera display to determine what setting to use, because it can't show you how much detail you're losing; look at the final results in a print or on the computer screen (depending on how you plan on viewing your photos). The ability to switch to lower quality settings can also be useful if you're running out of storage space in the middle of nowhere: better to have the last couple dozen pictures taken at a less-than-ideal quality setting, than to run out of exposures before you reach home.

Film

Not only do film cameras tend to be less expensive in general, you can get real bargains buying used equipment from owners who have decided to switch to digital models, and a cheap camera is less of a loss if broken or stolen. Many models will run for months of use on the same little battery. Standard 35mm film can usually be replenished if you run out, and offers resolution roughly equivalent to a 10 to 22 megapixel digital camera. However, the cost of film and developing photos may quickly exceed any price difference with a digital camera.

Film can be fogged - or even ruined - by x-rays. Most modern airport x-ray machines use low enough intensity beams that a dose or two probably won't show up in your photos, but it's better to be safe than sorry. Also, older x-ray machines used in some countries might not be as film-safe. As a general rule-of-thumb, most x-ray units used for carry-on luggage are film-safe, while most units used for checked luggage are not. When flying, keep your camera and your film in your carry-on luggage, and give it to security to inspect by hand instead of running it through the x-ray machine. Note that in many airports, all carry-on material including films must be x-rayed.

Film comes in different film speeds, referring to their sensitivity to light, and therefore the shutter speeds you can use with them. Relatively "slow" film varieties (ISO 100-200) produce the highest quality images, but don't work as well indoors or in other low-light situations, where they require either the use of a flash or slow (blurry) shutter speeds. Higher speeds (ISO 400-800) are better in low light, but the images can look more "grainy". Since you probably won't have the luxury of changing film depending what conditions you're in at the moment, try to anticipate how much you'll be in each; if you're going to be in low-light situations much, a high-speed film will be more flexible... but a little more expensive.

There are also different types of film: color print, color slide, and black and white print film.

Color print film is the most popular option, producing a stack of printed photos that are easy to pass around.

Color slide film (aka "transparency film") is cheaper to have developed than print film, because it doesn't require the second step of putting the images on paper, and for this reason many pros use it, and only have selected images printed. However, slide film has less exposure latitude, so light areas are more likely to end up washed out, and dark areas turn out too dark to see anything.

Black and white print film was used for many of history's most famous news photos and candid street shots; some photographers will want to emulate these. However, this is not a popular option, largely because doing it really well requires doing your own printing in a darkroom, and because of its "specialty" nature, having black and white film developed by a modern commercial photo lab might actually end up costing more than color.

Lenses

For professional and prosumer cameras with interchangeable lenses, the choice of lenses to bring along becomes crucial. Many come with a standard kit lens that covers the range from wide-angle to short-telephoto. For a high-end digital SLR this might be in the range of 18-70mm; for a 35mm SLR 28-100mm would be equivalent. (The magnification strength of lenses on digital SLRs varies from that of 35mm film, and even from camera to camera.) However, due to their moving parts zooms are more prone to breaking, and a sturdy and fast 50mm prime lens is a popular (and compact) backup.

Often the kit lenses are designed more for low cost than high quality; in particular they are generally quite slow. Professionals tend to buy either "prime" fixed focal length lenses or much more expensive high-end zooms.

If you intend to photograph far-away objects - typical examples include going on safari or birdwatching - you will also need a strong telephoto lens. If space is at a premium, you may be tempted to ditch the kit lens and instead go for a superzoom lens that covers the full range from wide-angle to to 200 or even 300mm; however, picture quality on these will suffer noticeably and you'll be stuck using a physically big lens all the time. A smaller-range 75-200mm or a fixed-focal length telephoto will offer better quality.

At the other end of the scale, if you expect to take a fair amount of panoramic landscapes or want to be able to fit a busy city square into the frame in close quarters, supplementing a normal-to-tele zoom with a strong wide-angle lens (e.g. 24mm or less for 35mm film) might be useful.

People with several interchangeable lenses sometimes carry two or more bodies with different film, or even a digital and a film body. A camera body that uses film can be an advantage for wide-angle lenses, because the larger format widens the angle that lens captures. Put a lens from a film camera on most digital bodies and the angle of view decreases; a 24mm lens on a digital camera might have the limited angle of view of a 38mm lens on a film SLR. Why not load some film into another body and use the lens as real wide-angle optics? This may give pictures that your digital rig can't capture.

If you are going on a safari for two weeks, you might consider renting a lens. Lens rental can cost about 10% the cost of the lens for a 2 week rental, and you can always have the right lens for your style of trip.

Focus

Consumer-grade cameras usually handle focusing in one of two ways. Fixed-focus snapshot cameras are quickest and easiest to use. They have a lens that's pre-set to get everything more than a meter or two away roughly in focus. They rely on bright light and/or flash to pull this off. Auto-focus cameras tend to produce sharper images and allow you to work in somewhat dimmer light, but can be a little slower to react. This can be a problem when taking pictures of quick-moving subjects like your boyfriend running with the bulls in Pamplona. Professional- and prosumer-grade cameras usually offer the choice of manual or auto focusing.

Zoom

Film cameras may include zoom capability, which is handy for getting a closer shot of something in the distance. (One of the most common errors of inexperienced photographers is not getting close enough.) Digital cameras usually have zoom, but only one of two kinds they feature is "real". Digital zoom doesn't capture any additional detail at high magnification; it reprocesses the same information for a larger image, or just crops off the edges for you. If you have photo editing software on your computer, you can do a better job of that at home. Optical zoom actually changes the magnfication of the lens, and is better for getting sharp close-up shots of distant subjects. This is the kind of zoom worth paying extra for, and a built-in high-ratio optical zoom (e.g. 10x) distinguishes some prosumer-grade digital cameras.

Most photographers today use at least a zoom lens or two, but some feel that the extra weight, extra complexity, and the drop in image quality are not worth it. Consider a 70-200 mm zoom vs an 85 mm fixed lens. The 85 will be considerably smaller and lighter, will take sharper pictures at 85 mm, and will be probably be much faster, so usable in lower light. As for the photos where you want a 200 mm lens, either use a teleconverter or just shoot at 85 and enlarge it more. You lose convenience but are better off overall in terms of weight, reliability, and low light performance. Whether you get better image quality depends on the specific lenses in question.

Batteries

Batteries are an important thing to think about, because it can be extremely frustrating to run out of battery power right in the most exciting part of your trip. If your camera uses a non-standard battery type (especially common with digital cameras), be sure to bring extras or a recharger and use it regularly. Don't wait for your power to run out before deciding to recharge.

Some cameras normally use higher-capacity batteries (CR-V3 lithium are common), but can run on standard AAs (with more frequent changes) if needed. The ability to use AA batteries - readily available anywhere from Tibet to Togo to Tuvalu - is a great safety net.

Battery chemistry makes a big difference, and even something as standard as AA batteries come in several varieties. A rechargeable NiMH battery usually lasts longer (even without recharging) than even the best lithium battery, and its reusability will pay for itself in the long run. The main drawback of rechargeables is that they lose their charge even just sitting for a few weeks. Don't use NiCd batteries in a digital camera (except in emergencies); they simply won't last.

If you're leaving civilization behind altogether, consider an old-fashioned mechanical film camera that can be run without battery power, or a not-quite-so-quaint electronic film camera which uses so little battery power (e.g. for the light meter, to time the shutter speed) that it can run for months on a single button-size cell. Most manual-exposure 35mm cameras from the 1970s and earlier will run battery-free; auto-exposure 35mm cameras from the 1980s merely sip from their batteries, and a few (e.g. Pentax ME series) can even continue working (on manual) without.

The largest battery drains on a digital camera are the preview screen, and the sensor. Many will last for thousands of shots if you disable the screen and use a manual viewfinder (if available).

Accessorize

Many photographers carry along a tripod, and even a little pen-sized model can come in handy if you want to set up timed shots of yourself and yours. If weight is an issue (e.g. when hiking), consider a monopod instead. Bogen/Manfrotto even makes a line of well-regarded monopods that double as hiking sticks, although they're rather pricy. Alternatively, shop for hiking sticks with camera mounts hidden under the top knob. However, bear in mind that many (if not most) museums and tourist attractions do not permit tripods or monopods.

Sometimes breaking out the tripod will put you in the "professional" category, and you suddenly need copyright permissions for what the owners of the place now consider commercial photography. An ultraviolet filter comes in handy, not just for blocking ultraviolet (which can cut down on distant "haze" in landscape photos) but also for protecting your lens from dust, grime, and scrapes. A USB-enabled SD Card will save having to bring an adapter and can transfer photos straight onto a laptop.

Pack

With expensive photography gear, packing it properly becomes an issue. Specialized cases specifically for packing cameras and lenses are available, but they are bulky and inconvenient. If travelling light, it's better just to bring along the original leather pouches for your lens and camera. A T-shirt folded and wrapped around a lens provides some impact protection and guards it from prying eyes.

Wipe down your camera and lenses with tissue after use, before you put them away. In particular, zoom lenses in dusty environments should be extended fully, wiped off, and allowed to dry before packing them, as grit will wreak havoc on the delicate mechanisms inside.

Moving Pictures

With fragile Super-8 film cameras and bulky VHS cameras receding into ancient history, compact videotape and digital cameras have made it more practical than ever to take moving pictures of your travels. These can be more entertaining to look at (for you and your friends), and better capture the grandeur of a panoramic view or the excitement of a helicopter ride. But video is also harder to do well than still shots, and bumpy recordings that cut abruptly from one scene to the next can be more disorienting than informative. Movie-editing software can help turn your raw footage into a slick presentation, but it's additional work after you get home.

Some digital still cameras have the ability to record video, but many have quality limitations. Try out the feature before you buy.

Respect

Be aware that people in other cultures may view being photographed differently from you. In some countries, it is illegal to take pictures of individuals without their consent. Some Brazilian indigenous groups, for instance, believe their souls are captured when they are photographed. Members of some religious sects (e.g. the Amish) consider having their picture taken an act of impious vanity, and although they may permit it they don't welcome it. Cameras may also not be welcome during some religious rituals, in certain religious buildings, or at certain cultural events. Such particular views on photography should always be taken into account when deciding whom, what, and when to photograph. When in doubt, it is always better to ask before taking a photo.

There are various situations in which flash photography may be inappropriate. Sometimes it will not be permitted, either to preserve a solemn atmosphere, or to protect antiquities from the damaging effects of bright light. Keep in mind that flash usually won't illuminate things more than a few meters away, so taking flash photos of the roof of a cathedral would be both distracting and ineffective. Flash also tends to spoil the natural appearance of the things you're trying to photograph, and if the object is behind protective glass, then your camera may end up blinding itself with the reflection of its own flash. So if you can disable your camera's flash and shoot by natural light (holding the camera very steady to compensate for slow shutter speeds), it may very well be worth the effort.

Stay Safe

Photography equipment can be expensive and the pictures you've already taken at any point in your trip are effectively irreplaceable, so it's always wise to consider their safety when traveling. Besides theft and accident human-caused damage, natural issues like extreme heat and cold may have a significant impact on your equipment. If rain is likely, a weatherproof camera might be a good investment.

Don't flash your camera around any more than necessary. If you take it out of your bag, wrap the strap around your wrist a few times and hold it firmly in your hand. Walking around with an expensive SLR hanging from a neck strap is an invitation to motorcycle thieves. When walking in a city, keep not just the camera but also the bag holding the camera on the side of you facing away from the road. Brand-name camera bags advertise what's inside them. You may be safer carrying your camera in an old rucksack or even a shopping bag, perhaps padded with some clothes.

Avoid photographing government buildings (other than obvious tourist landmarks), military installations, or other plausible targets of political violence. In areas with ongoing military conflicts and/or heightened alertness for terrorism, this can get you unwelcome attention - or worse - from anxious security personnel.

Pose

Some people get their family or other travel companion(s) into every picture. Others focus exclusively on the places. Try to strike a balance. Including members of your group (especially if they're your kids) can add some fun and personality to your photos. But a litany of "Here's Stan standing in front of the Eiffel Tower. Here's Stan standing in front of Notre Dame. Here's Stan standing in front of..." can get tedious, not just to say but to look at. Try to capture your human subjects in the process of exploring the environmental subjects; a shot of Stan gazing into the sunset captures the experience better than him standing in front of it.

Similarly, share the camera, so that sometimes Stan is behind it and you get in some of the pictures too. Asking another camera-toting traveler to snap a picture of both/all of you (with your camera, not his), in exchange for returning the favor, helps to establish that you were in fact there together (though it puts you at the mercy of their ability to work your camera). Likewise, if you're traveling alone, either get someone to take a shot of you at various locales, or if that's not practical, at least try setting up a shot or two with a self-timer to prove to everyone that you really went there. Note that it's usually advisable to ask someone with a camera at least as expensive as yours - less of a temptation.

One of the most practical things to remember with a camera, is that you are capturing "light". If you are photographing outside, make sure the sun is to your back. If you are shooting into the sun it will throw off the automatic settings on your camera and you will have a very dark image. The same applies to shadows. Sitting someone in shadows and standing in the light to photograph them will likely be disappointing. Same applies to inside photography. Taking a photo with an outside window in the frame will throw off the automatic settings and result in a dark image of what's in front of the window.

Running

Running as part of a vacation has seen strong growth in recent years. Individuals wanting to complete marathons in different cities, states, or countries can do so with the numerous marathons offered all over the world. Companies such as Marathon Tours and Travel operates tours that take traveling marathoners around the globe.

Marathons are not the only option for running on a vacation - both endurance races and shorter distance runs are also possible. Run the World operates interesting culture/running tours to international destinations, and allows a traveller to run, but still soak in a large part of culture, which is often missed on a marathon trip.

The Hash House Harriers are a running club that originated among expats in South-East Asia but has since spread widely, with well over a thousand groups in many countries. They do a weekly hare-and-hounds run, followed by a gathering at a local eatery. There are frequent regional gatherings called "interhashes".

Guided running tours are a new category of adventure travel. Experienced runners take clients on great routes and allow them to maintain a running routine while traveling on business or pleasure. In San Francisco, check out American Running Guides. They bring runners all over the city and across the Golden Gate Bridge for some trail running in Marin County.

Destinations

Here are some of the best places in the world for travellers to run; that is, routes that lend themselves to both sightseeing and a good jog:

Vancouver - a gentle 8km loop around Stanley Park will take you around downtown Vancouver's coastal rain forest, totem poles and the best views of the Coastal Mountains rising out of the sea. For some extra distance, continue down the sea wall around False Creek and into Granville Island. For those who like a companion or a guide around Vancouver, executiveRUN provide guided running tour around Downtown Vancouver.

Singapore - the pedestrian friendly pathways will take you past most of Singapore's most famous landmarks including the Merlion, Clarke Quay and the Singapore River.

United States - the Boston, New York and Chicago marathons are three of the largest in the country. Not surprisingly, Honolulu is a top marathon destination of choice as well, due to Hawaii's travel appeal.

Ottawa - enjoys a lovely greenbelt that traces over the city. Of particular interest is the river valley and Rideau Canal where a 10km loop will take you past such national landmarks as the Supreme Court, the Parliament Buildings, the landmark hotel Chateau Laurier, down the Rideau Canal, loop back across the canal on the heritage Pretoria Lift bridge, past the National Gallery of Canada and over the Ottawa River into Hull, Quebec, where you'll run along the river past the Museum of Civilization and finally cross back into Ottawa past the War Museum.

Golf

Golf is a game that is variously considered a pastime, recreation, sport, profession, religion or an obsession. The apparent object is to knock a small hard ball into a designated hole, using only a minimum number of blows of a stick or club, while avoiding the hazards of the terrain such as vegetation, water, soft ground and loose sand. While this may appear frustrating to some, the pleasure that so many people do derive from working out their frustrations in the course of this game means that golf and visiting the golf courses where the game is played is a significant reason for travel.

Understand

Golf originated at Saint Andrews, in Scotland. Because of this, Scotland, and in particular the Old Course at St. Andrews, is considered the traditional home of Golf, and the standard to which all other Golf Courses are compared.

Golf spread throughout the British Isles, and by 1829, beyond them with the establishment of the "Royal Calcutta Golf Club" in

India. By the end of the 19th Centuary, Clubs in Ireland, The United States of America, and Wales had come together to organise the sport at their respective national levels. Scotland and England followed after the First World War. Golf has two global Governing Bodies, the "R&A" at St Andrew's, Scotland and the "United States Golf Association" which work closely in partnership, for example in agreeing to changes to the "Rules of Golf". This joint approach helps to ensure that golf has not suffered the fate of other sports and split between a "British" sport, (e.g. Soccer and Cricket) and an "American" analogue (e.g. American Football and Baseball). Golf is golf wherever you play in the world, with the same standard rules, which is particularly useful if you want to play the sport outside your own country.

Today, perhaps one of the first two things that developers consider when wanting to attract more tourism to a destination is where to put the (next) golf course to go with the hotel they are wanting to develop.

Destinations

Europe

Golf as we understand it originated in Scotland, although it is probable that ancestor games to modern golf originated on the Continent. However both the insular and continental European golfers do not let such matters divide them too much, when it comes to the Ryder Cup. That biennial trophy succeeds every two years to unify the Europeans in a way that has so far eluded the European Union.

The British Isles remain the main focus of golf in Europe. Throughout the British Isles you will find many good quality courses. The Celtic countries, Scotland, Ireland and Wales, in particular hit above their weight in terms of the courses they offer. This is due to the fact that their extensive coastlines offer ample opportunities to build links courses. Their larger neighbour England also has many fine courses. The most famous course undoubtedly would be the Old Course at St Andrews.

Iberia offers also offers the second most important focus for European Golf. Golf courses have developed in both Spain and Portugal, particularly in coastal areas. Valderama is probably the most famous of the continental courses the venue of the only European Ryder Cup held on Mainland Europe.

Other destinations have also developed golf courses. In France courses seem to be located disproportionately in the West of the country, in particular in Brittany. The Czech Republic for example has seen new courses open since the fall of communism, and the Scandanavian countries offer the opportunity of around the clock golf during the summer months.

In the current economic climate due to the relative weakness of Sterling, England, Northern Ireland, Scotland and Wales probably offer better value than Eurozone destinations.

Scotland

The legendary home of golf and home to the one of the game's two co-governing bodies, the R&A. Scotland and St. Andrews in particular is a must for any golfing enthusiast and is estimated to have around 400 course - not all are open to the public and so the real figure is unknown.

Courses in Scotland include

St Andrews - where else but...

Carnoustie in Angus - venue for the 2007 Open Championship (and 6 previous Opens)

Gleneagles in Perthshire

Royal Troon - Open Championship course on the beautiful Ayrshire Coast

Royal Dornoch - One the trickiest course available

Turnberry in Ayrshire - A newer (1903) Open Championship course attached to a world class hotel

Muirfield - A highly rated championship course

The South Fife coast - Not an individual course but more of an experience. An area near St. Andrews where every town and village has its own course (no-matter how small). While they may vary in standard it is interesting to play in an area where the game is universally popular.

Trump International Golf Club Scotland A 1400 -acre stretch of spectacular sand dunes at Balmedie Beach on Menie Estate to the north of [Aberdeen] is controversially slated to have this huge golf resort built on it.

The Scottish Execitive's official golf tourism website gives details of all courses in Scotland.

England

See Golf in England for further details.

England has a long golfing history.

Courses include.

Royal Birkdale

Royal Liverpool, Hoylake, Wirral

Royal Lytham and St Anne's

Royal St George's, Sandwich, Kent

The Belfry- Venue for a number of Ryder Cups

Wentworth- Venue for the World Matchplay Championship

Ireland

Scotland may be the home of golf, but Ireland was in fact the first country to organise golf on a national level. It has been one of the more popular golf destinations in recent years. It's popularity has pushed prices up, and playing golf in Ireland is relatively expensive compared with other destinations.

Famous courses include:-

The K Club, in the Republic, venue for the 2006 Ryder Cup

Royal Portrush, in Northern Ireland, the venue for the only Open Championship not held in Great Britain.

Killeen Castle, in the Republic, venue for the 2011 Solheim Cup.

The Island of Ireland's official golf tourism website gives further details.

Portugal

Portugal is an important golf destination on the European Mainland.

In this domain Praia d'el Rey Golf & Beach Resort is reputed to be one of Portugal's finest. Designed by Cabell Robinson, it is a championship course that boasts marvelous fairways and perfectly manicured greens. Even the bunkers are pro-active: left to their own devices, sunbathers tend to stretch out in them, risking the wrath of Caddie Master, Jim Lambert.

Roughs are made rougher by the presence of a sponge-like grass that insidiously attempts to digest anything that lands in it. Jim advises taking the strokes rather than adding up two-digit scores.

From Number 12 through 15, play is overlooking the Atlantic: sometimes windy, always stunning. The last three holes are all uphill to the 18th green and the way is not without potential disaster. A gap to the 16th green is narrow, requiring painstaking accuracy. Further challenge is added by Number 17, a 523-metre hole that is one of the longest Par 5s in Portugal; 17 is regarded as the most difficult hole on the course.

Spain

Spain is the major golf destination on the European mainland. It is the only country in continental Europe, as well as the only non-English-speaking country, to have hosted to the Ryder Cup.

Courses in Spain include

Valderrama Golf Club (in Sotogrande)

Wales

Wales like the other British Isles countries has a long golf history. It has approximately 150 golf clubs.

Wales has often been one of the earlier adopters of innovations in the game. Wales was the third country to start organising golf on a National Level, and indeed in 2007 both Men's and Ladies' golf came under the same organisational umbrella. The Stableford Scoring Systerm, used by most amateur club golfers also originated in Wales.

Wales has produced two Ryder Cup winning captains, Dai Rees and Ian Woosnam. Wales hosted the competion in 2010, at the Celtic Manor Resort, Newport.

Despite the prestigious golfing heritage, Wales' courses remain relatively undiscovered by international visitors. This however has its advantages, since it offers the visitor high quality courses, at prices generally lower than elsewhere in Western Europe, and crowding on Welsh fairways is thankfully rare. Wales is growing in popularity as a golfing destination, and the 2010 Ryder Cup is expected to generate further international interest.

The Welsh Assmebly Government's official golf tourism website gives details of all courses in Wales.

The more prestigious Courses in Wales include.

Aberdovey (Gwynedd) - Links course adjacent to the village of Aberdyfi

Conwy- A Venue for 2006 Final Qualifying for the Open.

Nefyn & District, Lleyn- offers arguably the some of the most spectacular holes in world golf.

Machynys Peninsula, Llanelli, Carmarthenshire- Wales's only Nicklaus Designed Course.

Royal Porthcawl, Porthcawl- Venue for the 1995 Walker Cup, the defeated USA team included Tiger Woods

Royal St David's, Harlech- Links course overlooked by the famouse Harlech Castle

The Wales National, Vale Hotel, Golf & Spa Resort, Hensol, Pontyclun

The Twenty Ten, Celtic Manor Resort, Newport- Venue of the 2010 Ryder Cup

Africa

South Africa

Gary Player Country Club, Sun City

Sun City Golf Course, Sun City

Glendower Golf Course, 20 Marias Rd,Dowerglen ext 2, Johannesburg, +27 (0)11 453-1013,

Steenberg Golf Course, Tokai Road, Tokai, Cape Town, +27 (0)21 715-0227 (mailto:reservations@steenberghotel.com),

Durban Beachwood Course, Durban

Humewood Golf Course, Marine Drive, Port Elizabeth, +27 (0)41 583-2137,

ASIA

Thailand

Thailand has about 200 golf courses where more than 100 of them are met international standards. Some of them are even recognized international for outstanding quality and standards.

Nearly 50% of all golf courses are found in and around the city of Bangkok, all reachable within 2-3 hours drive from Bangkok. Generally, courses in Bangkok are highly utilize and cost more than those courses that are further away with the exception of courses in Phuket. As such, golfers without pre-booking are more likely to get tee-off times for courses further away from Bangkok, even during weekdays.

Famous golf courses and more information:

Alpine Golf & Sports Club This venue located in the province of Pathum Thani, is usually for members only and is rated to be one of the most challenging courses in Thailand. They have hosted many international competitions including the prestigious Johnny Walker Classic and the 13th Asian Games.

Thai Country Club Not only is this course one of the finest in Thailand but also one of the best in Asia. It has been voted Thailand's Best Golf Course 2001-2007 and Best Golf House in Asia 2000-2007. They have been host to many major competitions such as the Johnny Walker Super Tour, Asia Honda Classic and Volvo Masters Asia.

Oceania

New Zealand

There are over 400 registered New Zealand golf courses from local clubs to internationally renowned golf resorts. These include;

Carrington Club - Northland. Oceanside location but plays like an inland golf course complete with rolling hills, vales and natural water hazards.

Kauri Cliffs - Northland. Designed by David Harman, the course is stunningly situated overlooking the Cavalli Islands on 4000 acres of rolling coastal farmland.

Gulf Harbour Country Club - Auckland. Designed by Robert Trent Jones Jr. this oceanfront course was the scene of the 1998 World Cup of Golf.

Formosa Auckland Country Club - Auckland. Situated on the beautiful Pohutukawa Coast and designed by Sir Bob Charles the course was modeled on the Augusta National Golf Course home of the US Masters.

Wairakei International Golf Course - Taupo. Rated by US Golf Digest to be in the Top 20 courses in the world outside the USA.

Cape Kidnappers - Hawkes Bay. Tom Doak designed, on a special site with links to New Zealand's important Maori culture.

Paraparaumu Beach Golf Course - Wellington. A true links test with the best in design, shot making and world class greens. It has been the scene of the NZ Open on ten occasions.

Clearwater Resort - Christchurch. The home of the NZPGA championship and was designed by John Darby and Sir Bob Charles.

Terrace Downs - Canterbury. Close to high country sheep farms and in amongst the Southern Alps.

Millbrook Resort - Queenstown. Designed by NZ's golfing great Sir Bob Charles and set amongst exquisite mountain scenery.

North America

Canada

Mountains, oceans and Arctic tundra form the backdrop to challenging fairways and immaculate greens. Celebrated names like Nicklaus, Thompson, Robinson, Furber and Whitman loom large on world-class courses. Play all night under the warm glow of the midnight sun in the Far North. Or putt your way around beautiful Prince Edward Island in full view of the sparkling Atlantic. In Canada, spectacular golfing is just par for the course.

United States of America

The United States is a major golf destination, it has more golf courses than any other country, (approximately 10,000 Golf Courses).

The United States also has a surprisingly long golfing tradition. The formation of the United States Golf Association in 1894 was predated only that of by Ireland's Golf Union. Indeed the United States Golf Association, as well as acting as National Golf Association for the United States, is one of the worldwide game's co-governing bodies.

The United States has for many years produced many of the world's best golfers, and remains a golf superpower, despite recent Ryder Cup defeats to the Europeans. The USA hosts the event in years divisible by 4; the next Ryder Cup to be held in the U.S. will be in 2012 at Medinah Country Club in suburban Chicago.

Two other major team events are alternately hosted by the U.S. The Solheim Cup is the women's equivalent to the Ryder Cup, featuring teams from the U.S. and Europe. The Presidents Cup is a men's event that features a U.S. team facing an "International" team made up of golfers ineligible for the Ryder Cup. Both events are held in odd-numbered years, and the U.S. hosts both in the year after it hosts the Ryder Cup, meaning that the next editions of both competitions in the U.S. will be in 2013. The next Solheim Cup in the U.S. will be held at Colorado Golf Club in the Denver suburb of Parker, Colorado, and the next Presidents Cup in the U.S. will be held at Muirfield Village in the Columbus suburb of Dublin, Ohio.

Three of the four major golf tournaments for both men and women, as well as four of the five major tournaments for men 50 and over, are played in the United States. Some of the most famous, and best, courses can be found there.

Florida is an important national and international golf destination. At the other extreme Alaska offers the possibility of late night golf during the summer.

Caribbean

Somewhat surprisingly, challenging courses and major tournaments are hosted in the Caribbean. Some of the main courses include:

Tierra Del Resort Spa and Country Club, Aruba - This course was designed by Robert Trent Jones Jr., and includes 18-holes, par-71 course totals 6,811 yards in length, with its highest tee at over 95 feet above sea level. The Aruba International Pro-AM Golf Tournament is a major tournament that takes place on this course.

Temenos Golf Club, Anguilla - Opened by Cap Juluca in 2009, this 18 hole course includes challenging holes and breathtaking views.

Half Moon, Jamaica- Caribbean World Magazine named this course the "Best Caribbean Golf Resort". The course is appropriate for both novice and advanced golfers. Half Moon is also home to David Leadbetter Golf Academy.

South America

Golf is an increasingly popular sport in Argentina, thanks in part to the success of Argentinian players such as Angel Cabrera, Andres Romero and Eduardo Romero. There are currently around 280 courses in the country, most located around Buenos Aires and including such well-known names as the Jockey Club, Olivos and Hurlingham. On the Atlantic coast in Mar del Plata are a couple of courses that have held international events, and Patagonia has excellent resort courses such as Llao Lloa, Arelauquen and Chapelco (a Nicklaus design) as well as the 9-hole course in Ushaia.

Buy

At larger and more popular courses, the on-course Pro Shop will normally be able to supply all the necessary accessories.

Eat

Many golf courses have a Clubhouse that serves meals. Some provide a full service restaurant.

Drink

Most Clubhouses have a bar; such establishments are colloquially known as the 19th hole.

Stay safe

Golf is the sort of game that can be played in all sorts of weather conditions, especially if one wants a challenging game. However, lightning and severe storms are contraindications for safe play.

Consider golf insurance. This will pay out in the event of a hole-in-one, or if you injure other golfers.

Tipping

If you use a caddies (and in many places you have no choice), you may be expected to tip them. In other places tipping is not permitted. You should ask when you book your round what the expected tip is.

Get out

Once you have finished playing be sure to clean your equipment. If you are crossing borders with your gear be sure to declare it, particularly where countries have biosecurity controls to limit the importation of equipment that has been in contact with farmland and the like. Otherwise you might find you are delayed while the equipment is cleaned, or worse, confiscated.

Canyoning

Canyoning combines elements from swimming, climbing and jumping--but requires relatively little training or physical shape to get started (compared to rock climbing, scuba diving or alpine skiing, for example).

There are several kind of techniques in a canyon, which are also features of a specific canyon:

sifons (dive-under)

vertical rappeling (or abseiling)

horizontal abseiling: moving over a rope above a river from one side of canyon to another

jumps

slides (toboggan in Spanish)

Plus trivial techniques which are used in virtually every canyon with water: walking, swimming, climbing to large stones.

Other characteristics of a canyon are length, duration, altitude difference; time to get in to a canyon start and to get out from its finish.

HOT DESTINATIONS

Asia

Vietnam

Dalat

Australia and New Zealand

Australia

Blue Mountains (available from Wentworth Falls)

New Zealand

Queenstown (see also Nine days in New Zealand's South Island)

Europe

Austria

near Salzburg

near Salzkammergut

Croatia

near Omiš

France

Alpes Maritimes

Pyrenees, though shorter than in Spain

Vercors

Provence-Alpes-Côte d'Azur

Hautes-Alpes

around St-Clément-sur-Durance

Germany

Bad Reichenhall

Kempten (Allgäu) in Bavaria

Greece

Acheron (available from Paramythia)

Enippeas in Larissa Prefecture, Thessaly

Slovenia

near Bled

Bovec (Sušec stream, other canyons)

Spain

Alava

Andalucía:

Sierra Nevada

Aragon:

Sierra de Guara (available from Alquezar)

Pyrenees (available from Alquezar)

Asturias

Burgos

Cantabria

Galicia

Guipúzcoa

León

Mallorca

Navarra

Vizcaya

Switzerland

Interlaken

Turkey

near Ka?

Yazili in Isparta Province

United Kingdom

Wales:

Brecon Beacons

North America

United States

California:

Los Angeles

South America

Brazil

Cassorova Valley in Bahia (from Brotas)

São Paulo:

Fortaleza Mountain (available from Caconde)

Chapada dos Veadeiros

10

FUTURE OF URBAN TOURISM

Without good transport facilities and basic infrastructure, one cannot think of bright future of urban tourism. A large majority of European citizens live in an urban environment, with over 60% living in urban areas of over 10.000 inhabitants. They live their daily lives in the same space, and for their mobility share the same infrastructure. Urban mobility accounts for 40% of all CO_2 emissions of road transport and up to 70% of other pollutants from transport.

European cities increasingly face problems caused by transport and traffic. The question of how to enhance mobility while at the same time reducing congestion, accidents and pollution is a common challenge to all major cities in Europe. Congestion in the EU is often located in and around urban areas and costs nearly 100 billion Euro, or 1% of the EU's GDP, annually. Cities themselves are usually in the best position to find the right responses to these challenges, taking into account their specific circumstances.

Efficient and effective urban transport can significantly contribute to achieving objectives in a wide range of policy domains for which the EU has an established competence. The success of policies and policy objectives that have been agreed at EU level, for example on the efficiency of the EU transport system, socio-economic objectives, energy dependency, or climate change, partly depends on actions taken by national, regional and local authorities. Mobility in urban areas is also an important facilitator for growth and employment and for sustainable development in the EU areas.

The European Commission's first policy proposals in the area of urban mobility, the "Citizens' Network", date back to 1995 and 1998. They resulted in the launch of a series of initiatives based upon a "best practice" approach.

As a follow-up to the mid-term review of the 2001 Transport White Paper 'European transport policy for 2010: time to decide', the European Commission adopted the Green Paper "Towards a new culture for urban mobility" on 25 September 2007. This consultation document opened a broad debate on the key issues of urban mobility: free-flowing and greener towns and cities, smarter urban mobility and urban transport which is accessible, safe and secure for all European citizens. Based upon the results of the consultation, the European Commission adopted the Action Plan on urban mobility on 30 September 2009.

The School of Architecture and Planning is one of three schools at MIT taking part in a global collaboration with the National Research Foundation of Singapore to develop new models and tools for the planning, design and operation of future urban transportation.

The central theme of the effort is to bring together recent advances in information technology and transportation science to increase the efficiency of urban transportation systems while at the same time ensuring a sustainable and livable environment - first in Singapore, and ultimately on a global scale.

At the heart of the project is SimMobility - a simulation platform with an integrated model of human and commercial activities, land use, energy use, transportation and environmental impacts - linked with a range of networked computing and mobility innovations.

The modeling initiative is akin to a new project recently funded by the MIT Energy Initiative on reducing urban energy consumption. Led urban planning professors Carlo Ratti and Christopher Zegras, working with Moshe Ben-Akiva of Civil and Environmental Engineering, that project aims to develop an integrated model of land use, transportation and energy use that will enable evaluation of a range of policies and projects for reducing energy consumption in metropolitan areas.

Did you know ten percent of the entire global workforce is employed in tourism? Many countries are experiencing a shortage of trained, knowledgeable travel professionals due to this high growth industry.

Below are excerpts from research studies by the World Travel & Tourism Council; the results of a survey by Statistics Canada and Conference Board of Canada, Canadian Travel Distribution Report; and TICO, the Travel Industry Council of Ontario on the growth of tourism locally and around the world.

Quotes from The World Travel & Tourism Council (WTTC):

- "Global Travel and Tourism Exceeded US$6 Trillion in 2005; "We are witnessing the power, speed and vitality of Travel & Tourism and how they can bring economic opportunity and jobs to people and economies seeking sustainable development,"
- "The industry is expected to grow 4.6 per cent (real terms), to US$6.5 trillion in 2006
- The global Travel & Tourism industry is expected to produce 2.5 million new jobs in 2006, comprising 76.7 million jobs, or 2.8 per cent of total world employment.
- Travel & Tourism are expected to create nearly 10 million new jobs globally, for a total of 234.3 million jobs or 8.7 per cent of total employment."
- Richard Miller, Executive Vice President of WTTC said, "Although events like the tsunami, bombings and hurricanes, as well as a major increase in the price of oil, could have dampened demand, it appears that consumers are becoming more resilient, and Travel & Tourism continue to be a significant part of everyday life."

A survey by Statistics Canada showed 37% of people online window-shopped for travel services, and 55% of Canadians, or more than 6 out of 10 purchased directly from a travel agency.

A study by Conference Board of Canada, Canadian Travel Distribution Report finds an even higher percentage of travellers use the services of a travel agency.

TICO, the Travel Industry Council of Ontario reports Ontario travellers spent over $4 billion in overseas travel.

Cruises, weddings, honeymoons, luxury and adventure travel (all ages) are fast growing travel markets.

Role of the Internet....

The Internet is a great way to research information however for many, the amount of information has become totally overwhelming, time consuming and at times unreliable. Customer care may be a concern as the internet is impersonal. When there is a question or concern about a product and/or service purchased online it is often difficult to secure assistance making it time consuming to resolve matters (if at all) without a 'live' person to deal with. Some companies are unresponsive to customer concerns and instead choose to "hide" behind the Internet.

Further, booking travel over the internet may be quite complex as products are not always clearly described in an accurate way; consumers do not have the advantage of best product and price comparisons without knowledge of all possible travel suppliers; insurance options are often inadequately described or explained; as is entry requirements e.g. passports, visas, health and security policies and procedures. Highly trained professional travel agents ensure important information is provided and understood by their client prior to travelling.

Highly trained professional travel agents ensure important information is provided and understood by their client prior to travelling. These are excellent reasons for travellers to use the personal services of an agent rather than book over the Internet..

Providing credit card and personal information on the Internet is required when booking online, this should be a concern to everyone. Regardless of security and firewalls, many corporations simply can't keep up with hackers and scammers.

Role of Professional Travel Agents....

The services of a professional travel agent is invaluable. They are trained to research and price compare for the best tour, cruise, airline, hotel etc. and to provide information on travel insurance options; climate, entry requirements (e.g. passport, visa and health requirements) before recommending and booking the best travel product to their client.

There is a shortage of well trained staff in the travel industry due to high growth therefore career opportunities should continue to increase.

Over the past two decades, Indonesia's coal industry has transformed itself from being an unknown, minor player in Asia's coal markets to the world's largest exporter of steam coal. The study argues that key physical and technical factors, along with regulatory and political factors, have acted as the primary drivers of the industry's phenomenal growth over the past two decades and will be the most important factors for consideration over the next two decades.

It also discusses current estimates of Indonesia's coal resources and reserves, the role played by location and geological factors in the development of its coal resources, the future impacts of the passage of Indonesia's Mining Law of 2009 and its related implementing regulations, and how these issues might affect the coal industry's structure and performance before 2020.

Increasingly, cities and urban regions compete with other places for attention, investment, visitors, shoppers, talent, events, and the like. Accelerated and intensified globalisation has lead to a situation where the main competition is no longer the city down the road or the town across the bay, but where competitors are places half a world away. And this global competition is no longer limited to the capital and big cities; it now directly affects all cities and concentrations of urban settlements. A city brand is its promise of value, a promise that needs to be kept.

Sustainable City

A sustainable city or eco-city is a city designed with consideration of environmental impact, inhabited by people dedicated to minimization of required inputs of energy, water and food, and waste output of heat, air pollution - CO2, methane, and water pollution. Richard Register first coined the term "ecocity" in his 1987 book, Ecocity Berkeley: building cities for a healthy future.

Other leading figures who envisioned the sustainable city are architect Paul F Downton, who later founded the company Ecopolis Pty Ltd, and authors Timothy Beatley and Steffen Lehmann, who have written extensively on the subject. The field of industrial ecology is sometimes used in planning these cities.

A sustainable city can feed itself with minimal reliance on the surrounding countryside, and power itself with renewable sources of energy. The crux of this is to create the smallest possible ecological footprint, and to produce the lowest quantity of pollution possible, to efficiently use land; compost used materials, recycle it or convert waste-to-energy, and thus the city's overall contribution to climate change will be minimal, if such practices are adhered to.

It is estimated that around 50% of the world's population now lives in cities and urban areas. These large communities provide both challenges and opportunities for environmentally conscious developers. In order to make them more sustainable, building design and practice, as well as perception and lifestyle must adopt sustainability thinking.

INTERNATIONAL EXAMPLES

Australia

Melbourne

- City of Moreland. The City of Moreland in Melbourne's north, has programs for becoming carbon neutral, one of which is 'Zero Carbon Moreland', amongst other existing sustainable implementations and proposals.
- City of Melbourne. Over the past 10 years, various methods of improving public transport have been implemented, car free zones and entire streets have also been implemented.
- City of Greater Taree. The City of Greater Taree North of Sydney has developed a masterplan for Australia's first low-to-no carbon urban development.

Brazil

Southern cities of Porto Alegre and Curitiba are often cited as examples of urban sustainability.

Canada

In 2010, Calgary ranked as the top eco-city in the planet for its, "excellent level of service on waste removal, sewage systems, and water drinkability and availability, coupled with relatively low air pollution." The survey was performed in conjunction with the reputable Mercer Quality of Living Survey.

China

- China is working with investment and technology supplied by the Singapore government to build an ecocity in the Coastal New District of Tianjin City in northern China, named the "Sino-Singapore Tianjin Eco-city".
- Dongtan Eco-city is the name of another project on the third largest island in China at the mouth of the Yangtze River near Shanghai. The project was scheduled to accommodate 50,000 residents by 2010, but its developer has currently put construction on hold.
- Huangbaiyu is another major eco-city being built by China.
- As of April 2008, an ecocity collaboration project is being proposed for a district in Nanjing, the capital city of Jiangsu Province on the Yangtze River, just west of Shanghai.
- Rizhao mandates of solar water heaters for households, and has been designated the Environmental Model City by China's SEPA.:108

Denmark

The industrial park in Kalundborg is often cited as a model for industrial ecology.

Ecuador

Loja, Ecuador won three international prizes for the sustainability efforts begun by its mayor Dr. Jose Bolivar Castillo.:25

Estonia

Oxford Residences for four seasons in Estonia, in development by the Oxford Sustainable Group, winning a prize for Sustainable Company of the Year, is arguably one of the most advanced sustainable developments, not only trying to be carbon neutral, but already carbon negative and considering factors such as economic, financial, social development of the surroundings, environmental, food, energy, government policy, local residents, education, in fact more than most other development.

Germany

No other country has built more eco-city projects than Germany. Freiburg im Breisgau is often referred to as green city. It is one of the few cities with a green mayor and is known for its strong solar economy. Vauban, Freiburg is a sustainable model district. All houses are built to a low energy consumption standard and the whole district is designed to be carfree.

Another green district in Freiburg is Rieselfeld, where houses generate more energy than they consume. There are several other green sustainable city projects such as Kronsberg in Hannover and current developments around Munich, Hamburg and Frankfurt.

Hammarby Sjöstad, Stockholm

United Kingdom

- St Davids the smallest city in the United Kingdom aims to be the first carbon neutral city in the world.
- Leicester is the United Kingdom's first environment city

United States

- Arcosanti, Arizona
- Treasure Island, San Francisco: is another project that aims to create a small eco city.
- Coyote Springs Nevada largest planned city in the United States.
- Babcock Ranch Florida a proposed solar-powered city.
- Douglass Ranch in Buckeye Arizona
- Mesa del Sol in Albuquerque,New Mexico
- Sonoma Mountain Village in Rohnert Park, California.

BIBLIOGRAPHY

- Adams, J.Q.; Pearlie Strother-Adams (2001). Dealing with Diversity. Chicago, IL: Kendall/Hunt Publishing Company. ISBN 0-7872-8145-X.

- Alon, Ilan, ed. (2003), Chinese Culture, Organizational Behavior, and International Business Management, Westport, Connecticut: Praeger Publishers.

- Armstrong, Michael (2006). A Handbook of Human Resource Management Practice (10th ed.). London: Kogan Page. ISBN 0-7494-4631-5. OCLC 62282248.

- Beaver, Allan (2002). A Dictionary of Travel and Tourism Terminology. Wallingford: CAB International. p. 313. ISBN 0851995829. OCLC 301675778.

- Becker, B. and Gerhart, B. (1996) 'The impact of human resource management on organisational performance' Academy of Management Journal 39 (4) 779-801

- Caitlin A. Johnson (April 15, 2007). "For Billionaire There's Life After Jail". CBS News. http://www.cbsnews.com/stories/2007/04/15/sunday/main2684957.shtml. Retrieved 2009-12-29. "Alfred Taubman is a legend in retailing. For 40 years, he's been one of America's most successful developers of shopping centers."

- Clack, George, et al. (September 1997). "Chapter 1". One from Many, Portrait of the USA. United States Information Agency. http://usinfo.state.gov/usa/infousa/facts/factover/ch1.htm.

- Delery, J. and Doty, H. (1996) 'Modes of theorizing in SHRM' Academy of Management Journal, 39(4), 802-835

- Encyclopædia Britannica (kl ed.). "Personnel administration is also frequently called personnel management, industrial relations, employee relations".

- Golding, N. (2010) "Strategic Human Resource Management" in Beardwell, J. and Claydon, T. (2010) Human Resource Management A Contemporary Approach, FT Prentice Hall

- Hine, Darlene; William C. Hine, Stanley Harrold (2006). The African American Odyssey. Boston, MA: Pearson. ISBN 0-12-182217-3.

- Jefferson, Thomas (1904). The writings of Thomas Jefferson. Thomas Jefferson Memorial Association of the United States. pp. 119.

- Kochan, T. and Barocci, T. (1985) Human Resource Management and Industrial Relations, LittleBrown

- Marsden, George M. 1990. Religion and American Culture. Orlando: Harcourt Brace Jovanovich, pp.45-46.

- Paauwe, J. (2009) 'HRM and Performance: Achievement, Methodological Issues and Prospects' Journal of Management Studies, 46 (1)

- Semiannual Report of the War Relocation Authority, for the period January 1 to June 30, 1946, not dated. Papers of Dillon S. Myer. Scanned image at trumanlibrary.org. Accessed 18 September 2006.

- Theobald, William F. (1998). Global Tourism (2nd ed.). Oxford [England]: Butterworth–Heinemann. pp. 6–7.

- U.S. Census Bureau, educational attainment in the U.S. 2003" (PDF). http://www.census.gov/prod/2004pubs/p20-550.pdf.

- Wilkerson, Chad (2003). "Travel and Tourism: An Overlooked Industry in the U.S. and Tenth District". Economic Review **88** (Third Quarter): 45–72.

INDEX